Lore of the Bambino

LORE OF THE BAMBINO
100 Great Babe Ruth Stories

JONATHAN WEEKS

LYONS
PRESS

Guilford, Connecticut

An imprint of Globe Pequot, the trade division of The Rowman & Littlefield Publishing Group, Inc.
4501 Forbes Blvd., Ste. 200
Lanham, MD 20706
www.rowman.com

Distributed by NATIONAL BOOK NETWORK

British Library Cataloguing in Publication Information available

Library of Congress Cataloging-in-Publication Data

ISBN: 978–1-4930–6140–2 (paperback)
ISBN: 978–1-4930–6694–0 (ebook)

♾™ The paper used in this publication meets the minimum requirements of American National Standard for Information Sciences—Permanence of Paper for Printed Library Materials, ANSI/NISO Z39.48-1992.

CONTENTS

Introduction

More than 70 years after his death, people still talk about Babe Ruth. No other Yankees player has ever been as idolized. Though Joe DiMaggio and Mickey Mantle may have come close in their respective eras, both men paled in comparison to Ruth. DiMaggio was quiet, remote, and relatively dull. Mantle had a vibrant personality, but a string of injuries prevented him from putting up the kind of epic numbers generated by the Sultan of Swat.

The Babe was light years ahead of his time. He transformed baseball from a ponderous game of strategy to an explosive exhibition of raw power. He could alter the final score with a single swing. When he retired in 1935, he owned dozens of statistical records and his 714 homers were more than double the output of the next closest competitor.

Beyond the ball field, Ruth was approachable, friendly, fun-loving. He autographed a myriad of baseballs, befriended sportswriters, and raised bundles of cash for charity. In an era when heroes were in great demand, he fit the bill. He understood what he meant to people (especially children) and went out of his way to bring them joy.

As a role model, he was imperfect. He broke rules, got suspended, and struck out often. But when the game was on the line, he almost always rose to the occasion in dramatic fashion. Over time, he became part god and part mortal—a mythical man-child who propelled baseballs farther than any player of the Lively Ball Era. He got more attention than US presidents and was just as newsworthy as a world war or economic depression. Everyone wanted a small piece of him. And everyone who met him had an interesting story to tell.

Though he was generous to a fault, Ruth didn't need credit for his good deeds. Sportswriter Grantland Rice remembered driving sixty miles with the Babe before a World Series game in Chicago to visit a sick boy. Afterward, the slugger told Rice that he would punch him if Rice included the story in one of his columns.

In later years, when Ruth's skills were in decline, he continued to draw people to the ballpark in great numbers. He became an outsider after he retired—rejected by club owners in his efforts to secure a big-league managerial position. It weighed heavily upon him. But he carried on, maintaining a special bond with the fans who still worshipped him. He came from humble beginnings and shared a simple message: "You just can't beat the person who never gives up." He never did. Even when his body was ravaged by cancer, he found the strength to attend Babe Ruth Day at Yankee Stadium and issue a final farewell during the venue's 25th anniversary celebration. In death, it remained his home. It belonged to him just as he belonged to it: The House That Ruth Built—a cenotaph and a shrine.

FROM WRITERS
"He was a perfect fit for the times—a man of mighty appetites and unrestrained desires. The Babe was a metaphor for the big, broadening shoulders of America."—Steven Stern

"No novelist or Hollywood screenwriter at the furthest extremes of their imagination would have dared to invent somebody like [Ruth]. This was science fiction."—Donald Honig

"He changed the extent of the appeal of baseball for all time. I don't know of anyone in any other sport who as an individual had as much of an effect on the popularity of the game."—Leonard Koppett

"It was a time when heroes were created from common men. Ruth seemed to embrace it vigorously and to shake every ounce of life out of the twenty-four hours in a day."—Steve Hundt

"He understood that people came to the ballpark to be entertained. That may be his legacy: that he was the first guy who figured it all out. That this was a stage, it was an act, this was Broadway, this was the theater. I think that's why we're talking about Ruth now in a new millennium."—William C. Rhoden

FROM PLAYERS

"What a warm-hearted, generous soul [Ruth] was—always friendly, always time for a laugh or wisecrack. The Babe would give you the shirt off his back. All you had to do was ask him."—Jimmy Austin, St. Louis Browns

———

"I still can't believe what I saw: this nineteen-year-old kid, crude, poorly educated, only slightly brushed by the social veneer we call civilization, gradually transformed into the idol of American youth and the symbol of baseball the world over.... I saw a man transformed from a human being into something pretty close to a god. If somebody had predicted that back on the Boston Red Sox in 1914, he would have been thrown into a lunatic asylum."—Harry Hooper, Boston Red Sox

———

"He was my idol. He was a picture up there at the plate. What a ballplayer. And such a sweet guy, too. I tried to copy everything he did."—Goose Goslin, Washington Senators

———

"When Ruth's time at bat is over and it's my turn, the fans are still buzzing about what the Babe did regardless of whether he belted a home run or struck out. They wouldn't notice if I walked up to home plate on my hands, stood on my head, and held the bat between my toes."—Lou Gehrig, New York Yankees

———

"I've seen them: kids, men, women, worshippers all, hoping to get his name on a torn, dirty piece of paper, or hoping for a grunt of recognition when they said " 'Hiya, Babe.' He never let them down, not once. He was the greatest crowd pleaser of them all."—Waite Hoyt, New York Yankees

FROM RUTH

"I swing big, with everything I've got. I hit big or I miss big. I like to live as big as I can."

———

"Never let the fear of striking out get in your way."

———

"If I had tried for them dinky singles, I could have hit .600."

———

"Gee, it's lonesome in the outfield. It's hard to keep awake with nothing to do."

———

"If it wasn't for baseball, I'd be in either the penitentiary or the cemetery."

Part 1:
A Chronological Journey Through the Babe's Life and Career

A Troubled Childhood

Ruth's mother had several children, but only two survived infancy. Very little is known of Kate Schamberger. Aside from a single photo in which she is holding her famous son as a toddler, there is virtually no tangible evidence of her association with the boy who later became the most revered ballplayer of his time (and perhaps of all time). Ruth's sister Mary once disclosed that Kate was not well but offered no specifics regarding her physical or mental condition.

George Herman Ruth Sr., the Babe's father, is a somewhat less obscure figure. In August of 1918, he was tending bar in his Baltimore saloon when a fight broke out between two of his brothers-in-law. He fell and hit his head during the brawl, sustaining a fatal skull fracture. Earlier, he had owned several other taverns and worked in the lightning rod business. Those who frequented his establishments would likely have described him as a stern individual well-suited to handling rough alehouse crowds.

George Jr. was raised in a tough Baltimore neighborhood known as Pigtown—aptly named for the herds of swine that were paraded through the streets on their way to a local slaughterhouse. His stomping grounds included an area known as Ridgely's Delight, which was located between the docks of the central harbor and terminals of the Baltimore & Ohio Railroad. By his own admission, he was a poorly behaved child. He once stated candidly, "Looking back on my boyhood, I honestly don't remember being aware of the difference between right and wrong."[1] He developed a taste for chewing tobacco during his elementary school years and was known to sample alcohol from the glasses left on his father's barroom tables. He was habitually truant from school and some of his favorite leisure-time activities included stealing food from lunch counters and throwing assorted projectiles at moving vehicles or policemen. He also pilfered money from his father's till.

In June of 1902, Kate and George Sr. granted custody of their seven-year-old son to the Xaverian Brothers of St. Mary's Industrial School for Boys—a Catholic reformatory offering housing to more than eight hundred troubled youths. Under the watchful eyes of the Brothers, young George was guaranteed much-needed structure and discipline. Schedules at St. Mary's were tightly regimented, rules were strictly enforced, and corporal punishment was a natural consequence for those who misbehaved.

Ruth would remain at St. Mary's until the age of nineteen. Though he was reunited with his parents on multiple occasions, he always ended up in some kind of trouble that resulted in his return to the school. Boisterous and hyperkinetic, he was probably suffering from some form of ADHD (which would not be officially recognized as a disorder until long after his death). His boundless energy and fun-loving nature endeared him to a majority of his peers.

Ruth was introduced to baseball by Brother Matthias Boutlier, who served as St. Mary's prefect of discipline. An intimidating presence at 6-foot-6, the charismatic monk was simultaneously feared, respected, and admired by the children. On Saturday evenings, he put on hitting displays in the schoolyard with a fungo bat. The kids—gathering in groups of several hundred—marveled at how far the balls traveled. Ruth is said to have developed his passion for hitting from watching Brother Matthias's powerful swing.

St. Mary's offered a number of sports, including football and wrestling, but baseball was by far the most popular. In 1909, there were more than two dozen teams on campus. Brother Herman, who was in charge of athletics, gave George a mitt designed for right-handed catchers. A natural lefty, Ruth had to take the glove off in order to throw. But he made it work. After mastering most of the other positions, he became an exceptional pitcher. It happened by accident. As the story goes, he was taunting a schoolmate who was having a rough time on the mound one afternoon. Brother Matthias stopped the game and invited George to take over if he felt he could do a better job. Never one to back down from a challenge, Ruth accepted. It was soon discovered that he could throw harder than most of the other boys on campus. With practice, he mastered the fundamentals—how to hold runners on base, switch speeds, and spot his pitches. In 1913, he struck out 22 batters in a game. Word of his talent began to spread, and he got his first big break the following year.

In the early part of the 20th century, the Baltimore Orioles were a top-level minor-league team affiliated with the International League. Orioles owner Jack Dunn, who had aspired to a brief career in the majors in spite of a partially paralyzed arm, was known to play hunches when it came to signing prospects. After receiving a scouting report on the 19-year-old Ruth, he asked St. Mary's officials for permission to meet with the budding star. There are conflicting reports as to whether Ruth was asked to demonstrate his pitching skills or if he was offered a contract on the spot, abilities unseen. Either way, the Brothers vouched for his vast potential as a pitcher and hitter. Since he was still legally a minor, custody had to be turned over to Dunn before he officially left the reformatory.

In March of 1914, Ruth took his first-ever train ride to Fayetteville, North Carolina, where Orioles spring training was being held. It was the beginning of an illustrious career. He attended many benefits and exhibitions at St. Mary's after he became rich and famous. And he maintained a close bond with Brother Matthias, who he once referred to as the greatest man he had ever known. When some of the school's buildings burned down years later, Ruth arranged for the St. Mary's band to tour American League cities with the Yankees, holding concerts to raise money for reconstruction. He never spoke ill of his parents for giving him up during his childhood. And he never forgot his humble beginnings—or the fact that baseball had, in many respects, saved his life.

FAST TRACK TO THE MAJORS

Ruth's gullible nature made him the brunt of numerous practical jokes during his first spring training. But he took it all in stride, grateful for the opportunity to play ball. Enamored with Ruth's vast potential, Jack Dunn took a paternal interest in his development. Though multiple stories exist as to how the rookie southpaw got his enduring nickname, the most popular account alleges that coaching assistant Scout Steinman instructed Orioles veterans to take it easy on Ruth because he was one of "Dunnie's babes."[2] He was not the first "Babe" in baseball, nor would he be the last. In the first several decades of the 20th century, a number of professional players shared the moniker.

Ruth provided sporadic glimpses of his magnificent power in the spring of 1914. During a split-squad practice at the team's training camp in Fayetteville, he hammered a shot that was estimated to have traveled around 400 feet—a remarkable achievement in an era when baseballs didn't carry well and home runs were somewhat rare.

When he wasn't stationed in the outfield or at shortstop (a position traditionally assigned to right-handers), the Babe was honing his pitching skills. He had added a curveball to his repertoire during his St. Mary's days and was faring pretty well with it in practice sessions. He got his first trial against big-league hitters in an exhibition game on March 18. The Philadelphia Phillies had a formidable lineup that year, gathering more homers than any team in the majors while compiling the third-best collective batting average in the National League. Summoned to face them in relief, Ruth was conspicuously nervous, surrendering a pair of singles and a walk before recording the first out of the inning. With the bases loaded, he induced a harmless pop-up followed by a serviceable double play ball to shortstop. Unfortunately, infielder Claud Derrick misplayed it, scoring leadoff man Hans Lobert. A bit rattled, the Babe then coughed up another single for the second Phillies run of the afternoon. He escaped without further damage and tossed two hitless innings afterward as the Orioles rallied to win, 4–3.

Ruth returned to the mound the next day against the same opponents. With the O's trailing 6–0 in the sixth, Dunn called upon his boy wonder to subdue the Phillies attack. Again, the Babe was up to the task, striking out both batters he faced that inning. He followed with three scoreless frames as the Orioles staged a remarkable comeback, edging the Phillies, 7–6.

Ruth's first professional start took place on March 25. He was assigned the daunting task of facing the Philadelphia Athletics—winners of three World Series in a four-year span. The A's roster featured a trio of .300 hitters, two of whom were bound for the Hall of Fame—second baseman Eddie Collins and third sacker Frank "Home Run" Baker. The Babe yielded 13 hits to baseball's reigning world champions but repeatedly pitched out of trouble in a 6–2 win.

Dunn arranged for Ruth to square off against the A's again in a rematch the following week. Though he got hammered in a 12–5 loss, major-league opponents were beginning to take notice of his abilities. Collins told reporters, "Ruth is a sure comer. He has the speed and a sharp curve, and believe me, he is steady in the pinches."[3] Phillies coach Pat Moran remarked, "Ruth is a marvel for a kid just breaking in. I predict that within a few years [he] will be one of the best southpaws in baseball."[4] After an exhibition win over the Brooklyn Robins, Hall of Fame manager Wilbert Robinson predicted that the Babe would rise to prominence even sooner.

Ruth had assembled an 11–7 record by the end of June. But the Orioles were struggling financially in spite of his success. The short-lived Federal League (considered a third major league) had opened for business in 1914 with a team stationed in Baltimore. Instead of giving the Orioles some breathing room, owners of the new club built their stadium right across the street. As the inaugural Terrapins squad remained in pennant contention throughout the season, fans began to gravitate toward Federal League games.

In July, Dunn met with a group of Virginia investors who were interested in purchasing a share of his ailing franchise. The group wanted to move the Orioles to Richmond, but Dunn refused, walking away from the bargaining table. In order to stay afloat, he began selling off his top players. After arranging a pair of deals with the Yankees and Reds, he approached A's owner/manager Connie Mack about Ruth. Mack agreed that the young hurler was a can't-miss prospect but explained that he couldn't meet Dunn's asking price since his current roster—already crowded with superstars—was costing him a virtual fortune. The straight-shooting Mack suggested that Dunn speak to Red Sox owner Joe Lannin, who had money to spare in spite of carrying one of the best outfield tandems in history (Tris Speaker, Harry Hooper, and Duffy Lewis). As it turned out, Lannin was interested. Dunn sweetened the deal by including pitcher Ernie Shore and catcher Ben Egan.

The Babe was dumbstruck when he received the news. Though his Red Sox contract included a pay increase, he wanted to stay in Baltimore where most of his friends lived. Dunn offered his condolences and wished Ruth the best of luck. On July 10, 1914, the Babe found himself on a train to Boston accompanied by Shore, Egan, and Orioles press secretary Bill Wickes, who had been charged with the responsibility of protecting all three players from potential Federal League contract offers. Ruth didn't realize it at the time, but he would soon become one of the biggest names in sports.

THE TRAGIC DEATH OF HELEN RUTH

On the morning of July 11, 1914, the Babe stepped off a train at Back Bay Station in Boston and had breakfast with Ernie Shore at a nearby diner. It was there that he met his future bride, a 16-year-old waitress named Helen Woodford. Born and raised in East Boston, Helen (by most accounts) was the daughter of native Newfoundlanders. Whatever words passed between Ruth and the teenage hostess that day have been lost to the mists of time. But details of Ruth's Red Sox debut have not. After a brief stop at the team offices on Devonshire Street, the Babe headed across town to Fenway Park. While being fitted for a uniform, he learned that he was scheduled to start against the Indians that afternoon. He turned in a solid effort, yielding eight hits and two earned runs over seven innings for his first big-league win.

The Red Sox were well stocked with talented pitchers, and Ruth ended up on the bench before being transferred to the Providence Grays—Boston's newly acquired minor-league affiliate. By season's end, he had won more than 20 International League games. He had also established himself as a potent offensive threat. His first professional homer was a titanic shot that cleared the right field fence at Hanlan's Point Stadium in Toronto and splashed down in Lake Ontario.

Ruth asked Helen Woodford to marry him at some point during the busy 1914 campaign. In mid-October, the couple drove to Ellicott City, Maryland, to tie the knot. In another interesting development, the Babe was reunited with his father, whom he hadn't seen in several years. The newlyweds spent the winter living above George Sr.'s tavern on Conway Street in Baltimore.

After securing a starting position with the Red Sox in 1915, Ruth moved to Cambridge, Massachusetts, with his adolescent bride. In a rookie class that included three other future Hall of Famers, he emerged as one of the game's most promising young stars, compiling an 18–8 record and .315 batting average. His contributions helped the Sox win a tight pennant race over the Tigers. However, when the World Series arrived, manager Bill Carrigan limited him to a single pinch-hitting appearance in Game 1. Carrigan later claimed that he didn't want to start a green southpaw against a Phillies lineup stacked with right-handed batters, but most insiders realized that there were underlying disciplinary issues.

Just 20 years old and experiencing big-city life for the first time as an adult, the Babe had become an incorrigible party animal. Though he was seen with Helen at various public functions, he secretly maintained a bachelor's lifestyle, bingeing on food, alcohol, and sex. His insatiable appetites prompted teammates to refer to him unflatteringly as the Baboon or Tarzan, King of the Apes behind his back.[5] Helen kept up appearances for many years but grew increasingly unhappy over time.

Traded to the Yankees in 1920, the Babe had an affair with a model named Juanita Jennings, who gave birth to his daughter Dorothy. Adopted by the Ruths in 1921, Dorothy grew up believing that Helen was her biological mother. By 1925, the Babe's marriage was falling apart. Though Helen had previously been in the habit of staying in Manhattan during baseball season, she moved to Sudbury full-time while the slugger remained in New York. In 1927, the year that the Big Bam reached the peak of his career with a record 60 home runs, Helen (now separated from her famous husband) began cohabitating with a childhood friend named Edward Kinder. Kinder, a veteran of World War I, had graduated from Tufts University and opened a dental practice in Boston. For all intents and purposes, the couple carried on as man and wife.

On the night of January 11, 1929, Kinder attended a boxing exhibition at Boston Garden. Helen spent the evening alone and turned in early with the aid of some sleeping pills. At around 10:00 p.m., neighbors reported smoke coming from the windows of the Kinder home. By the time fire trucks arrived, flames had reached the second floor, where Helen lay incapacitated by the pills she had taken. She succumbed to smoke inhalation.

When police contacted Kinder at the Boston Garden, he told them that the woman who had died in his home was his wife. The story appeared in multiple newspapers and, recognizing her picture, members of Helen's family reached out to authorities. Burial plans were temporarily put on hold as a preliminary investigation revealed that shoddy electrical repair work had likely caused the fire.

Upon learning of Helen's passing two days after the fact, Ruth contradicted the statement made by Kinder on the night of the blaze. He explained that although he and Helen had lived apart for quite some time, they were still legally wed. Kinder ended up being summoned to the Watertown police station, where he altered his story, insisting that he had never claimed to be married in the first place. By then, members of the Woodford family had become suspicious and were demanding a full inquiry.

Circumstantial evidence implicated both Kinder and Ruth in devious subplots. According to Nora Woodford (Helen's sister), Helen had requested a $100,000 divorce settlement from the Babe a month before the tragedy. The slugger's agent, Christy Walsh, had tried to facilitate an amicable agreement, but Ruth refused to pay. Painting him as a villain, Nora claimed that the Babe had threatened Helen with a shotgun at the couple's Sudbury home prior to their separation.

Meanwhile, Helen's brother Thomas—a Boston police officer—was entertaining serious doubts about the circumstances surrounding the fire. He believed that since the Kinder home was relatively new, there should not have been any problems with the wiring. And he considered Kinder's absence at the time of the disaster to be highly suspect. When rumors surfaced that the dentist had been supplying Helen with opium, a team of Harvard pathologists was summoned to perform an autopsy. Additionally, narcotics officers were sent to search Kinder's office.

In the end, authorities reported no traces of opium or evidence of foul play. The case was officially closed on January 16. Helen's funeral was held the following day with Ruth in attendance. The *Boston Globe* reported that he was visibly shaken during the service. "His great chest rose and fell, he gulped audibly and his eyes filled as he dabbed at them with his big hands," the article read. "For fully five minutes, he struggled for control of his feelings and emotions."[6]

A NEW WORLD SERIES PITCHING RECORD

Though pitchers have historically proven to be somewhat inept at the plate, the game has seen a fair share of hard-hitting moundsmen. George Uhle compiled a .289 batting average over seventeen seasons. Wes Ferrell smashed 38 homers during his fifteen-year career. And Red Lucas, known colorfully as the Nashville Narcissus, set a major-league record (since broken) for pinch-hits with 114. Of all the pitchers who have emerged as double threats over the years, Babe Ruth is generally considered to be the most proficient.

The Babe compiled some impressive numbers before his mighty bat drove him off the mound and into the daily lineup. During the three seasons in which he made at least 30 appearances as a pitcher (1915–1917), he gathered 37 extra-base hits and 50 RBIs while hitting at a .302 clip. In 1918—when Red Sox manager Ed Barrow began using him primarily as an outfielder—he led the American League with 11 home runs. He blasted 29 the following year while winning 9 of 14 pitching decisions.

Ruth established dozens of statistical records over the course of his storied career. But since a majority of his greatest feats were accomplished in the batter's box, his adventures on the mound have been largely forgotten. In 1916, he came out on the winning end of the longest World Series game of the 20th century. Two years later, he stretched that performance into the second-longest scoreless streak in the history of the Fall Classic.

After being snubbed by Bill Carrigan in the 1915 World Series, Ruth turned in the finest single-season pitching performance of his career. Had there been a Cy Young Award in 1916, the Babe would likely have won it with his league-leading 1.75 ERA and nine shutouts. His 23 wins ranked third in the AL. The Red Sox encountered stiff competition from the White Sox and Tigers that year but came out on top at season's end. Hoping to enhance postseason revenue, the Sox hosted their World Series games at Braves Field, which had a much larger seating capacity than Fenway Park. On the heels of a 6–5 Boston win in the opener, Carrigan handed the ball to Ruth in Game 2.

Ruth's opponents that day were the Brooklyn Robins, who had held onto first place for four consecutive months despite a historic 26-game winning streak by the New York Giants. The Babe appeared to be in top form at the start of the game, retiring the first two Brooklyn hitters he faced. But the cavernous dimensions of Braves Field were a looming hazard. With two outs, centerfielder Hi Myers drove a pitch into the alley in right-center field—a 550-foot expanse. Known for his peculiar style of running with his arms held straight at his sides, Myers circled the bases with Brooklyn's only run of the afternoon.

Boston evened the score in the bottom of the third as Ruth helped his own cause with an RBI groundout. Both pitchers settled down after that, staging an iron-man contest the likes of which have rarely been seen in postseason play. After shutting out the Red Sox for 10 straight innings, Brooklyn southpaw Sherry Smith (whose career was otherwise unremarkable) faltered in the bottom of the 14th. A leadoff walk and a successful sacrifice put the Robins in jeopardy with one out. Going for the win, Carrigan inserted a pinch-runner and replaced Larry Gardner—who was 0-for-5 at the plate—with utility man Del Gainer. The gamble paid off as Gainer delivered the game-winning hit in what was undoubtedly the finest outing of Ruth's pitching career. The fourteen-inning contest was the longest in World Series history until the Red Sox and Dodgers battled for 18 innings in Game 3 of the 2018 Fall Classic.

Ruth waited two years to return to the October stage. By then, the United States was embroiled in a war overseas. Since baseball was considered nonessential, the regular season was preempted on Labor Day. A majority of the Babe's appearances had been outfield assignments, but given his reputation as a big-game pitcher, he was chosen as a surprise starter in the series opener against Chicago. He continued his postseason mastery, scattering six hits over nine frames and extending his World Series scoreless streak to 22 innings.

While celebrating with teammates on the train from Chicago to Boston, the Babe—forever a child—got into a playful wrestling match with rookie hurler Walt Kinney. He smashed his pitching hand on the wall of the train car, and by the following morning, his middle finger was swollen to twice its normal size. With the Sox holding a 2-games-to-1 advantage, Ruth was selected to start Game 4. Boston's trainer slathered the Babe's left hand with iodine, but it did nothing for the inflammation. The ailing hurler later complained that he had difficulty gripping the ball. He held the Cubs scoreless through seven innings in spite of the handicap.

Things finally began to unravel for Ruth in the eighth. Catcher Bill Killefer led off with a walk. Claude Hendrix followed with a single to left field. Losing his composure, the Babe unleashed a wild pitch, advancing both runners. He got the next two hitters on groundouts, but a run scored on the latter play, ending his scoreless streak at 29.2 innings. It was a record that stood until 1961, when Yankee ace Whitey Ford completed a string of 33.2 scoreless frames.

By the time he retired, Ruth had established more than twenty postseason precedents, including most runs scored (37) and most home runs (15). Buried beneath a plethora of offensive feats, his World Series pitching line is as follows:

GS	W	L	IP	H	BB	R	ERA
3	3	0	31	19	10	3	0.87

Pretty remarkable, to say the least.

THE INFAMOUS COMBINED NO-HITTER

Not all of Ruth's marvelous feats were particularly marvelous. Though box scores indicate that he participated in a no-hitter during the 1917 campaign, teammate Ernie Shore did most of the work. In fact, the Babe threw only four pitches prior to being ejected from one of the most unusual games in major-league history.

Ruth entered the contest with a 12–4 record—among the best marks in the majors. The game, originally scheduled for April 26, had been postponed due to extremely cold weather. When it was incorporated into a June

23 doubleheader, more than 16,000 fans turned out at Fenway Park to see Boston's most popular hurler face the lowly Senators, who were floundering in seventh place.

The Babe had trouble locating the plate from the onset. When his first three pitches to second baseman Ray Morgan (a .266 hitter that year) were determined to be outside the strike zone, he stomped around the mound and barked at umpire Clarence "Brick" Owens to open his eyes. Owens had little tolerance for insubordination. His nickname was derived from an ugly incident in which he had been hit in the head with a brick hurled by a disgruntled fan. And he had accumulated so many scars from altercations dating back to his minor-league days that NL president Harry Pulliam—upon offering Owens a job in 1908—bluntly asked the arbiter if he had been in a train wreck. Owens ordered Ruth to settle down and he did—for one more pitch at least. But when the next offering resulted in a leadoff walk, the sulky hurler stalked toward home plate and swore at Owens, drawing an ejection. Catcher Pinch Thomas tried to step between the two men, but Ruth swung away, missing with a left and following with a wild right that caught Owens in the back of the neck. Realizing that things had spiraled out of control, Red Sox player-manager Jack Barry rushed over from his infield post to help restrain the Babe. In the end, a police officer came out of the stands and escorted Ruth off the field.

Faced with an unexpected dilemma, Barry summoned Ernie Shore to take over. Shore was relatively unaccustomed to working on short rest, but he had some prior experience dealing with Ruth's disorderly conduct. During their brief stint as roommates, Shore had complained repeatedly about the Babe's unpleasant habits, which included walking around naked, cavorting with prostitutes, and rarely flushing the toilet. Barry initially asked Shore to muddle through one inning. When it became apparent that the hurler had supreme command of his pitches, he remained on the mound for the duration.

After Morgan was thrown out on an attempted steal by Sox backup catcher Sam Agnew (who had entered the game following the ejection of Thomas), Shore retired the next 26 batters he faced. There is no official count for the game, but the right-hander later claimed that he threw fewer than 75 pitches and hardly broke a sweat. The entire affair, including the first inning dustup between Ruth and Owens, lasted just one hour and forty minutes.

Shore's masterpiece was threatened on several occasions. In the fifth inning, Charlie Jamieson hit a hard smash that was deflected by Shore to the left side of the infield. Shortstop Everett Scott—among the top defensive specialists of the era—made a nice one-handed pickup and nailed the speedy Jamison at first base. In the seventh, Boston's Duffy Lewis climbed the steep ten-foot embankment in front of Fenway's left field wall (appropriately nick-named "Duffy's Cliff") to snare a long drive off the bat of Ray Morgan. And in the ninth, Lewis saved the day again, racing in to grab a sinking liner hit by Senators catcher John Henry. Left fielder Mike Menosky tried to catch Shore off guard with a swinging bunt on the last pitch of the game, but the rangy moundsman fielded it cleanly and threw to first to complete the historic gem.

The Babe was suspended for ten games, fined $100 and forced to issue a public apology. When he finally returned to the mound, he lost two consecutive starts. His name was associated with a perfect game until 1991, when MLB commissioner Fay Vincent assembled a "committee for statistical accuracy." The eight-man panel downgraded Shore's perfect game to a combined no-hitter. Harvey Haddix was another victim of the committee's actions, getting stripped of a no-hitter in which he had tossed 12 perfect innings.

Shore lasted just six seasons in the majors, missing the entire 1918 campaign while serving in the US Naval Reserve. He finished his career with the Yankees, retiring with a 65–43 record and a 2.47 earned run average. He was even better in World Series action, winning three of four decisions while posting a 1.82 ERA. He later became sheriff of Forsyth County in North Carolina—a position he held for more than three decades. He never tired of talking about the greatest game of his career, which indelibly linked him to one of baseball's greatest players.

THE BIG BAM VERSUS THE BIG TRAIN

During Ruth's pitching days, he shared the spotlight with several Hall of Fame hurlers. Though the careers of Chief Bender, Eddie Plank, and Ed Walsh were winding down as the Babe was approaching his peak years, Ruth had the opportunity to face three other mound masters in their prime: Walter Johnson, Red Faber, and Stan Coveleski. Faber, a two-time ERA leader who spent his entire career with the White Sox, was among the last legal spitballers in the majors. Coveleski, another member of that slippery group, enjoyed his best years in Cleveland, helping the club to its first World Series title. Though Faber and Coveleski were undoubtedly among the top pitchers of the era, Johnson (known to many as "the Big Train") was in an entirely different class.

Johnson has often been referred to as the greatest American League pitcher of all time. The ultimate sportsman, he never argued with umpires, yelled at teammates for mistakes, or brushed back hitters. Ty Cobb once famously remarked that Johnson's fastball appeared to be about the size of a watermelon seed and made a hissing sound as it crossed the plate. Various technologies were employed to measure the velocity of his pitches, which reportedly traveled at speeds ranging from 83 to 99 miles per hour. Using a windmill windup and sidearm delivery, the mild-mannered right-hander captured five ERA titles and three Triple Crowns while setting an all-time record for shutouts. Perhaps the most remarkable statistic of Johnson's career is that he won 417 games for a Senators team that finished out of contention more often than not.

In glaring contrast, Ruth was boisterous and cocky. He enjoyed being the center of attention. He didn't have the patience to develop a pregame strategy. Though he was able to identify the idiosyncrasies of various hitters, he couldn't commit their names to memory. He referred to everyone as "Kid" or "Doc." And he approached every at-bat the same way, treating opponents to a steady diet of high, inside fastballs offset by curveballs, low and outside.

High-strung and prone to emotional outbursts, Ruth's temper tantrums were the stuff of legend. Though he was relatively durable, he had a tendency to run out of gas in late innings. He was also known to lose the plate on bad days. On his best afternoons, he had an above average fastball, an effective curve, and a penchant for hitting his spots with mechanical precision.

Although Ruth really let himself go in later years, he arrived in the majors as a broad-shouldered, muscular bruiser standing 6-foot-2 and weighing roughly 200 pounds. One writer remarked that he looked more like a boxer on the mound. He was a smart—if not moderately adept— fielder. He wasn't a remarkable glove man, but he knew exactly what to do with the ball if it came his way. It has been said many times that he never threw to the wrong base.

Ruth's biggest detriment as a pitcher was his lifestyle. Even with curfews enforced by team officials, he was known to pull all-nighters before his scheduled starts. And his gluttony was notorious. He consumed massive quantities of hot dogs, beer, and steak (which he preferred raw). When manager Bill Carrigan introduced a rule prohibiting food in the dugout, Ruth smuggled it into the clubhouse. Yet somehow—in spite of all the alcoholic binges and food orgies—he managed to get the job done more often than not.

Showdowns between the free-spirited Ruth and the genteel Johnson were among the many highlights of the Deadball Era. Over the course of five seasons, the Babe locked horns with the Big Train on eight occasions. Though logic dictates that Johnson should have gotten the best of these encounters, the historical record reveals a very different story.

The two men squared off for the first time during the second half of the 1915 campaign. Ruth surrendered three runs that afternoon, two of them on account of an uncharacteristic error by centerfielder Tris Speaker, who led the AL in fielding percentage seven times. Johnson was less than spectacular, coughing up four earned runs on eight hits as the Red Sox prevailed, giving the Babe his eleventh win of the season.

There were five encounters between the two rivals in 1916, which was the Babe's finest campaign as a pitcher. Ruth went 4–0 in those meetings with one no-decision—a 4–3 Boston loss marred by a late-inning bullpen implosion. The most hotly contested game of the 1916 set occurred at Fenway Park on August 15, when the duo battled for 13 innings. Ruth held the Senators scoreless throughout while Johnson faltered in the final frame. After Jack Barry led off with an infield hit, Johnson retired the next two Sox batters. A single by Tilly Walker chased Barry to third and, with the crowd on its feet, Boston's Larry Gardner lofted a game-winning hit into right-center field.

The Big Train had two more chances to beat the Bambino in 1917. After another tough-luck loss on May 7, he finally had his comeuppance. Ruth, perhaps feeling the strain of more than 320 innings of work, stumbled against the Senators in his final start of the season, giving up 6 runs on 11 hits. Johnson—more accustomed to a heavy workload—turned in a stellar performance that day, earning his twenty-third win with a complete game shutout.

Though the Babe was credited with six victories in eight showdowns, Johnson's numbers paint the picture of a dominant hurler deserted time and again by an anemic offense. The Senators managed just 15 runs and were shut out four times as the Big Train posted a miserly 1.68 ERA. Ever the gentleman, Johnson harbored no hard feelings toward Ruth. In a 1920 article for *Baseball* magazine, he wrote flatteringly: "Ruth is still a young fellow with his best years ahead of him. There is no pitcher who can stop him or prevent him from making his long hits. As a veteran pitcher with most of his career behind him and a rather uncertain future ahead of him, I can only say that every time I am called on to face Ruth, I shall do my best to get an extra hop on my fastball. Whatever happens, I wish Babe Ruth the best of luck."[7]

On the topic of dangerous hitters, the Babe fared pretty well against them during his pitching career. In addition to Ty Cobb (who fashioned an extravagant .366 lifetime batting average), Ruth was challenged by some of the most capable batsmen in baseball history, including George Sisler, Tris Speaker, and Shoeless Joe Jackson. He held opponents to a cumulative .223 batting average. Though it will never be known how Ruth would have fared on the mound during the second phase of his career, it has been argued by many that he was on a trajectory to Cooperstown even before he became a full-time outfielder.

NEW JOB, NEW HOME

When the US government announced an impending military draft in September of 1917, players from both leagues flocked to local reserve units and war-related manufacturing jobs to avoid being recruited for combat. The Red Sox lost several key players as a result. Though Boston owner Harry Frazee orchestrated some savvy deals with the Philadelphia A's, the roster was still a bit thin when spring training arrived in 1918. Seizing the opportunity, Ruth began clamoring for more playing time.

Sox manager Ed Barrow, who had been hired to replace Jack Barry, did not want to risk an injury to his best pitcher by inserting him into the lineup every day. But he knew he was obligated to placate Ruth to an extent, so he offered the Babe a few scattered appearances as an infielder during exhibition games. In spite of his .429 performance in Hot Springs (which included four homers), Ruth was still officially a member of the starting rotation when the regular season began.

At some point during the spring, Boston captain Harry Hooper noticed that attendance was higher whenever Ruth was on the mound. Since the staff included several other quality pitchers, he reasoned that it must be the Babe's hitting that was drawing fans to the ballpark. The Sox were off to a decent start but couldn't seem to gain a comfortable lead in the standings. Realizing that another productive bat might give them an edge, Hooper approached Barrow about installing Ruth in the outfield. The answers was no—initially. But Barrow warmed to the idea in the days that followed.

Beginning with his first start of the season, the Babe reached base in fifteen straight games. By the second week of May, he was playing regularly on afternoons he wasn't scheduled to pitch. His finest day at the plate came on May 9 against the Senators, when he went 5-for-5 with a triple and three doubles. He ended up as the AL leader in multiple offensive categories, including home runs, extra-base hits, and slugging percentage.

On the heels of a World Series victory over the Cubs (Boston's third championship in a four-year span), Barrow was completely on board with the idea of using Ruth as an outfielder. But assorted issues with the pitching staff forced the hard-hitting southpaw into double-duty again during the first half of the 1919 campaign. As the Babe griped incessantly about being fatigued, Barrow responded by enforcing evening curfews. This led to an epic confrontation between the two men during a team meeting. Ruth threatened to punch Barrow in the nose, receiving a one-game suspension for his actions. He later issued a heartfelt apology and agreed to leave a note in the manager's mailbox on game days, informing his boss what time he had gotten back to the team's hotel.

The Babe's performance in 1919 changed the game of baseball. Not only did he establish a new single-season record for homers, but he put up stand-out numbers in several other statistical departments. His performance ushered in what would come to be known as the Lively Ball Era—a period of steep offensive production in the majors. As players began to hammer balls out of stadiums with regularity, various old-school strategies such as bunting, stealing, and sacrificing were employed less frequently. The rise in offense was accompanied by an increase in player salaries. Once again, Ruth pioneered the movement.

Prior to 1919, the Babe had asked for $15,000 per year. He settled for $10,000 a few weeks before Opening Day. After his blockbuster season at the plate, he told Frazee that he wouldn't play for less than $20,000 per season—a salary proportionate to that of baseball's most prolific hitter, Ty Cobb. While waiting for Frazee to make up his mind, Ruth maintained a busy schedule, participating in a series of exhibition games that netted him $500 apiece. He bragged monotonously to the press about his accomplishments while asserting that he deserved to be paid more than any player in the game.

Frazee eventually grew tired of Ruth's remarks and fired back. He assured writers that he was willing to part with any member of his club except for Harry Hooper. Backing up that statement, he met with Yankee owners Cap Huston and Jacob Ruppert to hash out a plan for the sale of Ruth. In the end, the Babe was sold for an unprecedented total of $125,000. The agreement included a $300,000 loan to Frazee that gave the Yankees a mortgage on

Fenway Park. Had Frazee defaulted on the loan, Ruppert and Huston would have owned the legendary Boston venue.

Justifying the transaction, Frazee told reporters, "I do not wish to detract one iota from Ruth's ability as a ballplayer nor from his value as an attraction, but there is no getting away from the fact that despite his 29 home runs, the Red Sox finished sixth in the race last season. What the Boston fans want, I take it, and what I want because they want it, is a winning team, rather than a one-man team which finishes in sixth place."[8]

Realizing he had pulled off the deal of the century, Ruppert assured fans that his primary objective as owner was to bring a pennant to New York. "I think the addition of Ruth to our forces should hold greatly along those general lines," he added. "We are going to have the best team that has ever been seen anywhere."[9] The Babe, who was not present during the negotiations, said he was not at all surprised by Frazee's failure to meet his salary demands.

As the deal was analyzed and interpreted exhaustively by the press in the months that followed, the *New York Times* issued a cautionary statement, proclaiming, "Neither club can be blamed for its part in this affair, but it marks another long step toward the concentration of baseball playing talent in the largest cities, which can afford to pay the highest prices for it. That is a bad thing for the game."[10] Furthermore, the Times article proposed that Ruth had sent a troubling message to established stars playing on small-market teams—that if they complained loud enough and long enough, their services might be sold to the highest bidder. The statement proved to be prophetic, especially when free agency arrived during the 1970s.

THE CURSE OF THE BAMBINO (AND MORE THAN A DOZEN OTHER PLAYERS)

Most people with a rudimentary knowledge of the game have heard a little something about the Babe Ruth curse. For anyone new to the topic, the thumbnail version is as follows: After the Babe was sold to the Yankees, the Red Sox failed to win another World Series for the remainder of the 20th century. They had some great teams and marquee players. They had their fair share of opportunities, capturing four pennants between 1946 and 1986. But something always happened on the road to baseball's most coveted title. When conventional wisdom failed to properly explain the second longest dry spell in major-league history (behind the long-suffering Chicago Cubs), sportswriters began to consider the supernatural.

The initial idea of a curse was disseminated by *New York Times* sportswriter George Vecsey in the wake of Boston's heartbreaking loss to the Mets in 1986. The Sox had been on the verge of clinching the series before a routine grounder went through the legs of sure-handed first baseman Bill Buckner in the tenth inning of Game 6. Vecsey's proposed curse gained momentum in 1990, when *Boston Globe* columnist Dan Shaughnessy published his seminal work, *The Curse of the Bambino*. From that point on, the concept became firmly embedded in popular culture. In 2001, it became the subject of a musical, which was produced again in subsequent years. In 2005, it served as the backdrop of a romantic comedy starring Jimmy Fallon and Drew Barrymore. When the script for the film *Fever Pitch* was originally written, it was assumed that the Red Sox would continue their losing ways. But when the team executed an efficient sweep of the Cardinals in the 2004 World Series, the ending had to be revised.

With the 86-year drought behind them, the Sox quickly became one of the winningest teams in the majors, running their cumulative championship total to nine (as of 2021)—third most in history behind the Yankees and Cardinals. Though no one talks much about the Curse of the Bambino anymore, it's interesting to note that Ruth was not the only player generously donated to the Yankees by the Red Sox under owner Harry Frazee. In fact, Frazee's frivolous trades kept the New Yorkers in contention for many years.

Before assuming a controlling interest in the BoSox, Frazee made a fortune in the performing arts. He opened a Chicago theater in 1907 and followed with the construction of a New York City venue a few years later. He also gained control of Boston's Arlington Theater, producing a string of hit musicals. In 1916, he expanded his interests to the world of baseball.

Putting things in proper perspective, the "curse" actually began in December of 1918, when Frazee traded pitchers Ernie Shore and Dutch Leonard to the Yankees along with left fielder Duffy Lewis in exchange for several low-impact players and $15,000 in cash. Though Leonard never threw a single pitch for the Yankees and Shore was past his prime, Lewis had two fairly remarkable seasons in New York before a subsequent trade sent him to Washington.

The second phase of the "curse" was invoked in July of 1919, when Frazee parted with one of his top pitching stars—right-hander Carl Mays. A 20-game winner for Boston in 1917 and 1918, the ornery Mays used a submarine delivery to mow down opponents. In 1920, he permanently mowed down Indians shortstop Ray Chapman with a wild pitch—an incident that haunted him for the rest of his life. He had several excellent seasons in the wake of Chapman's death, winning 80 games for the Yankees over portions of five campaigns.

After the earth-shattering sale of Ruth, Frazee continued to help build a Yankee dynasty, sending Waite Hoyt and Wally Schang to New York before the 1921 campaign. Used as a swingman in Boston, Hoyt forged a Hall of Fame pitching career in the Big Apple, winning 157 games over a 10-year span. Schang, one of the best offensive catchers of the era, hit .297 in five seasons, topping the .300 mark twice.

December of 1921 brought more charitable gifts from Frazee. This time, it was Everett Scott, Joe Bush, and Sam Jones who joined the exodus out of Boston. Scott, a slick-fielding shortstop, served as captain of the Yankees and BoSox while leading the American League in fielding percentage eight times. Before Lou Gehrig, he was baseball's reigning iron man, appearing in 1,307 consecutive games. Bush, nicknamed "Bullet Joe" for the speed of his fastball, threw his arm out in 1919 then revived his career with the development of a new pitch known as the forkball (which is similar to the splitter). His .788 winning percentage in 1922 was tops in the AL. Jones, who had a peculiar habit of never throwing to first base to keep runners in check, averaged 13 wins per season during his five-year stint in the Bronx. He tossed a no-hitter in 1923.

Not quite finished stocking the Yankees with exceptional talent, Frazee traded Joe Dugan in July of 1922 and Herb Pennock in January of the following year. Dugan was a staple at third base for seven seasons in New York. He hit .286 in that span while emerging as a clutch World Series performer. Pennock, a notoriously slow worker who frustrated hitters with his various quirks on the mound, won no fewer than 16 games in six consecutive seasons, securing himself a spot in the Hall of Fame.

Frazee's dealings with the Yankees were not limited to player transactions. Realizing that the Sox were headed for a fall, Boston skipper Ed Barrow approached Jacob Ruppert and Cap Huston about a job as business manager. After securing a release from Frazee, the Yankee owners welcomed Barrow to New York, granting him free rein over player contracts. Barrow faithfully served the organization from 1920 to 1945, assembling a long-running dynasty that included fourteen pennants and ten world championships.

In all, Frazee's transactions netted him over $300,000—an enormous sum in those days. But there were disastrous repercussions. As the Yankees became a dominant force in the American League, the Red Sox sank like a stone, finishing in fifth place or lower for fourteen consecutive seasons. By the time the new millennium arrived, the Yankees had won twenty-five world championships compared to Boston's five.

Over the years, Red Sox supporters resorted to a number of outrageous stunts in order to shake the alleged curse. Exorcists were hired and occult ceremonies were performed. One fan—acting on advice from a Buddhist monk—left a BoSox cap at the top of Mount Everest after burning a Yankees cap at base camp. In spite of all the lunacy, most level-headed folks realized that the Sox just needed the right combination of players at the right time to bring a championship to Boston. Even horror writer Stephen King—a proponent of many far-flung theories in his novels and short stories—knew the idea was nonsense. After the release of Shaughnessy's landmark book, King proclaimed, "There is no Curse of the Bambino. I, who was writing about curses and supernatural vengeance when Mr. Shaughnessy was still learning to eat the ends of Crayolas, tell you that it's so."[11]

How Ruth "Saved" Baseball in 1920

The Babe made his presence known immediately upon arriving in New York before the start of the 1920 campaign. A meeting at the team offices in late February included a memorable exchange. When Yankee co-owner Cap Huston spoke at length about the slugger's need to tone down his self-indulgent habits, Ruth responded with characteristic brashness.

"Look at you," he said to Huston. ". . . Too fat and too old to have any fun."

He then gestured toward Jacob Ruppert.

"That goes for him too."

The owners were flabbergasted.

"As for that shrimp," Ruth continued, looking directly at manager Miller Huggins (who was scarcely over five feet tall), "he's half-dead right now."[12]

The Babe had a talent for speaking his mind then walking away unrebuked—yet another effect of his thunderous bat. Just minutes after insulting team executives, he climbed aboard a train headed for spring training in Jacksonville, Florida. Though he was new to the club, there were plenty of familiar faces around. He had played with Ernie Shore, Carl Mays, Duffy Lewis, and Bob McGraw—a right-handed reliever—in Boston. Ruth would never have felt out of place anyway. He made friends wherever he went.

The Yankees were a team on the rise, having placed a distant third in 1919—their best showing in almost ten years. With Ruth aboard, the club remained in contention throughout the summer of 1920, ultimately falling just three games behind the Indians. In spite of another third-place finish, the Yankees generated the highest attendance in the majors, surpassing the Giants by more than 350,000 admissions (a figure that infuriated manager John McGraw and indirectly led to an eviction from the Polo Grounds, which the Giants rented to Ruppert and Huston).

It was a rough year for baseball. In August, Indians shortstop Ray Chapman was struck and killed by a Carl Mays pitch. The sound of the ball hitting Chapman's skull was reportedly so loud that Mays assumed the offering had made contact with the infielder's bat. When the ball rolled toward him, the Yankee hurler actually scooped it up and threw to first base. Chapman collapsed, dying hours later at a nearby hospital. Mays had established a reputation for throwing at hitters, and in the wake of the incident, other teams threatened to boycott games in which he was scheduled to pitch. Deeply shaken by the tragedy, he told reporters, "I would give anything if I could undo what has happened. Chapman was a game, splendid fellow."[13] Though he became a pariah around the league, he weathered the storm somehow, winning 26 games that year.

Things took another ominous turn during the season's final month when a grand jury was convened to investigate claims that members of the White Sox had conspired with gamblers to throw the 1919 World Series. On September 28, Chicago pitcher Eddie Cicotte admitted his role in the affair and implicated several teammates. It couldn't have happened at a worse time. Scheduled to face St. Louis in a three-game set, the ChiSox had a chance to sneak past Cleveland into first place. After Cicotte and his coconspirators were suspended by Chicago owner Charles Comiskey, the club dropped two of three to the lowly Browns and finished second. Eight players were permanently banished in the wake of the scandal, including "Shoeless Joe" Jackson, who had set a record in the series with 12 hits. On an interesting side note, Ruth once claimed to have modeled his batting style after Jackson, who he said was the greatest hitter he had ever seen.

During baseball's darkest hour, the Babe was among the few bright spots. But it took a while for his bat to heat up. The Yankees sought to cash in on Ruth's name immediately, billing spring training games as a chance to see baseball's mightiest slugger in person. Unlike his previous managers, Huggins did not enforce curfews and the Babe took full advantage of it. When outfielder Ping Bodie was asked by reporters what it was like sharing a room with Ruth during training camp, he responded comically, "I don't room with Ruth. I room with his suitcase." (Several versions of the quote exist.)[14]

The Babe—either due to overindulgence or lack of conditioning—failed to hit a home run outside of batting practice during the entire month of March. It was a tremendous disappointment to fans, many of whom attended games for the sole purpose of watching him knock the ball out of the park. During a late March exhibition, one unruly patron kept needling Ruth from the grandstand, reportedly calling him a "big piece of cheese."[15] The Babe, who had an extremely low tolerance for verbal abuse, climbed into the crowd looking for a fight. Newspapers reported that the excitable Yankee outfielder restrained himself when he realized that his tormentor was nearly a foot shorter at 5-foot-4, but the fact that the fan pulled out a knife probably influenced Ruth to a greater extent. Either way, the Babe was rescued by teammate Ernie Shore, who hauled him back onto the field before things got out of hand.

Silencing his critics, Ruth's first homer of the spring finally came on April 1—a tape measure shot off Brooklyn Robins hurler Al Mamaux. His bat remained relatively silent for another month. On opening day in Philadelphia, he was held to a pair of singles. During the home opener in New York, he sustained an injury during batting practice and saw limited action for the next week. He finally returned to form in May, fashioning a .329 average with 12 homers and 26 RBIs during the month. By early September, he had broken the professional record for home runs in a season, set by Western League slugger Perry Werden in 1895. It's worth mentioning that Werden had the benefit of playing his home games at Athletic Park in Minneapolis, where the foul poles were situated less than 250 feet from home plate.

As Ruth's assault on the record books progressed, beat writers began adding colorful nicknames to the existing vernacular. The Babe carried more than two dozen alliterative monikers at various points in his career, including "The Rajah of Rap," "The Caliph of Clout," and "The Mammoth of Maul." Attendance records for games at the Polo Grounds were broken many times during the 1920 campaign. And as Ruth's star burned brighter than ever before, movie companies began courting his services. In August, he began work on a silent film entitled *Headin' Home*, which was a fictionalized version of his life story. He received a $15,000 advance—equivalent to nearly $200K nowadays.

By season's end, the Babe was among the most recognizable public figures in the country with a massive fan base. Evaluating his performance against the backdrop of the Black Sox scandal, author Leigh Montville wrote, "The show was too exciting, too compelling, for a scandal to stop it. The Babe—though he probably would get too much credit for saving baseball from a crisis that never really developed—certainly was a huge part of that show."[16] On an interesting final note, Ruth was later forced to negotiate with the studio that had made *Headin' Home* for the unpaid balance on his movie contract. The check he received bounced.

THE BABE'S RECKLESS DRIVING

Growing up as a poor kid in Baltimore, Ruth had always wanted a bicycle. While training with the Orioles in Fayetteville before the 1914 campaign, he saw children pedaling to the ballpark and bought himself a bike. The Babe had an innate tendency to push the limits in any given situation, and before long, he was speeding recklessly through the North Carolina streets. According to multiple sources, he came tearing around a corner one day and almost flattened Orioles owner Jack Dunn. He ended up crashing into the back of a hay wagon and tumbling to the ground, shaken but essentially intact. Relieved that his top pitching prospect had avoided injury, Dunn allegedly quipped, "If you want to go back home, kid, just keep riding those bikes."[17]

As Ruth's salary increased, he set his sights on more expensive forms of transportation, purchasing a number of fancy sports cars. Like most things he owned, he used them up very quickly. He had little regard for the rules of the road, parking his vehicles wherever he pleased, driving them too fast and smashing into things repeatedly. His carelessness nearly killed him multiple times and eventually led to an arrest.

While barreling through downtown Boston in October of 1917, Ruth hit a trolley car hard enough to derail it. Authorities arrived on the scene and found him with a woman who was not his spouse. Though he walked away unharmed, the woman ended up in a nearby hospital. When the story hit the newspapers, Ruth's wife was justifiably angry. A passionate apology and sincere promise to be faithful from that point forward helped smooth things over (for a little while at least). But it was not the end of the Babe's extramarital affairs or his misadventures behind the wheel.

On July 7, 1920, Ruth was driving from Washington to Philadelphia after a 17–0 rout of the Senators. The game had featured a wild fifth inning in which the Yankees had scored 14 runs. Members of Ruth's traveling party, which included his wife, outfielder Frank Gleich, catcher Fred Hofmann, and coach Charlie O'Leary, were in a particularly jovial mood after the blowout victory. As the story goes, there was much merriment and several stops were made for moonshine along the way. (It could only have been moonshine since Prohibition had begun several months earlier.) While traveling on wet roads near Wawa, Pennsylvania, Ruth took a corner too fast. He applied the brakes, but his $10,000 Packard skidded into a ditch and flipped over. Helen and O'Leary were ejected from the vehicle while the Babe (according to various accounts) was trapped in some capacity. His teammates had to reposition the car with a mighty push in order to extricate him. Miraculously, no one was seriously injured, though O'Leary was knocked unconscious. In most retellings of the story, the Yankee third base coach woke up disoriented and exclaimed, "What happened—where the hell is my hat?"[18] Battered and a bit traumatized, the party fled the scene to a nearby farmhouse, where they were taken in for the night. Ruth told a local mechanic in the morning to keep the car because it had outlived its usefulness to him. The group caught a train to Philly as newspapers mistakenly published reports of the slugger's demise. It would not be the last time that deaths were presumed in association with Ruth's careless driving.

On September 10, 1920, rumors spread that Ruth had broken both legs in another car wreck. Teammates Bob Meusel, Del Pratt, and Duffy Lewis were said to have died in the crash. The story was debunked when all four players showed up at League Park in Cleveland that day. Ruth hit his 48th homer of the season and ran his average up to .374 as the Yankees prevailed, 6–1.

Having learned nothing from prior mishaps, the Babe ended up in hot water again the following year. On June 8, 1921, the Yankees were trailing the first-place Indians by just a game and a half. Scheduled to play against them at 3:15 that afternoon, Ruth decided to pass the morning hours by taking his roadster out for a spin. While cruising up Riverside Drive in Manhattan, he was apprehended for speeding and taken directly to traffic court. The magistrate—noting that the slugger had committed a prior transgression that year—sentenced him to a day in jail. Recognizing his value to the Yankees, police officials agreed to release him at 4:00. By then, word of his arrest had drawn a crowd of curious bystanders to the station on Mulberry Street. The throng—numbering roughly a thousand—was dispersed and the Babe was given a motorcycle escort to the stadium. One observer reported that he made the nine-mile trip to the ballpark in 18 minutes. If that report is accurate, then he was actually speeding again!

The Yankees won the game thanks to a ninth-inning rally, but Ruth's contributions were minimal. Inserted as a pinch hitter in the sixth inning, he walked and was stranded at third. He batted again in the eighth, grounding out to second base. The rest of the regular season went splendidly as the Yankees won the pennant and Ruth broke his own single-season record for home runs, pushing the mark up to 59.

THE 1921 SUBWAY SERIES

Describing the Babe's physical condition during the 1921 campaign, author Glenn Stout wrote colorfully, "Ruth was at his peak, a strapping 6-foot-2 and 220 pounds of still mostly muscle. His youth and exuberance burned off extra calories and alcohol. He had the constitution of a Clydesdale and had yet to gain that weight that would later make him look cartoonish."[19] Though Ruth's speed on the basepaths is seldom mentioned, Yankee skipper Miller Huggins identified him (in his prime) as the second fastest player on the team behind outfielder Bob Meusel. Huggins's endorsement more or less cemented the slugger's status as a five-tool player.

The Babe drew an incredible total of 145 walks over the course of his epic 1921 season. And he flirted with the .400 mark in September, peaking at .386. A walk to Ruth only invited trouble for opposing pitchers with Meusel waiting on deck. Playing in his second season, "Silent Bob" (named for his stoic persona) slugged 80 extra-base hits and drove in 138 runs. Though the duo combined for an unprecedented 169 strikeouts, they amassed more than 80 homers and 300 RBIs—numbers that were off the charts at the time.

The Yankees took the American League lead on the first of September and held on the rest of the way. Meanwhile, the Giants outpaced the Pirates by four games, earning the right to battle their intracity rivals for major-league supremacy. The 1921 World Series was significant in many respects. It was the first for the Yankees and the first to be played at a single site. Although this was often referred to as baseball's inaugural Subway Series, the term is not ideal since the prefix implies two teams sharing a city but maintaining separate addresses. Semantics aside, the clash in Gotham was also memorable in that it was the last application of a best-of-nine format. When attendance sagged by more than 10,000 in the final game, owners from both leagues voted to reinstate the standard seven-game arrangement. In the wake of the decision, one writer remarked, "Going back to the seven game series will make a lot of people believe that baseball is something of a sport rather than a purely commercialized form of entertainment."[20]

While it's true that the affair may have become a bit tiresome by the time the eighth game rolled around, it began with tremendous hype and fanfare, drawing people from every corner of the United States. The New York and Pennsylvania railroads made arrangements to add cars to their trains and run them in sections to handle extra traffic. Scalpers purchased tickets in large blocks and as rumors of a sellout swept the city, many fans shied away from the opening game. The crowd was actually well below capacity that day.

Though the Babe had appeared in three prior Fall Classics, it was his first in pinstripes. Owing much to Ruth's historic performance during the regular season, the Yankees entered the series as favorites. Living up to their billing, they won the opener and followed with another victory in Game 2. It came at a tremendous price. Taking no chances against the most feared hitter in baseball, Giants starter Art Nehf walked Ruth three times. Trying to make something happen, the Babe stole two bases in the fifth inning. While sliding into third, he twisted his leg to avoid the glove of the Giants' Frankie Frisch, scraping his elbow on the ground and tearing off a large chunk of skin. He finished the game, but by the following morning the wound had become infected.

A tough customer, Ruth soldiered on, delivering a big two-run single that gave the Yankees an early lead in the third contest. Unfortunately, starter Bob Shawkey couldn't find the plate, loading the bases then walking in a pair of runs. The bullpen was horrific in a 13–5 Yankee loss. Even worse, the Babe banged his elbow again during another attempted steal and ended up on the bench.

Ruth's wound was so badly inflamed before the start of Game 4 that doctors had to lance it. Though it was initially believed that he wouldn't play, he delighted fans at game time by jogging out to his defensive post with his arm swaddled in gauze. Incredibly, he banged out a pair of hits—one of them a ninth-inning solo homer off starter Phil Douglas. Ruth's blast brought the Yankees within two runs, but the last two batters went quietly, giving the Giants a series-tying 4–2 win.

The Babe's arm was worse than ever the following day and a tube was inserted to drain off the fluid. On the verge of being incapacitated, he played anyway, bunting safely for his only hit of the afternoon. A solid performance from Waite Hoyt gave the Yankees a 3–1 win, but it was all downhill from there. Limited to a single pinch-hitting appearance in the final meeting, Ruth watched his club drop three straight, handing the series to the Giants.

Rubbing salt in the Yankees' wounds, a writer from the *Sporting News* crowed, "The fans who shrieked their heads off last summer every time the Yankees knocked the cover off the ball had their eyes opened to the fact that it wasn't real hitting and it wasn't the lively ball that enabled the Hugmen to break all home run records during the American League race. Punk pitching was the real reason."[21]

Though the "punk pitching" theory is greatly exaggerated, offense in both leagues increased significantly during the 1920s. By the end of the decade, the single-season home run record in the National League had been increased to 43. And collective batting averages in the majors ranged from .276 to .292. By way of comparison, averages in the previous decade had peaked at .263.

THE SUSPENSION AND THE CAPTAINCY

The term "barnstorming" first appeared during the early 19th century in reference to theatrical troupes that traveled the country performing in assorted venues. In rural communities, these acting companies frequently staged their shows inside rented barns. Though the phrase did not appear in respect to baseball until the early 1900s, the convention began long before then. Beginning in 1860, major-league teams held contests in various cities on the way from spring training to Opening Day sites. Postseason exhibitions became popular as well.

Over the years, baseball's barnstorming tours have featured a wide variety of participants including women's teams (known as "Bloomer Girls"), bearded religious sects (the House of David squads), and Negro League clubs such as the Kansas City Monarchs. But major-league tours were not always permitted. In 1903, Pittsburgh Pirates owner Barney Dreyfuss forced his players to scrap plans for an exhibition trip in the wake of the club's World Series victory over Boston. Dreyfuss was not alone in his opposition to the practice as other owners soon began issuing assorted fines to barnstormers. In 1910, a clause was included in all big-league contracts prohibiting players from engaging in exhibitions without written consent from team owners. Justifying the rule, AL president Ban Johnson asserted, "It doesn't look good for a professional baseball player to be beaten by an amateur or semi-professional. It discredits the league."[22]

In 1916, the Fraternity of Professional Baseball Players fought back, challenging the rights of owners to punish major leaguers for barnstorming. "The players have, of course, no right to represent any club without the consent of its owner," said fraternity president David L. Fultz, "but as long as they trade upon their own personal reputations they are clearly within their rights."[23] Controversy continued to swirl as a new directive was added to the official major-league code of conduct forbidding members of pennant-winning teams to compete in exhibition games after the World Series. Ruth, who had a lifelong disregard of rules and regulations, decided to challenge the status quo in October of 1921.

When the slugger announced his intention of leading the Babe Ruth All-Stars on a barnstorming tour, Commissioner Kenesaw Mountain Landis advised players against it. Though the projected roster included Carl Mays and Wally Schang, both men backed out, leaving Ruth, Bob Meusel, and pitcher Bill Piercy to carry on without them. Another Yankees hurler named Tom Sheehan was recruited, but since he had not appeared on the World Series roster, his involvement was not in violation of major-league guidelines. The Babe understood the potential consequences of his actions, stating openly, "I am doing this with the full knowledge of what it may mean. When the bell rings after the World Series, why should I or any other player be kept from earning money?"[24] It was a fair question. Aside from Ruth and Cobb— the game's highest-salaried stars—most players worked in the offseason to make ends meet. But still—rules were rules. And Landis was committed to maintaining control in the wake of the Black Sox scandal.

The Yankees offered the Babe a bonus if he agreed to cancel the tour, but he declined. When he learned that the commissioner intended to enforce the rule laid out in section 8B, article 4 of the major-league code, he reportedly sniped (off the record), "Tell the old guy to go jump in the lake."[25] The tour lasted roughly a week and was highlighted by a heated exchange between the two rivals. "This case resolves itself into the question of who is the biggest man in baseball, the Commissioner or the player who makes the most home runs," said Landis. Ruth responded, "I am not in any fight to see who is the greatest man in baseball. . . . I am out to earn an honest dollar and at the same time give baseball fans an opportunity to see the big players in action."[26]

Again, Ruth had made a fair point. In the early 1920s, fans who lived a considerable distance from major-league ballparks were forced to rely on newspapers or magazines to follow their favorite players. Even radio was in its infancy then. Though the 1921 World Series was broadcast on multiple stations, announcers were not actually present at the games. Play-by-play accounts were re-created from live reports relayed by telephone.

At some point during the Babe's all-star tour, he had an unexpected change of heart and quit. An attempt to settle his dispute with the commissioner by phone was rebuked. While waiting to see what penalty he had incurred, he signed a contract to tour with a vaudeville troupe. Landis waited nearly two months to issue a ruling, fining Ruth, Meusel, and Piercy the entire amount contained in their World Series bonuses. Additionally, he suspended all three men for forty days—a sentence that lasted until May 20.

Landis was fair-minded enough to grant Ruth and Meusel permission to attend spring training with the Yankees. Piercy, on a different career path, ended up being traded to the Red Sox. In an attempt to bring about more ethical behavior from Ruth in the future, manager Miller Huggins handed him the honorary title of captain. It turned out to be the shortest captaincy in team history.

Before the Yankees broke camp, Landis announced that the Babe would not be automatically reinstated at the end of his suspension. He would have to file an application. Upon completing the process, the slugger returned to action on the agreed-upon date. He soon fell into one of the worst slumps of his career, going 3-for-30 at the plate in his first eight games. Overcompensating for his poor performance, he began pushing too hard.

In a game against the Senators on May 25, Ruth was tagged out trying to stretch a single into a double. The pressure on him was immense at that point and he lost his cool, throwing dirt at umpire George Hildebrand. He was subsequently ejected, inviting a hearty round of boos from the crowd. He might have exited the field without further incident had he not been treated to a stream of verbal abuse from a pair of Pullman conductors seated in the stands. "They can boo me all they want," he said after the game. "That doesn't matter to me. But when a fan calls you insulting names from the grandstand and becomes abusive, I don't intend to stand for it."[27] He didn't stand for it. In fact, he completely flew off the handle, climbing into the seats in pursuit of the hecklers. When he failed to get his hands on them, he jumped onto the dugout roof and challenged anyone in the stadium to a round of fisticuffs. There were no takers.

AL president Ban Johnson handed down a one-game suspension and $200 fine. Huggins stripped Ruth of his captaincy, which on paper had lasted for just six days. Though his bat eventually heated up, the Babe's unruly behavior persisted. On June 19, he was ejected for an angry tirade aimed at umpire Bill Dinneen. He was initially suspended for two games, but when he threatened the arbiter during batting practice the next day, he drew an extended penalty. He ended up sitting out five games without pay. The Yankees posted an 11–15 record for the month.

Though Ruth told reporters that his days of arguing with umpires were over, he contradicted himself on August 30, getting kicked out of another game for debating a called third strike with Tommy Connolly, who was actually renowned for his diplomacy. The Babe incurred his fourth suspension of the season as a result. In spite of his unsportsmanlike conduct, the Yankees took possession of first place on September 8 and remained there until season's end.

Ruth and Meusel led the team in most slugging categories, combining for 51 homers, 184 RBIs, and a .317 batting average. But that success did not carry over into the postseason. In a rematch against the Giants, the pair was limited to a collective 8-for-37 showing at the plate. Ruth was the goat, hitting .118 with just one RBI. Putting the finishing touches on a frustrating campaign, the Yankees dropped the series in five games.

THE 1922 WORLD SERIES (ATTACK OF THE BENCH JOCKEYS!)

Ruth had unintentionally exposed some glaring weaknesses during the 1922 campaign. Not only had he demonstrated a tendency to press too hard during batting slumps, but he proved that he was thin-skinned when it came to absorbing insults. Looking for any advantage against the Yankees in the World Series, the Giants chose to exploit the slugger's vulnerabilities.

Testing Ruth's patience, manager John McGraw ordered his pitchers to throw nothing but curveballs and to keep them out of the strike zone. Although the Babe drew 2,095 walks during his career (including the postseason), he preferred to swing the bat. Never was this more apparent than in the 1922 Fall Classic, when he walked just twice in 19 plate appearances.

The Giants verbally harassed Ruth throughout the series. His chief tormentor was Johnny Rawlings—a utility infielder who had sat out more than 60 games during the regular season. Rawlings had a penetrating voice and a vulgar vocabulary to go with it. Through the first three games, he rode the Bambino mercilessly. It achieved the desired effect as the Yankee superstar was limited to a double and a single in his first 13 trips to the plate. Rawlings's curses grew increasingly offensive as the series progressed and, by the end of the third meeting, the Babe was fed up. After venting his frustrations to teammates, he paid a visit to the Giants clubhouse accompanied by Bob Meusel. Rawlings was seated at his locker when the Yankee duo barged in.

"You little bastard!" Ruth growled. "If you ever call me that again, I'll choke you to death!"

Giants catcher Earl Smith, who had been in the bullpen during the game, asked what Rawlings had said.

"He called me a nigger," the Babe answered.

"That's nothing," Smith said matter-of-factly.

But it was to Ruth. During his early days at St. Mary's, schoolmates had saddled him with the pejorative moniker of "Nigger Lips." It had followed him for years and he despised it. He calmed down quickly after that and apologized for the intrusion. Before he left, he added, "I don't mind being called a prick or a cocksucker or things like that. I expect that. But lay off the personal stuff."[28]

By the end of Game 4, there was little need to taunt the Big Fellow any further. The Giants took a commanding lead in the series. And the Babe went out with a whimper, going hitless in his last six at-bats. His incompetence at the plate was somewhat overshadowed by a controversial development in the second contest.

The teams had battled to a 3–3 tie through ten innings when the umpires decided to call the game on account of darkness. This might have sat well with the 37,000 fans in attendance had it actually been dark at the time. According to numerous reports, the center field clock at the Polo Grounds displayed 4:40 p.m. as the official time when the game was stopped, and the sun was still shining. Fans let loose with a roar of disapproval as an angry mob surrounded Commissioner Landis's box. He required a police escort out of the stadium.

After the game, rumors swirled that the controversial tie had been a deliberate attempt to increase gate receipts. Landis acted quickly and decisively, declaring that the proceeds would be donated to various charities. Asked by the commissioner why the game had been called, umpire George Hildebrand said that a haze on the field had been affecting visibility. Sportswriter Grantland Rice was unsatisfied with that explanation, grumbling, "Due to the immense amount of money paid in and the great amount of gossip that baseball has drawn in the past few years, it would have been wiser to let the game run out at least another chapter to effectively stifle any shrill voice of indignant protest, fair or otherwise."[29]

It was not the first tie in series history—there had been two others in 1907 and 1912. But it was the last. A new rule was established soon afterward requiring all suspended games to be resumed at a later date.

RUTH'S SEXUAL ESCAPADES

Few players have enjoyed the nightlife as much as Ruth. Describing his voracious lust for women, booze, and entertainment, one researcher fittingly proclaimed: "Ruth grabbed life by the throat (or maybe it was another part of life's anatomy) and shook it up—frequently."[30] Though he was not handsome by traditional standards, he was a charismatic figure. He drew crowds wherever he went. Among those crowds were scores of female admirers.

In his biography *The House That Ruth Built*, journalist Robert Weintraub pointed out that "Ruth's effect on women was akin to the effect the Beatles would have forty years later—hysteria."[31] Indeed, women threw themselves at him constantly. And he lacked the moral fortitude to say no. Years later, Hall of Famer Waite Hoyt revealed that Ruth's personal magnetism benefited other members of the Yankees as well. The stacks of fan mail he received were filled with propositions from attractive females looking for a good time. Since Ruth rarely opened the letters, teammates often did the work for him, setting up trysts of their own.

While training in Hot Springs, Ruth frequently combed the Arkansas countryside looking for farmhouses advertising "Chicken Dinners." *New York Sun* writer Frank Graham, who accompanied the slugger on several of those excursions, explained: "What he really wanted was the chicken-daughter combo and he got plenty of them."[32] Ruth wasn't always very tactful about expressing his desires. During a lively party one night, he jumped up on a chair and announced crudely, "OK, girls—anyone who does not want to get fucked can now leave!"[33]

Ruth had no preference when it came to women. He liked them short or tall, slender or plump, attractive or homely. In addition to popular starlets, he frolicked with prostitutes. There was no shame in this for him. He habitually told St. Louis fans that he enjoyed visiting "The House of the Good Shepherd." While some of his Missouri followers assumed he was going to church, many of them realized he was actually referring to a notorious brothel. Putting it bluntly—the Babe loved sex. And he didn't care if the women he hooked up with were spoken for. This led to multiple run-ins with jilted lovers and enraged husbands.

During a spring training trip to New Orleans in 1921, Ruth was spotted by several sportswriters running naked through a train car. The reporters scarcely had time to process what they were witnessing before a naked lady wielding a knife appeared on the scene in hot pursuit. Details of the woman's backstory vary slightly. Some sources claim that she was married to a Louisiana politician. Others allege that she was unattached. In every version of the tale, she believed that the Babe was in love with her and that their relationship was exclusive. Since Ruth was friendly with the journalists on the train, the incident was kept out of the newspapers (as was the custom with many sports heroes of the era). But in 1923, the slugger's indiscretions were thrust into the spotlight.

As the Babe was leaving an Elks Club function in November of 1922, he received a summons to appear in court. A pregnant teenager named Delores Dixon had filed a $50,000 paternity suit against him. Ruth initially denied ever having met the nineteen-year-old plaintiff and then later acknowledged that he had become acquainted with her at the Manhattan department store where she worked. A host of sordid details were leaked to the public in the months that followed. According to Dixon's lawyer (a man named George Feingold), Ruth had sexually assaulted the girl multiple times in his car. Making the case even more compelling, Feingold claimed that Dixon had become "sick and disabled" in the wake of the experience.[34]

Attempting a bit of damage control, Ruth invited photographers to his New Orleans hotel during spring training and allowed them to snap pictures while he rocked his daughter Dorothy to sleep. Portraying himself as the victim, he said, "Look, I'm no angel. But ever since I made my home run record I've been hounded by con-men, gamblers and scheming women."[35] He referred to Dixon's case as "a hold-up game" and asserted, "I've been behaving myself for a long time. Seems that as soon as a fellow gets a little bit famous, he gets himself into a lot of hot water. I'll fight that case to the last ditch."[36]

It's a good thing he did. During the ensuing trial, the Babe's legal team was able to convincingly discredit the claims made against him. Feingold revealed that there was no Delores Dixon—it was just a pseudonym. He later admitted that his client had been hoping to extort money from the Babe in an out-of-court settlement. At a posttrial press conference, Ruth's lawyer presented a signed agreement stating that the case was being dropped. As Ruth returned to form on the ball field in 1923, the incident quickly faded from public consciousness.

THE OPENING OF YANKEE STADIUM

For many years, a myth has persisted that Ruth's great slugging feats directly led to the Yankees' eviction from the Polo Grounds. While there is certainly a connection between the two, the story is a bit more complex. The Giants' decision to remove the Yankees from their rented space actually took place in May of 1920, when the Babe was new to New York. And though the Yankees outdrew the Giants during each of the three seasons that Ruth roamed the Polo Grounds (provoking the ire of manager John McGraw), the real point of contention was Sunday baseball.

At the dawn of the 20th century, blue laws were still in effect. These laws dated back to colonial times, when devout religious practices resulted in the prohibition of many recreational and commercial activities. In keeping with this theme, the National League prohibited Sunday games in 1878. Though the restrictions were temporarily lifted at different points in time, the Sunday ban was still in place at the turn of the century.

Change arrived very slowly. In 1902, Sunday games were legalized in Chicago, St. Louis, and Cincinnati. Five years later, an attempt to lift restrictions in New York stalled out on the State Assembly floor. The Giants and Reds played the first Sunday game at the Polo Grounds in 1917. Immediately afterward, both managers were arrested for violation of blue laws. The subsequent acquittal of McGraw and Christy Mathewson signified a shifting paradigm in the world of baseball. In 1918, the Senators, Indians, and Tigers all began playing Sunday games. The Giants, Yankees, and Brooklyn Robins got the green light the following year.

Playing on the Sabbath brought substantial financial returns for the Giants, but with the Yankees still holding a lease on the Polo Grounds (a ten-year agreement signed in 1913), the earning potential was significantly reduced. In 1919, the Yankees played more Sunday games than the Giants. And though McGraw's squad outdrew Huggins's club by a wide margin that year, things were about to change. As Ruth began breaking down fences with his powerful bat, attendance at Yankee games went through the roof. McGraw decided that something needed to be done.

On May 14, 1920, Giants owner Horace Stoneham—acting on advice from McGraw—decided to terminate the Yankees' lease. The decision was based on the premise that the eviction would allow the Giants to play six additional Sunday games at a profit of more than $100,000. McGraw, who was resentful of the Yankees' newfound success, must have been fuming two days later when a Yankees-Indians matchup drew more fans than the Giants' last postseason home appearance in Game 6 of the 1917 World Series.

In spite of a bitter dispute with Jacob Ruppert over the purchase of pitcher Carl Mays in 1919, American League president Ban Johnson united owners in support of the Yankees. Under pressure from numerous rivals, Stoneham and McGraw retracted the eviction, allowing Ruppert's troops to stay put until the lease ran out. But the Yankee owner had no intention of hanging around.

When their offer to purchase half a share in the Polo Grounds was ignored, Ruppert and co-owner Cap Huston began searching for a suitable location in Manhattan to build their own stadium. They eventually settled on a 10-acre plot located across the Harlem River in the Bronx. The site—which had at one time been a lumberyard—was a holding of the William Waldorf Astor estate. In February of 1921, the Yankee owners shelled out $675,000 to acquire the property. A few months later, they gave the White Construction Company a $2.5-million budget and an 11-month deadline to build a ballpark.

When the stadium opened in 1923, *Baseball Digest* writer F. C. Lane proclaimed, "Yankee Stadium is indeed the last word in ballparks. . . . From the plain of the Harlem River it looms up like the Great Pyramid of Cheops from the sands of Egypt."[37] More than 70,000 people came to see Major League Baseball's newest wonder on April 18. The governor, mayor, police chief, and commissioner of baseball were all on hand for the season opener against the Red Sox. Ruth told reporters before the game that he would give a year of his life if he could hit one out in the stadium's inaugural game. Most fans in attendance wanted nothing more than to see that happen.

They didn't have to wait very long. With the Yankees leading, 1–0, in the third, the Babe came to bat with Whitey Witt and Joe Dugan aboard. He blasted right-hander Howard Ehmke's 2–2 offering into the right field seats for a three-run homer—the first in the stadium's history. The ball landed about ten rows above the railing in front of the bleachers, and the ovation Ruth received, considering the size of the crowd, may have been the most deafening of his career. As he crossed the plate, he smiled and tipped his cap to the fans. It remains one of the most iconic moments in Yankees history.

Reports circulated widely that the new stadium had been built specifically as a launching pad for Ruth, but nothing could have contained the Bambino in his prime. He homered in twelve ballparks during his major-league career. As for the remaining four locations—he appeared in a combined total of just seventeen games there (most of those appearances coming during his final season with the Braves, when he was grossly out of shape). Ruth's most productive setting outside of Yankee Stadium or the Polo Grounds was Shibe Park in Philadelphia. He clubbed 68 homers there in spite of the vast dimensions. Interestingly, the Babe didn't love hitting at Yankee Stadium. "All the parks are good except the Stadium," he once said. "There is no background there at all. I cried when they took me out of the Polo Grounds."[38]

THE BETSY BINGLE, THE ARRIVAL OF GEHRIG, AND A CHAMPIONSHIP AT LAST

The Yankees dominated the American League again in 1923, building a 16-game lead over their closest rivals by season's end. It was a weird year for Ruth. Though he compiled the highest batting average of his career at .393 and regained the major-league home run lead (tying with Cy Williams of the Phillies), he fell into a series of mini-slumps along the way. During one particularly frustrating stretch, he went homerless with 3 RBIs in the span of eleven games. Looking to get the slugger back on track, former Tigers great Sam Crawford suggested that the Babe try one of the new bats he was marketing.

Among the most popular players in Detroit during the Deadball Era, Crawford set the all-time mark for triples with 309. He also established a single-season record for inside-the-park home runs, gathering 12 of them in 1901—an unusual feat that has not been seriously challenged in over a hundred years. Finished in the majors by 1918, "Wahoo Sam" (named for the Nebraska town he was born in) continued in the Pacific Coast League for four seasons. He began tinkering with experimental bat designs in his retirement. The prototype he offered Ruth was known as the Betsy Bingle. It consisted of four individual pieces of wood glued together as opposed to a single piece of lumber. Another striking difference from standard major-league models was that the grains of the Betsy Bingle were oriented sideways.

Ruth preferred to work with extremely heavy bats (typically in excess of 40 ounces) and initially ignored the much lighter ones donated to him by Crawford. But when his power outage continued, he decided to make adjustments. The results were dramatic. Using the Betsy Bingle, he assembled his longest hitting streak of the season and pushed his average into the .390 range. The experiment came to a screeching halt on August 11, however, when American League president Ban Johnson announced that he had inspected

Crawford's bats and found them to be illegal. The decision, which appeared petty and arbitrary on the surface, was immediately challenged by Miller Huggins, who pointed out that "the rules simply state that the bat must be round, made entirely of hard wood and conform to certain dimensions."[39] Johnson allowed the controversy to simmer for a few days before issuing a response. He explained that he had no issue with the shape or size of the Betsy Bingle. The problem was the glue, which (in his opinion) served to increase the velocity of struck baseballs. He further contended that if the American League were to allow the use of this latest innovation, then other contraband material might be placed inside bats in the future. Though Crawford abruptly found himself out of business, Huggins needn't have worried. Ruth kept on hitting without his temporary crutch, peaking at .405 on August 30.

While the Babe was stealing headlines as usual, another Yankees idol crept quietly into the picture. On a train ride to New Brunswick, New Jersey, for a game between the Columbia and Rutgers University teams, Yankee scout Paul Krichell ran into Columbia's head coach, Andy Coakley. They got to chatting about a talented left-handed pitcher who was equally skilled in the batter's box. The young man's name was Lou Gehrig. After watching the sophomore hurler slam a pair of homers in three at-bats that afternoon, Krichell met with Yankees GM Ed Barrow, claiming that he had stumbled upon the next Babe Ruth. Barrow later wrote in his memoirs, "I had a lot of faith in Krichell, but I thought he was going overboard."[40]

He wasn't of course.

Krichell, a former catcher responsible for signing Tony Lazzeri and Whitey Ford during a long, successful scouting career, attended the next Columbia University game. Playing against NYU, Gehrig stuck out eight batters and hit another home run—this one a memorable blast that sailed out of the stadium. Upon hearing the news, Barrow authorized a modest $2,000 salary offer with a $1,500 signing bonus. Gehrig, a mediocre student with no particular attachment to college life, left the school and joined the Hartford Senators of the Eastern League.

Called to New York in mid-June, the man who would come to be known as "The Iron Horse" made sporadic appearances as a late-game replacement. He got his first start with the Yankees on September 27, slamming a two-run homer against the Red Sox. He clubbed three doubles and gathered four RBIs the next day. Huggins attempted to add Gehrig to the postseason roster, but the move was thwarted by Giants manager John McGraw, who had been given veto power by Commissioner Landis. McGraw's decision fueled the ongoing enmity between the two clubs.

The Giants were front-runners in the NL all season, eventually capturing the NL pennant by four and a half games over the Cincinnati Reds. Having beaten the Yankees in both of their previous October encounters, they entered the series feeling extremely confident. Commenting on Ruth's impressive numbers during the regular season, McGraw blustered, "I believe the same system which nullified his presence in the batting order in 1921 and 1922 will suffice."[41]

He was mistaken.

The series opened in the Bronx, where a capacity crowd gathered in the hope of seeing Ruth hit the stadium's first postseason homer. With the game tied at 4 in the top of the ninth, Giants' outfielder Casey Stengel stole the Babe's thunder, driving a Joe Bush pitch into the left-center field gap. The ball rolled all the way to the wall, giving the slow-footed Stengel enough time to scamper around the bases with the deciding run.

Ruth reclaimed the spotlight in Game 2 at the Polo Grounds, blasting a pair of solo homers, but Stengel struck again in the third meeting, lifting a Sam Jones pitch into the right field seats. It was the only run of the game and it gave the Giants a 2–1 series advantage. Stengel later joked, "It's a good thing I didn't hit three homers in three games or McGraw would have traded me to the Three-I League [a minor-league circuit with teams based in Illinois, Iowa, and Indiana]."[42]

Stengel's heroics were not enough to carry the Giants. Art Nehf was brilliant in Game 3, but none of McGraw's other starters lasted beyond the fourth inning. Bob Meusel drove in eight runs and infielder Aaron Ward hit .417 as the Yankees claimed the first championship in franchise history. Showing patience at the plate, Ruth walked eight times and compiled a .368 average. His three homers were a World Series record that stood until 1926, when he increased the mark to four. Though he would take the field with a number of Yankees greats over the next few seasons (Gehrig, Lazzeri, and Earle Combs, to name just a few), the Babe would remain baseball's biggest attraction until the day he retired.

RUTH'S ONGOING FEUD WITH TY COBB

In twenty-four major-league seasons, Ty Cobb established himself as the greatest hitter of the Deadball Era. He won 12 batting titles and retired with the highest average of all-time at .366. But his intensity and viciousness on the ball field made him one of the most hated players of his generation. Even teammates disliked him.

In Lawrence Ritter's celebrated work *The Glory of Their Times*, Hall of Famer Sam Crawford recalled, "Cobb was a great ballplayer, no doubt about it. But he sure wasn't easy to get along with. He wasn't a friendly, good-natured guy like [Honus] Wagner was or Walter Johnson, or Babe Ruth."[43] Outfielder Davy Jones, who considered himself a friend of Cobb's, was inclined to agree. "Ty didn't have a sense of humor. Especially, he couldn't laugh at himself. Consequently, he took a lot of things the wrong way. What would usually be an innocent-enough wisecrack became cause for a fist fight if Ty was involved," said Jones.[44]

Cobb's volatility led to a long-running feud with Ruth. Explaining the animosity between the two men, sportswriter Dan Holmes asserted, "Every time the two squared off on a baseball diamond it was a clash of polar opposites, of two different philosophies. It was New World vs. Old World. . . . While Cobb and Tris Speaker and other champions of the Deadball Era were still playing the game according to the established strategy of one run at a time, Ruth was ushering in a new era of fence busting."[45]

As baseball began to change and Ruth attained folk hero status, Cobb became a faded reminder of drearier times. Fans grew increasingly tired of watching the game being played as a chess match. They wanted something more colorful and exciting. The Babe provided if for them. Even in Detroit, where Cobb was just as firmly established as the auto industry, Ruth received roaring ovations. As could only be expected, Cobb resented it immensely.

Though no specific incident can be pinpointed as the one that precipitated the feud, Cobb fared rather poorly against the Babe in the batter's box. In fact, he struck out far more often against Ruth than he did against other pitchers. That couldn't have sat well with the petulant outfielder.

In Cobb's mind, baseball was a war that was both physical and psychological. He tore wildly around the bases with spikes flying, slamming into anyone who stood in his path. In the dugout, he degraded opponents with insults and ethnic slurs. The Babe's paunchy appearance, dark complexion and prominent nose made him an easy target. "Ape," "Baboon," and "Gorilla" were just a few of Cobb's favorite barbs. But Ruth did not sit idly by and allow himself to be insulted. He needled Cobb every chance he got, often inspiring teammates to join in.

One of the earliest examples of outright hostility between the two rivals occurred on May 11, 1917. Ruth was looking for his seventh win of the season against the Tigers at Navin Field in Detroit. The Red Sox were clinging to a one-run lead as the game entered the bottom of the ninth. Players on both sides maintained steady banter throughout, prompting a *Boston Globe* writer to report, "The Red Sox bench warmers gave Tyrus a great riding, getting what they were after—his goat."[46] Cobb got more than a verbal jab when he led off the inning with a bunt single (his first hit of the afternoon) then brazenly tried to advance to third on a groundout. Covering the bag, Ruth knocked the Georgia Peach senseless with a hard tag. Cobb lay on the ground in a daze for a couple of minutes. After the 2–1 BoSox win, the same *Boston Globe* writer remarked, "Ruth made Tyrus look cheap."[47]

Tempers boiled over again on June 12, 1921, when Ruth—responding to an insult made by Cobb the previous day—refused to have his picture taken with the Tiger star. When Cobb received word of this, he stood in front of the Yankee dugout and rendered a passable impression of a gorilla. Ruth charged onto the field, but umpires prevented him from getting his hands on Cobb. As the game progressed, the two antagonists exchanged words every time they came within earshot of one another. At one point, they stood toe-to-toe in a fighting stance, but no punches were thrown. In the eighth inning, a fight between Detroit first baseman Lu Blue and Yankee catcher Wally Schang broke out after a collision at home plate. As the benches cleared, Ruth and Cobb went straight for each other. They were about to mix it up when Miller Huggins literally tackled the Yankee slugger to keep him out of trouble. Harry Bullion of the *Detroit Free Press* remarked in the colorful language of the times, "Close to 32,000 people were undecided whether to weep out of shame for the athletes, give vent to joy or feel insulted at the spectacle."[48]

More mayhem broke out between the two clubs on June 13, 1924. Cobb—37 years old and serving as a player-manager—was looking to close out his distinguished career with a World Series title. Having split the first two meetings of a four-game set, the Tigers were sitting in second place just one game behind the Yankees. Cobb wanted this one badly and was willing to resort to underhanded tactics for a win. When the Yankees exploded for three runs in the top of the third, Cobb was razzed by the New York bench jockeys as he removed right-hander Lil Stoner from the mound. He extracted revenge an inning later, bowling over shortstop Everett Scott during a successful steal of second.

Play got scrappier as the game progressed. Detroit third-sacker Ducky Jones elbowed Wally Pipp in the face on his way to first base. Yankee hurler Sad Sam Jones (no relation to Ducky) threw at catcher Johnny Bassler in retaliation. The Tigers tied the score in the sixth, but the Yankees built a four-run cushion an inning later. Ruth stiff-armed pitcher Bert Cole on his way to first base during the rally, setting the tone for a major fracas. In the ninth inning, the Babe came to the plate again against Cole. After a couple of brush-backs, he pointed to center field and shouted at Cobb. Players on the Detroit bench peppered him with verbal abuse as he popped out. Bob Meusel was up next. When Cole nailed him with a pitch, he flung his bat aside and stalked toward the mound. Pandemonium ensued.

Meusel took a roundhouse swing and missed as the umpires restrained him. Ruth rushed to the scene in defense of his teammate but immediately found himself surrounded by a pack of Tigers. Seeing the Babe in danger, Meusel broke free and rushed into the center of the mob. There was some pushing and shoving, followed by an eventual lull in the hostilities. Order was nearly restored before a snide remark sent Ruth barreling toward the Detroit dugout, where he and several other Yankees tangled with various opponents. Wally Pipp joined the fray armed with a bat. The field became a dangerous place at that point as fans came pouring out of the stands. Police surrounded the Yankee bench to protect players from being accosted. In the end, the game was forfeited to New York.

Though there were no further brawls while Cobb and Ruth were active as players, there was plenty of trash talk. During a series against the Browns in May of 1925, Cobb announced to reporter H. G. Salsinger, "I'm tired of reading stories that say I get my base hits on infield groundouts and little bunts. The big guy, oh you know, Babe Ruth, he socks those home runs! Well, I'll show you something today. I'm going for home runs for the first time in my career!"[49] Making it look easy, he blasted three of them that afternoon in a 14–8 slugfest. He added two more the following day before reverting back to his old hitting style.

By the time the Georgia Peach retired in 1928, he had grown to accept and even admire Ruth a little—in his own way. He grudgingly admitted that the Babe ran the bases pretty well in spite of being overweight. And in a 1941 *New York Times* article, he named Ruth to his all-time all-star team. Summing up his feelings about Cobb, Ruth said bluntly, "[Ty Cobb] is a prick. But he sure can hit. God Almighty, that man can hit."[50]

When the National Baseball Hall of Fame opened in 1939, Cobb officially put his issues aside and struck up a friendship with Ruth. Describing the paradoxical shift, author Charles Leerhsen wrote, "[Cobb] was rich and seemingly content, after all, and Ruth was openly bitter about no one asking him to be a manager. Plus, Ruth had received seven fewer Hall of Fame votes than he had—a fact that was very important to Cobb, and which he often mentioned."[51]

After Ruth received a cancer diagnosis in 1947, Cobb played in a two-inning old-timers' game at Yankee Stadium to raise money for Ruth's charities. Cobb, nearing his mid-60s by then, was still as competitive as ever. When he stepped in to hit, he advised catcher Wally Schang to back up because he hadn't swung a bat in years and was afraid it might slip out of his hands. Schang fell for the con and Cobb laid down a perfect bunt, making it to first base safely.

BACK ON THE BARNSTORMING TRAIL

With another highly successful season in the books, Ruth had every reason to feel optimistic about the 1924 campaign. During spring training, he told Marshall Hunt of the *Daily News* to deliver the following message to fans: "You tell those people in plain language that I have been working like a trooper all winter on my farm, that I have never felt better in my baseball career, that I'm almost down to playing weight right now, that I'll try very hard to be adjudged the most valuable player in the American League again this year, and that if I don't sock 60 home runs, I'll buy Judge Landis a new white hat."[52]

The Babe should have kept his mouth shut. Not only did he fall more than a dozen homers short of his target, but the League Award (established in 1922 as a precursor to the contemporary MVP Award) went to Walter Johnson. In a surprising turn of events, Johnson's Senators clawed their way to first place in late June and hung on for dear life. The Yankees closed out the season with a grueling eighteen-game road trip. Though they swept the Red Sox, Browns, and Indians, they dropped three in a row against Detroit, ultimately finishing two games behind Washington. Explaining the club's failure to bring a fourth consecutive pennant to the Bronx, Ruth told writers: "We just sort of loafed and lazied along when we should have been doing our stuff. I'm sure we were a better team than Washington, but [Bucky] Harris's Senators got playing together and his pitchers could be counted on every time they went to the rubber and so they beat us."[53]

Lou Gehrig—who hit .369 at Hartford—might have had a major impact in New York. But Miller Huggins waited until the end of August to call him up. With Wally Pipp firmly established at first base, the untested Gehrig didn't get a single start. He looked pretty good in limited duty, however, going 6-for-12 at the plate.

With an unexpected opening in his October schedule, Ruth decided to hit the road with his traveling "all-star" squad. The commissioner's war on barnstorming had ended a couple of years earlier and there was no opposition this time around. The trip spanned over 8,000 miles and attracted more than 125,000 fans. The Babe hit at a torrid pace throughout, slamming 17 homers in fifteen games. One of them—a mammoth clout in Dunsmuir, California—was allegedly measured by a surveyor and estimated to have traveled 604 feet. If that figure is accurate, then Ruth's Dunsmuir blast is one of the longest in baseball history.

The Babe was an extremely busy man during the two-month tour. He gave nearly two dozen speeches and headed four parades. He fraternized with boxing great Jack Dempsey and Hollywood icon Douglas Fairbanks. He autographed more than a thousand balls for the *San Francisco Examiner*, all of which were sold for charity. In Los Angeles, he nearly fell off a grandstand roof hitting autographed baseballs to an assembly of school kids.

The most memorable game of the trip took place on Halloween in Brea, California—a small oil town located in Orange County. It was there that the Babe squared off against longtime pitching nemesis Walter Johnson. The Big Train had spent his teenage years in nearby Olinda and starred for Fullerton High School. When word got out that he was coming home to face baseball's most heralded slugger, tickets sold out quickly. Additional seating was added to the Brea Bowl in order to accommodate a crowd of more than five thousand—an impressive number considering that the town's entire population at the time was less than half that size.

In addition to Ruth and Johnson, a number of other major leaguers suited up that day, including the Babe's traveling buddy Bob Meusel. Sam Crawford, officially retired by then, joined the action along with Browns slugger Ken Williams—a lifetime .319 hitter who had led the AL in homers and RBIs during Ruth's shortened 1922 campaign.

Representing the Anaheim Elks, Johnson grooved pitches to opponents all afternoon. Ruth crushed a pair of homers, including a tape measure shot that sailed over 500 feet. Taking the mound for his "all-stars," he was far less generous than Johnson, limiting the Elks to a single run in a

12–1 complete game victory. The day's activities were concluded with a festive Halloween parade.

When Ruth returned to his Sudbury home (nicknamed Home Plate Farm) on December 6, he appeared to be sitting on top of the world. But he was headed for a mighty fall.

THE BELLYACHE

Prior to spring training in 1925, Ruth traveled to Hot Springs, where he had worked out with the Red Sox every year during his tenure in Boston. Hoping to shed some extra pounds, he hit the golf course, jogged, and soaked in the hot baths. But the nights of self-indulgence did him no good. He was still grossly overweight when he reported to camp in St. Petersburg.

Evaluating the unfortunate series of events that followed, author Jane Leavy wrote, "The gastric crisis was inevitable. Inevitable because everything about [Ruth] had become overstated: the meals, beer, pounds, spending, and even the linguistic entitlements. He had begun speaking of himself in the third person, a disease that has become endemic to the modern locker room."[54]

Nothing seemed to go smoothly for the Babe from the moment spring training began. First it was alligators. He jogged to his outfield post one afternoon and found a large reptile in residence. Then his wife and daughter showed up at camp, limiting his social opportunities. Another stressor was that he was being sued by a bookmaker for more than $7,000 in unpaid gambling debts. As if that weren't enough to dampen his spirits, he broke a finger on his left hand in practice and was out of action for almost a week.

When the Yankees headed north on their annual exhibition swing, Helen and Dorothy went home. Ruth—making up for lost time—partied like a madman. Describing the Babe's wild behavior during the road trip, teammate Joe Dugan remarked, "He was going all night—broads and booze."[55] After one particularly unruly outing, he was confronted by Miller Huggins. He got angry and charged at the Yankee skipper, but catcher Steve O'Neill intervened. The incident served as foreshadowing for an even bigger clash later in the season.

Ruth played well in exhibitions despite a lingering cold. He drank copious amounts of bicarbonate to settle his stomach, which had been bothering him for weeks. During a game in Atlanta, he was pulled from the lineup after a first inning strikeout. He returned to action the following day, but later developed acute abdominal pain. Advised by a hotel doctor to get some rest,

Ruth insisted on accompanying the team to Chattanooga. He slept for the entire trip then cracked a pair of homers. Though he was spiking a temperature, he appeared to be on the mend.

During a game in Knoxville, the Babe hit a line drive homer that knocked a branch off a tree in which several young boys were sitting. The startled youths scrambled hastily to the ground. In spite of his stellar on-field performances, Ruth was in rough shape. By the time the Yankees pulled into Asheville, his stomach pains had worsened. He resigned himself to head back to New York, but as he was making his way off the train platform, he collapsed. He was transported to the team's hotel, where a physician diagnosed him with the flu and confined him to his bed.

The Yankees traveled to Greenville without Ruth, leaving him in the care of scout Paul Krichell. After resting for a couple of days, the Babe set off for New York with his escort. They missed a connection in North Carolina and were forced to take a later train. When the original train turned up in Washington without the slugger on board, a rumor spread that he had died. One newspaper ran a banner headline announcing his demise. During the final leg of his homeward journey, Ruth fainted twice. He hit his head on a washbasin the second time and was knocked unconscious.

The Babe had wired his wife, Helen, at some point with instructions to meet him at Penn Station in New York. When the train pulled in and Ruth didn't immediately appear, Helen began to panic. An ambulance was summoned from St. Vincent's Hospital, but it broke down on the way. A second ambulance was dispatched—this one from New York Hospital—but its siren was not functioning and police intervention was necessary to clear traffic. Ruth, now delirious with fever, began to convulse and thrash about. It took multiple injections to sedate him.

By the time Opening Day arrived, the Babe was still at St. Vincent's and running a high temperature. His personal physician—Dr. Edward King—diagnosed him with an intestinal abscess and determined that he would have to undergo surgery. This sparked an ongoing debate among sportswriters as to what had put him in his current state. Prior to King's pronouncement, newspapers had reported that Ruth was suffering from a variety of ailments, including boils and the flu. One journalist—a man named W. O. McGeehan—ridiculously proposed that the slugger had collapsed after eating too many hot dogs. Others suspected more nefarious causes. Yankee executive Ed Barrow confided to at least one insider that the Babe may have contracted a venereal disease. Given his proclivities, the theory seemed entirely plausible.

Whatever the root cause, the illness came to be identified in newspapers as "The Bellyache Heard 'Round the World."

Activated by the Yankees on May 26, the Babe took batting practice and worked on getting back in shape. By then, the team had slumped to sixth place and compiled a sub-.500 record. The return of Ruth didn't help much. In his regular season debut on June 1, he went 0-for-2 with a walk. Proving he had lost a step or two, he got thrown out trying to score from first base on a double by Bob Meusel. One writer remarked colorfully, "He landed on home plate like a seal on a sandbar at low tide."[56]

Ruth's struggles persisted throughout the season. Though he finally turned things around in September, he fell short of the .300 mark. And for the first time in a decade, he failed to lead the league in a single statistical category. The Yankees limped to a seventh-place finish, but there were a few bright spots. Meusel won the AL home run and RBI crown. Gehrig—playing in his first full season—collected 53 extra-base hits. And Earle Combs won a permanent roster spot with a fine all-around performance. Though few would have guessed it by season's end, the Yankees were on the cusp of a dynasty.

THE BABE'S TROUBLED RELATIONSHIP WITH HUGGINS

In 1918, Miller Huggins inherited a Yankees team that had been struggling for a very long time. Seven managerial changes in the span of a decade had done very little to improve the situation. Though the influx of several high-impact players from Boston helped turn things around, Huggins found himself facing unexpected challenges. Describing Huggins's struggles in New York, Philadelphia A's manager Connie Mack remarked: "There seemed to be an impression here and there that anybody could manage so great a team. That's wrong. It took Huggins to make those fellows fight and hustle."[57]

While Huggins assumed an active role in choosing new players for the Yankee roster, many of his acquisitions proved difficult to work with. Carl Mays was sour and egotistical. Waite Hoyt was resistant to all forms of pitching advice. Bob Meusel appeared indifferent to the happenings on the field. And Ruth was the most oppositional of all.

In his book *The Big Bam: The Life and Times of Babe Ruth*, author Leigh Montville offered the following insight regarding the slugger's animosity toward Huggins: "[Ruth] forever had a bias against small men. He tended to bully them, to make them the brunt of his practical jokes. He paid small men no heed, as if physical size were the answer in all arguments, the small man's opinion worth nothing without the bulk to back it up."[58]

Huggins had never allowed size to become a detriment. Though most databases list him at 5-foot-6, 140 pounds, he was actually quite a bit smaller. He found his way to the majors in spite of his slight frame, forging a thirteen-year career as a second baseman. With a law degree from the University of Cincinnati and an intricate knowledge of the game, he aspired to the role of player-manager with the Cardinals. After five seasons at the St. Louis helm, he accepted an offer from Jacob Ruppert to manage the floundering Yankees.

It took Huggins four seasons to bring a pennant to New York. His patience was tested repeatedly along the way. In spite of Ruth's stupendous batting feats, he posed an ongoing threat to Huggins's authority. He made constant references to the manager's diminutive size, using derogatory phrases such as "Little Boy," "Shrimp," and "Flea." The two argued incessantly—though some of their clashes were actually somewhat comical. During a rowdy pennant celebration that took place on a commute from Boston to New York, Ruth (along with a handful of coconspirators) knocked on the door of Huggins's compartment and drunkenly announced that he intended to throw the Yankee skipper off the train. The exchanges went on for years, typically ending with the slugger getting the last word and Huggins quietly tolerating any challenge to his masculinity or power. But Huggins finally attained mastery over Ruth in 1925.

In late August of that year, Huggins hired a private eye to follow the Babe during a road trip. According to the detective's report, it was a week of total debauchery that included trysts with numerous women. Ruth wasn't playing horribly, but he wasn't living up to his potential either. And the Yankees were well below .500 for the year. When the Babe showed up late for a game on August 29 after having stayed out all night, Huggins finally put his foot down, fining the slugger $5,000 and sending him home for the rest of the season. Ruth threatened to go to Ruppert, but Huggins assured him that the owner was on board with the punishment.

"Five thousand dollars? Fuck you, you little son of a bitch!" Ruth bellowed. ". . . Who the hell do you think you are? If you were even half my size I'd punch the hell out of you!"

Huggins stood his ground.

"If I were half your size, I'd have punched *YOU*," he fired back. "And I'll tell you something else, Mister—before you get back in your uniform, you're going to apologize to me for what you've said. . . . Now get out of here!"[59]

Huggins had arranged for the Babe to take a train back to New York, but the slugger went to Chicago instead, where he mouthed off to reporters, blaming Huggins for the Yankees slump. Asked about his future with the team, Ruth said, "I won't be playing with them next year if Huggins is still there. Either he quits or I quit."[60]

As the days passed, the Babe began to come to his senses. He spoke with Ruppert about being reinstated, but the owner assured him he could do nothing in the absence of a direct apology to Huggins. Ruth eventually went to the manager's office and humbled himself, but Huggins was not impressed. Finally, after a nine-day layoff, the Babe offered an earnest apology in front of the entire team. With his dignity and sovereignty restored, Huggins allowed Ruth to suit up against the Red Sox on September 7. The penitent outfielder went off on a tear, hitting .346 with 10 homers and 31 RBIs in the remaining 29 games. It was too little too late for the Yankees as they placed seventh in the AL, their worst finish since 1913.

In the years that followed, Ruth obeyed orders and heeded advice from the man he had previously held in contempt. It was good for everyone involved, as the Yankees won three more pennants before the end of the decade and Ruth entered the prime of his slugging career. Paying his former manager the ultimate compliment years later, the Babe remarked, "Huggins was the only one who knew how to keep me in line."[61]

A HOMER FOR A SICK KID

Helen Ruth reportedly suffered two nervous breakdowns during the 1925 campaign—the first one coming shortly after her husband was admitted to St. Vincent's Hospital for his infamous "bellyache." The second one came later in the season in the wake of the Babe's blowout with Miller Huggins. Doctors said that Helen's condition had been brought on by the continuous stress associated with her marriage. The latest rumors concerned the slugger's not-so secret affair with Claire Hodgson—the model and former chorus girl who would later become his wife. When newspapers began printing stories including photos of both Helen and Claire, the Babe became irate, chastening a group of reporters. "What really gets me sore is these stories about me and women, and the pictures," he groused. "Those stories and those pictures are what put [Helen] in her sick bed. So I'd be very much obliged if you boys stuck to my baseball troubles and left my marital affairs alone."[62]

By the time the new year arrived, Helen and the Babe had separated for good. The farm in Sudbury was sold and the two lived apart from that point forward. Ruth turned his attentions to Claire but continued to chase other women (albeit a bit more discreetly than before). He had told reporters at the end of the disastrous 1925 campaign, "I have been a babe and a boob. And I am through with the pests and the good-time guys. Between them and a few crooks, I have thrown away over a quarter million dollars."[63] In a later interview, he increased that estimate to half a million, which he said had been squandered on gambling, bad business deals, and frivolous spending.

The Babe's spending was definitely an issue. He was an overly generous tipper at restaurants, sometimes leaving as much as $100 after a meal. He loaned money to teammates constantly without keeping track of who owed him (though he was a notorious borrower as well). One day, after a spring training game was rained out, he went to the racetrack and won about $9,000. Players didn't get paid until the regular season in those days. None of them were making as much as Ruth and many were broke. After his big day at the track, the Babe strolled into the Yankee clubhouse and put the cash he had won on top of an equipment trunk to be divvied up. "Well, boys," he said to his teammates, "look what I found."[64]

Before spring training got underway in 1926, Ruth announced that he would not be making his annual trip to Hot Springs. He also made it known that he had established a series of resolutions for the season ahead. This included keeping his temper in check, following rules, and getting back into shape. Proving his sincerity, he began working out at Artie McGovern's gym on Madison Avenue. McGovern, a former prize fighter who catered to New York's elite, was a recognized authority on physical fitness. Under his supervision, Ruth shed more than forty pounds and showed up at St. Petersburg ready to play.

In spite of the Babe's apparent transformation, initial reports from spring training were not entirely positive. A writer from the *Sporting News* proclaimed that "the big boy seems to be infected with a determination that will not be denied."[65] Other correspondents were less optimistic. Syndicated writer Hugh Fullerton predicted an A's-Pirates World Series and remarked, "Ruth is back in top form, but it is doubtful he can last through a hard season."[66]

There were a number of other question marks as the Yankees kicked off their annual exhibition tour. Aside from Herb Pennock, the pitching staff had been woefully inconsistent during the 1925 campaign. Lou Gehrig and Earle Combs were relatively inexperienced. And the double play combination of

Pee Wee Wanninger/Aaron Ward had been replaced with a rookie tandem. Called up from the American Association in September of 1925, Mark Koenig was slated to become the Yankees' regular shortstop. Tony Lazzeri, who had set Pacific Coast League records for runs scored, homers, and RBIs, was installed at second base.

Any lingering doubts about the Yankees' ability to compete were laid to rest when they won eighteen consecutive exhibition games and took the American League by storm. By July, they had built a 10-game lead over their closest rivals. In his triumphant return to form, the Babe hit .372 with 47 home runs and 153 RBIs. He was especially adept in the clutch, compiling a .396 average with runners in scoring position. Instead of chasing balls outside the strike zone, he demonstrated remarkable discipline at the plate, leading the majors with 144 walks and a .516 on-base percentage. The Yankees stumbled down the stretch but finished three games ahead of the Indians, claiming their first pennant since 1923.

In the National League, the race was tight with three teams vying for supremacy. In the end, the Cardinals outpaced the Reds and Pirates for their first NL championship. The club was managed by Rogers Hornsby, who also served as a full-time second baseman. Among the most cantankerous figures in baseball history, he once professed, "I've always played hard. If that's rough and tough, I can't help it. I don't believe there's any such thing as a good loser. . . . If I hadn't felt that way, I would never have made it in baseball."[67] Many players became unhappy under his autocratic leadership. One writer remarked that he controlled the team like a Gestapo officer. Another stated bluntly, "He was frank to the point of being cruel and as subtle as a belch."[68]

Clubhouse dysfunction aside, the Cardinals posed a legitimate threat to the Yankees championship bid. In addition to Hornsby—a seven-time batting champion—the St. Louis pitching staff was anchored by future Hall of Fame veterans Jesse "Pop" Haines and Pete Alexander (who won four triple crowns during his career). Demonstrating his characteristic swagger, Hornsby boasted to reporters before the series got underway, "We're going to come through winners. We have a better pitching staff, the better hitters and greater experience. That's what it takes to win."[69] Huggins felt the same about his own club, commenting, "It'll be whichever team does the hitting and we're sure going to do it . . . all the boys are cocky and ready to go."[70]

The series was a tightly contested affair that saw the Cardinals win two of the first three before dropping a pair at home. Hornsby had instructed his pitchers to avoid throwing strikes to Ruth and the slugger ended up drawing

11 walks. He hit a fair share of bad pitches too, setting a new postseason record with four homers. Three of them came in Game 4—another record that has been tied several times but never broken. The story surrounding that epic performance has become more celebrated than the feat itself.

The Babe had legions of young admirers throughout the country, but the most famous of all was Johnny Sylvester. Hailing from Essex Fells, New Jersey, Sylvester was nicknamed "The Babe Ruth Kid" by schoolmates in recognition of his exceptional baseball skills. Injured in a fall from a horse during the summer of 1926, he developed a bone infection in his skull. He was also said to be suffering from a number of other ailments, including blood poisoning, a spinal infection, and a sinus condition. By the time the regular season was over, the 11-year-old Jersey boy was reportedly fighting for his life.

Sylvester's father was wealthy and well-connected. He worked as vice president of the National City Bank of New York. Looking for something to lift his son's spirits, he sent urgent telegrams to the Yankees in the hope of getting some autographs. In particular, he was aiming for Ruth's signature. Not long afterward, a package arrived at the Sylvester home via airmail with two balls in it. One was autographed by players from both World Series teams. The other had a personal message inscribed on it from Ruth. It said, "I'll knock a homer for you on Wednesday" (the day of Game 4).

The Babe fulfilled his promise in grand fashion. In the top of the first inning, he went deep against 20-game winner Flint Rhem. In the third, he victimized Rhem again with a blast that cleared the roof at Sportsman's Park. After drawing a walk in his next at-bat, he stepped in to face Hi Bell with one out and a runner on in the sixth. He worked the count full before launching a moon shot into the center field bleachers. The Westinghouse radio announcer remarked, "Wow! That is a World Series record. Three home runs in one World Series game and what a home run! That was probably the longest hit ever in Sportsman's Park. . . . That is a mile and a half from here."[71]

After Ruth's unforgettable performance, Sylvester's physical condition was said to have miraculously improved. Though many facts in the story have come into question over the years, the ball autographed by Ruth with his promise to hit a home run in Game 4 has been authenticated. It is currently on display at the Babe Ruth Museum in Baltimore.

Another verifiable fact, Pete Alexander ended up as the hero of the 1926 World Series—not Ruth. After pitching nine solid innings in Game 6, Old Pete was called to the mound the next day. With two outs in the bottom of the seventh and the Cards nursing a 3–2 lead, Hornsby decided to pull Jesse Haines, who had developed a blister on his pitching hand.

"Are you all right?" asked Hornsby as he handed the ball to Alexander.

"I'm okay," the aging curveballer assured him. [72]

Rumors have persisted that Alexander had been drinking the night before and was still intoxicated when he entered the game, but the hurler adamantly denied that this was true. Drunk or sober, he had his work cut out for him with Tony Lazzeri coming to the plate. The Yankee infielder had enjoyed a spectacular debut, driving in 117 runs during the regular season. Without any warm-up tosses, Alexander got two quick strikes. The second one was a close call as Lazzeri lifted a wind-blown foul to deep left field. Old Pete knew that the rookie would be expecting a fastball on the next pitch, so he offered up a slow curve instead. Lazzeri swung through it, extinguishing the Yankees rally.

The series ended on an anticlimactic note. Alexander got Earle Combs and Joe Dugan on groundouts in the ninth. Ruth came to the plate with a solo homer already to his credit that afternoon. On a 3–2 pitch, he got the benefit of a borderline call from umpire George Hildebrand, drawing a walk. Bob Meusel, who had belted a double and a triple against Alexander in Game 6, was up next. Taking a major gamble, Ruth tried to steal on the first pitch. Meusel swung and missed as catcher Bob O'Farrell made a timely throw to Hornsby at second. Just like that, Ruth was out and the series was over. Huggins absolved the Babe of any wrongdoing afterward, commenting to reporters, "We needed an unexpected move. Had Ruth made the steal, it would have been declared the smartest piece of baseball in the history of World Series play." [73] Most sportswriters agreed.

In the wake of the base-running faux pas, Ruth visited Johnny Sylvester at his home in Essex Fells. This time it was the boy who offered comfort, telling the Babe he was very sorry that the Yankees had lost. Two days after the series ended, Ruth hit what is believed by many to be the longest home run in baseball history. It happened during an exhibition game at Wilkes University's Artillery Park in upstate Pennsylvania.

After six innings, the Babe was 0-for-2. Fans wanted him to bat again, but the game was already running well behind schedule due to obligatory stoppages for autographs. Realizing that there was no time to get the full nine innings in, Ruth challenged local pitchers to a duel. When Larksville hurler Ernie Corkran took the mound, the slugger instructed him to throw his best fastball. Corkran toyed around with a few curves before offering up a heater. The Babe pounded it over the stadium's 400-foot fence in right-center field. According to multiple reports, the ball was still rising as it left the park. It sailed over a quarter-mile running track and hit a fence situated in front of a grove of trees. The *Wilkes-Barre Record* reported that it traveled 600 feet. The Associated Press said 650. Exaggerating a bit, the *Scranton Republican* raised the estimate to 700.

Since Ruth's feat had taken place during an exhibition game, the story lay buried for many years. While conducting research for a book about baseball's greatest distance hitters, author Bill Jenkinson attempted to unearth the truth. With the help of the Wilkes University staff, he was able to measure the distance from home plate to the spot where Ruth's homer had landed. He also established contact with a surviving eyewitness—a man named Joseph Gibbons, who had been 10 years old when Ruth visited Artillery Park in 1926. Highly skeptical of Gibbons's credibility, Jenkinson questioned him about the game's details and found him to be a reliable historian. Speaking to a group of reporters, Jenkinson concluded: "I think the people from this area can rightfully claim that the longest ball in competitive baseball history was hit here. I think we can fairly conclude that this ball traveled well over 600 feet. There's no question about where [it] landed."[74] Ruth knew he had accomplished something extraordinary at the time. It was the first time he had ever personally asked to have one of his drives measured.

The Johnny Sylvester story ended on a happy note. The boy fully recovered from his injuries and later graduated from Princeton University. He served in the US Navy during World War II, eventually moving on to a position as president of a New York City–based manufacturing firm. He passed away in 1990.

RUTH VERSUS THE CURTISS CANDY COMPANY

It took Ruth just three seasons as a full-time outfielder to establish himself as baseball's all-time home run leader. But even before he surpassed the lifetime totals of deadball superstar Roger Connor, he was among the most celebrated heroes in the world of sports. Looking to cash in on that fame, journalist Christy Walsh inserted himself directly into the slugger's orbit.

Originally trained as a lawyer, Walsh had worked as a reporter and cartoonist for the *Los Angeles Herald*. He began ghostwriting articles for various celebrities early in his career and later accepted a position as an adman for a Detroit-based automobile company. He turned to ghostwriting full time after being fired from that job. Hoping to sign Ruth as a client, he began hanging around the Ansonia Hotel in New York, where the Babe lived with his first wife. A chance encounter never materialized, so he allegedly disguised himself as a deliveryman to gain access to the outfielder's suite. He convinced Ruth to accept a sizeable advance for the use of his name in subsequent articles. It was the beginning of a long, lucrative relationship.

Walsh's clients later included Ty Cobb, Lou Gehrig, Dizzy Dean, and Walter Johnson (who accepted Walsh's proposal after being followed into the bathroom of a New Haven, Connecticut, train station). Since the Babe was very much in demand and unable to effectively handle his own publicity, Walsh was placed in charge of his bookings. He encouraged Ruth to lend his name and image to various commercial products. Beginning in the 1920s and continuing until his death in 1948, the slugger endorsed dozens of items in a variety of markets. This included a brief venture into the candy industry.

Founded in 1916, the Curtiss Candy Company was located a few blocks from Wrigley Field in Chicago. Their top-selling product was a treat known as the Kandy Kake, which featured chocolate, peanuts, and a pudding-filled center. As sales began to slump, owner Otto Schnering instructed his developers to reformulate the Kandy Kake recipe in an attempt to compete with enterprising rivals. What they came up with was a mixture of peanuts, caramel, and nougat smothered in chocolate. Schnering named it the Baby Ruth bar.

At five cents, Schnering's new product cost half as much as competitors. And with a single letter altered, the Curtiss company avoided having to pay royalties to baseball's reigning home run king. The general public assumed that the candy was named after the ballplayer, and within a few years, the Baby Ruth bar was raking in about $1 million per month. Things rolled along smoothly for Schnering until the slugger decided to break into the business.

Acting on advice from Walsh, the Babe lent his name to the George H. Ruth Candy Company. Packaged in a wrapper featuring the slugger's likeness, Ruth's Home Run candy hit the shelves in 1926. Schnering—recognizing this as a threat to his livelihood—sued for copyright infringement. Justifying the lawsuit, he explained that the Baby Ruth bar had been named after US president Grover Cleveland's daughter.

There were a few glaring issues with Schnering's claim. First of all, Ruth Cleveland had been born in 1891. Though newspapers focused attention on her during her father's second term in office, the commander in chief repeatedly refused photograph requests. So a majority of Americans didn't even know what Ruth Cleveland looked like during her lifetime. The oldest of five children born to the president and first lady, Ruth was a sickly child. She died of diphtheria in 1904—17 years before the introduction of the candy bar. And so, if Schnering's assertion was truthful, then the Baby Ruth had been named after a highly obscure and virtually forgotten historical figure—a dubious story at best.

Nevertheless, in the case of the *George H. Ruth Candy Company v. Curtiss Candy*, a US patent court sided with Schnering, contending that Ruth was trying to cash in on the similarity of his name to that of the renowned confection. Ruth's Home Run candy was forced off the market in the early 1930s. The Babe—in spite of this setback—maintained a handsome income from numerous other endorsements. He issued a gruff statement to Schnering in the wake of the fiasco: "Well, I ain't eating your damned candy bar anymore!"[75]

The Curtiss Candy Company continued to exploit its connection (either coincidental or intentional) to the Yankee superstar. After Ruth's alleged "called shot" in Game 3 of the 1932 World Series at Wrigley Field, Schnering had an enormous Baby Ruth sign installed on a neighboring rooftop beyond the ballpark's center field wall. It was visible to fans for decades. Though the company changed hands several times during the 20th century, executives continued to use the candy bar's association with baseball to an advantage. It became the official candy bar of Major League Baseball in 2006. By then, it was a Nestle product.

In her acclaimed work *The Big Fella: Babe Ruth and the World He Created*, author Jane Leavy quoted Kevin Goering, a sports litigation expert, on the topic of the landmark Baby Ruth case. "Ruth's attorneys were never able to argue the merits of the case or enter evidence of all the ways Curtiss profited from the presumption of his participation," said Goering. "This manifest injustice was a comedy of errors on the part of his lawyers, the courts and the undeveloped state of the law in 1926. The right of publicity should have been born right then."[76]

Many decades after his death, Ruth's name and image were still being licensed to more than a hundred companies and products, including trading cards, art prints, and teddy bears. In a 1989 interview, Mark Roesler, president of the Curtis Management Group, told a writer from the *Los Angeles Times*, "The legend of Babe Ruth is a very tangible thing. The Babe's image as the ultimate hitter, the ultimate superstar isn't going to change.... He's achieved his place in history. Current players have not."[77] In 1989, fees paid to the Ruth family, which included his surviving daughter, Julia Ruth

Stevens, were reported at $400,000. That revenue increased substantially in the years that followed.

RUTH HITS THE SILVER SCREEN

On the heels of the 1926 World Series loss, the Babe embarked on a two-week barnstorming trip. He followed with a three-month vaudeville tour that netted him $100,000—the largest sum ever paid to a headliner during the era. When the show hit the West Coast, he landed a deal with First National Pictures to star in a full-length silent film entitled *Babe Comes Home.*

Unlike the company that had gone belly-up after Ruth's 1920 starring role, First National Pictures was an industry leader. Founded in 1917, it became the country's largest theater chain. By 1924, it was the most important studio in the business. Some of the brightest stars of the silent film era worked for First National, including Charlie Chaplin and Mary Pickford, who cofounded United Artists with Douglas Fairbanks.

Ted Wilde, director of *Babe Comes Home,* was a veteran in the trade, having worked on multiple projects with renowned silent film comedian Harold Lloyd. The Babe's costar, a blonde bombshell named Anna Q. Nilsson, was a former model who had been named the "Most Beautiful Woman in America." Born in Sweden, she accumulated two hundred film credits during her career, hitting her peak before the introduction of sound. She was the first Swedish-born actress to get a star on the Hollywood Walk of Fame. Though she was reluctant to accept a role with Ruth as a leading man, she grew to enjoy working with him, remarking to members of the press, "What he lacks in polish and experience, he makes up in ardor and seriousness. . . . I really believe that when he is more accustomed to this sort of thing, he may develop into a screen Don Juan."[78]

Based on a short story by Gerald Beaumont, whose work was adapted into more than fifty film projects, *Babe Comes Home* had not been written with Ruth in mind. The script, which was originally entitled *Said with Soap,* had been purchased months earlier. It wasn't until Ruth came to LA with his vaudeville troupe that executives entertained the idea of casting him in the leading role. His contract stipulated that filming would not interfere with his off-season training. To get in shape for the 1927 campaign, he invited his personal fitness instructor, Artie McGovern, to join him in California. McGovern arrived to find Ruth already in excellent physical condition, eliminating the need for any rigorous routines.

An upbeat romantic comedy, *Babe Comes Home* tells the story of Babe Dugan, star of the Angels ball club. Dugan (played by Ruth) is a tobacco-chewing slob who always manages to get his uniform filthier than any of his teammates. Nilsson plays Vernie, the laundress who cleans the team's uniforms weekly. When she notices that one particular garment is constantly soiled with dirt and tobacco juice, she writes a note to the club owner. Dugan's response inspires Vernie to attend her first ballgame to see him in action. During the game, Dugan lifts a foul ball into the stands that hits the laundress and leaves her with a black eye. Feeling regretful, he visits her home with candy and flowers. A romance follows and the two are soon engaged to be married. Unable to deal with her fiancé's tobacco habit, Vernie vows to reform him. The slugger changes his ways but falls into a horrible batting slump. In the movie's climax, Vernie relents and gives Dugan a plug of tobacco. Like Popeye with his spinach, the fictional Babe smashes a big homer at a critical moment for his team.

The 60-minute silent comedy was shot in three weeks. The baseball scenes were filmed at Wrigley Field in Los Angeles—home of the Pacific Coast League Angels. The park, opened in 1925, was another holding of Chicago Cubs owner William Wrigley Jr. Designed as a smaller version of its big-league counterpart, the stadium had a seating capacity of 21,000. The producers of *Babe Comes Home* wanted to fill Wrigley Field with fans for the movie's pivotal scene. In order to recruit volunteers, they placed an ad in the newspaper announcing that the Babe would put on a hitting display before shooting began. As promised, Ruth stood at home plate swatting balls all over the park for a full hour. The pitcher hired for the occasion was instructed to throw nothing but strikes.

While the film was being shot, Jacob Ruppert mailed a contract proposal to the Babe, offering him $52,000 for the upcoming season. Having already received $100,000 for the vaudeville tour and over $70,000 for the movie deal, Ruth scoffed at the lowball offer. He sent the proposal back unsigned with a note asking for $100K per year over two campaigns. Interviewed during one of the Wrigley Field shoots, he said, "It would hurt me a lot to leave baseball. I've lived and breathed the game since I was a kid. . . . About the movies, I like the work. It gets rather tiresome at times, but if it was purely a financial question, they make the best bid."[79] Responding to his remarks, Ruppert explained that the contract had been mailed as a formality to avoid giving other teams a chance at signing him. When filming was wrapped in late-February, Ruth returned to New York and met with the Yankee owner, who increased his offer to $70,000 per year over three seasons. The slugger agreed, becoming the highest-paid player in the game.

When it debuted in May of 1927, *Babe Comes Home* had the misfortune of competing against two other popular baseball movies: Paramount's *Casey at the Bat* and Metro-Goldwyn-Mayer's *Slide, Kelly! Slide!* Ruth's project wasn't a commercial success, but it generated a few positive reviews. One critic wrote, "If [the Babe] wanted to quit the diamond and crash the movies for keeps, he would more than make good."[80] Not everyone agreed. A respected trade magazine referred to the film as "pretty vulgar stuff as a whole."[81]

Interestingly, *Babe Comes Home* was banned in areas of Chicago due to its graphic depiction of tobacco use. Studio executives were forced to negotiate a diplomatic resolution. Though Ruth made other film appearances in the years that followed, including the 1928 Harold Lloyd comedy *Speedy*, he never had a leading role in a full-length feature again.

MURDERER'S ROW

The 1927 Yankees have often been identified as the greatest team in baseball history. But no one seems to know precisely where the term "Murderer's Row" came from. The moniker, which predated the team itself, can be traced to at least two potential sources: a seedy backstreet in Manhattan where degenerates often congregated or a block of cells in a New York City prison (known as "The Tombs") that housed violent criminals. Both were dubbed "Murderer's Row" during the 19th century. In 1918, the phrase was used by a sportswriter to describe a mediocre Yankees lineup that included Frank "Home Run" Baker, Wally Pipp, and Del Pratt. It took on a whole new meaning in 1927, when Ruth and Gehrig were in their prime.

During the 1980s, statisticians began inventing new ways to effectively measure the performances of players. One method that has gained credibility in recent years is a metric known as Wins Above Replacement (WAR). Though not officially recognized by Major League Baseball, WAR scores appear on all the leading statistical websites and are commonly used by assorted baseball insiders. The WAR formula (which varies slightly from source to source) attempts to quantify a player's contributions to his team. It should come as no surprise that Ruth's lifetime WAR score is the highest of all time while Gehrig's is in the top twenty. But advanced statistics are not necessary to determine that the two luminaries were vital components of the Murder's Row Yankees. From 1927 through 1931, the duo combined for more homers and RBIs than any pair of teammates in the American League. The other "murderers" in the New York lineup have captured far less attention over the years.

Earle Combs, known to many fans as "The Kentucky Colonel," was New York's leadoff man. An excellent bunter with a keen bating eye, he kept his on-base percentage around .400 throughout his career. He retired with a lifetime batting average of .325. Defensively, he was among the best in the game, leading the American League in putouts twice. On a personal level, he was a pleasant, unassuming man who gave teammates most of the credit for the Yankees' success. In his 1970 Cooperstown induction speech, he said, "I thought the Hall of Fame was for superstars, not just average players like me."[82]

Mark Koenig batted second. Though he played for five different teams, he gave his best years to the Yankees. During the four seasons in which he was New York's primary shortstop, he hit .290, averaging 82 runs scored and 58 RBIs per year. Forever grateful for the opportunity to wear a Yankees uniform during the Ruth era, he admitted humbly, "If I had joined another club during that time, I wouldn't have lasted a year. I was lucky to be on that club. They could have played a midget at shortstop."[83]

Bob Meusel appeared fifth in the order behind Ruth and Gehrig. Identified by Miller Huggins as the fastest player on the team, he spent significant portions of time in both right and left field, where his strong, accurate arm was highly respected by opponents. He hit .313 or better in seven of his first eight seasons. And his cumulative RBI total during the 1920s was second most for a right-handed hitter. Because he was extremely quiet and unnaturally calm, he was sometimes perceived as being lethargic or antisocial. Journalists looking for useable quotes generally avoided him.

Though Tony Lazzeri could have batted cleanup on almost any other club, he was relegated to sixth in the Yankees order. That didn't stop him from driving in runs. He gathered 102 RBIs in 1927 and 82 the following year despite missing more than 30 games with a shoulder injury. Unbeknownst to most of the general public, he suffered from epilepsy—a condition that prompted several teams to pass on his services despite a record-setting performance in the Pacific Coast League (he collected 60 homers and 222 RBIs during the 1925 campaign). Yankee GM Ed Barrow was willing to take a chance on the future Hall of Famer, commenting, "As long as he doesn't take fits between three and six in the afternoon, that's good enough for me."[84] Lazzeri remained a staple at second base for twelve seasons in New York and never had an epileptic seizure on the diamond. Like Meusel, he was extremely reserved, prompting one reporter to grumble, "Interviewing that guy is like mining coal with a nail file."[85]

The bottom of the batting order was less intimidating with third baseman Joe Dugan in the seventh slot followed by whoever happened to be catching that day. Before Hall of Famer Bill Dickey became a full-time Yankee backstop, Miller Huggins employed a tandem of Benny Bengough, Pat Collins, and Johnny Grabowski. The trio hit at a collective .259 clip over several seasons—significantly below average compared to many catchers of the era. But despite his ongoing knee problems, Dugan was far more competent at the plate, gathering close to 800 hits (nearly 200 of them going for extra bases) in six full campaigns with New York.

While the 1927 Yankees were capable of scoring runs in bunches, their pitching staff was adept at shutting down opponents. Veteran starters Waite Hoyt and Herb Pennock combined for a 41–15 record and a 2.80 ERA. Wilcy Moore, a thirty-year-old rookie acquired from the South Atlantic League, was brilliant in a swingman's role, making 50 appearances as a starter and reliever. He led the league with 13 saves and a 2.28 earned run average. Adding depth to the rotation, right-handed junk-baller Urban Shocker finished among the league leaders in wins and shutouts. Shocker, who had begun his career with the Yankees in the Deadball Era, became a star for the St. Louis Browns before returning to New York in 1925. Among the most resilient players in history, he suffered from a serious heart valve ailment that (according to multiple sources) forced him to sleep in an upright position. He soldiered on, winning 20 games in four consecutive seasons before the illness finally killed him in 1928.

With an unparalleled assortment of talent, the Yankees won 110 games in 1927, breaking an American League record set by the 1912 Red Sox. They finished 19 games in front of the A's—the biggest lead by any pennant-winning club since the 1906 Cubs. They led the league in more than a dozen offensive categories, doubling the home run output of every big league team except the Cardinals and Giants. In the pitching department, Yankees hurlers posted the lowest ERA in the majors while ranking second in hits and walks allowed.

The NL champion Pirates, despite the presence of three Hall of Famers, proved to be no match for the Yankees in the World Series. An enduring legend maintains that Pittsburgh players were mentally defeated as they watched the Yankees take batting practice at Forbes Field prior to Game

1. According to multiple sources, Ruth drove five consecutive pitches into the park's deepest recesses. He was followed by Gehrig and Meusel, both of whom put on similar displays of power. Even Johnny Grabowski knocked several balls out. "Have you ever seen such hitting?" Pirates third baseman Pie Traynor allegedly said. "They're even better than they're advertised."[86] Sapped of their confidence, Bucs hitters managed a feeble .223 collective average against New York moundsmen. The result was a brisk series sweep. After a four-year absence, the Yankees were back on top.

"60"—The Magic Number

Long before Mantle and Maris's celebrated home run duel in 1961, another pair of Yankee idols engaged in an epic bid for immortality. Entering the 1927 campaign, Ruth was baseball's undisputed home run king with 356 lifetime blasts. His closest competitor was Cy Williams of the Phillies, who had amassed 204 to that point. Though the Babe was unaccustomed to being challenged in the annual home run race, he encountered plenty of opposition in 1927 as Lou Gehrig had a breakout season.

Unlike Ruth, the 24-year-old Gehrig was a manager's dream. He played hard and made strenuous efforts to learn from his mistakes. He steered clear of alcohol and observed evening curfews. Unwaveringly polite, he never bragged about himself or complained about teammates. Compared to the Babe, he was milquetoast—the kind of player who was seen but rarely heard.

Though many had predicted that the A's would win the 1927 pennant, the Yankees coasted through the summer months with a comfortable lead, outscoring their opponents by a total of 376 runs. The only player who wasn't hitting at all was right-handed swingman Wilcy Moore. The hurler was so incompetent in the batter's box that Ruth offered him a friendly wager—$15 at 20-to-1 odds if he could gather more than two hits before season's end. Moore's pitiful attempt to win the bet kept teammates amused all year. After going hitless in his firsts 31 at-bats, he rapped out a pair of singles against the Tigers on July 8. And then—nearly two months later, he tapped a slow roller that settled on the infield grass at Navin Field in Detroit for his third hit of the season. After the game, he remarked humorously, "This is just an easy park to hit in."[87] Ruth paid him $300, which the rookie used to purchase a pair of mules for his Oklahoma farm.

While Ruth and Moore were engaged in a lighthearted rivalry, Gehrig was threatening to steal the 1927 home run crown away from the

Babe. The two sluggers were tied with 25 bombs apiece at the end of June. Things heated up in July, when Gehrig pulled ahead by one. Avidly following the race, Dan Daniel of the *New York Telegram* wrote, "If Gehrig could master the trick of pulling his drives to dead right, there would be no real contest with the Babe. Lou would hit at least sixty-five homers this season."[88]

By late August, the home run chase was deadlocked at 40 without a third contender in sight. But a mighty push from the Bambino during the last few weeks of the regular season left Gehrig in the dust. In a doubleheader against the hapless Red Sox on September 6, Ruth went deep three times. He added two more shots the following day, effectively ending the race. Gehrig's mother had fallen ill, creating a tremendous distraction for the Iron Horse, who managed just two homers in the final two weeks of the season. On September 29, the Babe hit number 58 against Hod Lisenbee of the Senators. Later in the game, he homered off rookie Paul Hopkins, tying the record he had set in 1921. (Interestingly, it was Hopkins's first major-league appearance—what a way to break in!)

There was a surprisingly small crowd on hand at Yankee Stadium the following day as Ruth set out to make history. Tom Zachary, who had yielded a pair of homers to the Babe earlier in the year, got the start for Washington. During their first encounter of the afternoon, the veteran southpaw worked carefully around Ruth and advised him to start swinging because he wouldn't be getting anything good to hit. After walking on four pitches, the Bambino treated Zachary to a stream of profanity, which the hurler responded to in kind. With the game tied at 2 in the bottom of the eighth, Zachary made a critical mistake, offering the slugger his best fastball. Ruth hammered it into the right field seats for a game-winning homer, prompting Yankee coaches Art Fletcher and Charlie O'Leary to throw their caps in the air. It was an unusual gesture for O'Leary, who was extremely self-conscious about his baldness. As fans waved handkerchiefs and littered the field with scraps of paper, Gehrig greeted the Babe at home plate with an enthusiastic handshake and pat on the back. In the clubhouse after the game, Ruth uttered one of his most famous statements, "Sixty! Count 'em, 60! Let's see some other son of a bitch match that!"[89] Years later, Zachary was still regretting his decision to throw a fastball in the strike zone. "I've been wishing ever since I'd stuck that pitch in his ear," he said.[90]

THE BABE'S GREATEST WORLD SERIES

Before the 1928 campaign, Ruth predicted that he would hit 61 home runs. "With Gehrig following me at the bat, most of the intentional pass stuff is eliminated," he told a reporter. "And as long as pitchers will pitch to me, I see no reason why I shouldn't break my record."[91] He collected 30 blasts before July arrived, but fell off the pace in August and September, coming up several homers short. It was a remarkable season nonetheless.

After the Yankees swept the Pirates in the 1927 World Series, Ruth hit the barnstorming trail with Gehrig (who had officially become a client of Christy Walsh). The tour, which included stops in 21 cities, pitted Ruth's "Bustin' Babes" against Gehrig's "Larrupin' Lous." Occasionally, the two idols pooled their efforts against other teams. One of the most interesting games took place in Asbury Park, New Jersey, where a crowd of roughly 7,000 grew restless waiting for Ruth's all-stars to take the field against the Brooklyn Royal Giants—an all-black team affiliated with the Eastern Independent Clubs. The Babe was holed up in the Berkeley-Cataret Hotel awaiting a check from the promoter. When the payment finally arrived, he made his way to the ballpark. By then, police had been called to control fans—some of whom had become unruly during the hour-long delay.

As was common in barnstorming games, children wandered onto the field repeatedly. Ruth honored their autograph requests, resulting in multiple interruptions. The ballpark was adjacent to a man-made body of water known as Deal Lake, which drains into the Atlantic Ocean. Organizers supplied the teams with a few dozen baseballs, but without any fences to contain them, many ended up in the water and were lost. Ruth hit two long homers that splashed down in the lake—the first one prompting a boy to leap from a canoe in pursuit of it. The game ended early when Gehrig deposited the last available ball into the field's soggy perimeter. None of the fans who had retrieved baseballs as souvenirs offered to return them so that play could continue. It became a common occurrence during the tour as most of the games were preempted due to unforeseen events. By the time it was over, Ruth had hit 20 home runs to Gehrig's 16 (according to Walsh's report).

Ruth went hunting in December and shot a goose, which he personally delivered to GM Ed Barrow at the Yankees office. He also took up the saxophone and learned a couple of songs. Fitness guru Artie McGovern worked with the slugger to get him in shape for the coming season. At 33 years of age, the Babe had gained some weight he couldn't shed. When spring training began, he tipped the scales at around 240 pounds.

It was turbulent year for the pitching staff. Waite Hoyt was a spring holdout. Though he was eventually signed, Urban Shocker became too ill to play and swingman Wilcy Moore was ineffective—the result of an undisclosed arm injury sustained in a fall from the roof of a barn. The Yankees had picked up Hall of Fame spitballer Stan Coveleski in the offseason and promoted right-hander Hank Johnson from the American Association, but neither was terribly reliable. Johnson struggled with his control and Coveleski got hit hard, eventually earning his release. While Hoyt picked up a lot of slack along with Herb Pennock, right-hander George Pipgras enjoyed one of the finest seasons of his career.

Known for his lively fastball, Pipgras had been kicking around the minors since 1921. After a couple of unsuccessful call-ups, he found a permanent home in New York during the 1927 campaign. He was a workhorse the following year, tossing more than 300 innings while posting a career-best 3.38 ERA. He also won 24 games—tops in the American League. Asked about his Yankees experience many years later, he remarked, "When we got to the ballpark, we knew we were going to win. That's all there was to it. We weren't cocky. I wouldn't call it confidence either. We just knew. Like when you go to sleep you know the sun is going to come up in the morning."[92]

A 13-game Yankee lead began to evaporate in the second half as injuries to key players took their toll. Joe Dugan's ongoing knee issues limited him to 94 appearances. Tony Lazzeri tore a muscle in his right shoulder, forcing him out of action for an extended period. Leo Durocher, who would gain far more acclaim as a manager years later, served as a reliable defensive replacement. But his hitting left something to be desired. A late July road trip proved disastrous for the Yankees as they dropped 11 of 17 games to noncontenders. Around the same time, the A's went off on a tear, winning 10 straight. By the end of August, Philly had pulled to within two and a half games of New York.

While the defending American League champions were desperately trying to fend off the A's, Herbert Hoover was running for president. During the heart of the pennant race, a newspaper incorrectly reported that Ruth was backing Hoover. Setting the record straight, the Yankee outfielder declared his support for the Democratic candidate—New York governor Al Smith. When Hoover visited Yankee Stadium on September 1, members of his publicity team requested a photo op with Ruth. "No sir," the Babe answered candidly. "Nothing doing on politics. Tell him I'll be glad to talk to him if he wants to meet me under the stands."[93] The candidate politely declined. And when details of Ruth's snub were released, Republican-based newspapers threatened to cancel the slugger's syndicated column (which was ghostwritten). Christy Walsh issued an apology of sorts and arranged for the Babe to have his picture taken with Hoover. He had already posed for multiple photos endorsing Smith, one of which included several teammates and a bat boy.

Nursing a slender half-game lead, the Yankees hosted the surging Athletics on September 9. Pipgras got the start against a powerful lineup that featured several future Hall of Famers. Rising to the challenge, the Yankee ace tossed a complete game shutout. It proved to be the turning point of the season as the Yankees won 12 of their last 18 games, capturing another pennant. Celebrating the occasion, Ruth threw a party at the team's hotel in Detroit. Three additional rooms were rented with adjoining doors so that waiters could wander freely about serving food and bootleg liquor.

In the World Series, the Yankees squared off against St. Louis for the second time in three years. Though the Cardinals had survived a tight pennant race, their aging pitching staff was not prepared to handle the combined forces of Ruth and Gehrig. None of the games were close. The Yankees won all four by at least three runs. While Gehrig launched four homers and drove in nine runs, Ruth set a series record with a .625 batting average—a mark that stood for more than 60 years. By the time the last pitch was thrown, the Babe had reached base safely in 11 of 17 plate appearances while striking out only twice. He saved his best performance for the finale.

Facing elimination in Game 4 at Sportsman's Park, the Cardinals sent 21-game winner Bill Sherdel to the mound. Among the shortest pitchers in the majors at 5-foot-8, the crafty right-hander had developed an assortment of slow curves and changeups that frustrated opponents. He held the Yankees scoreless until the fourth inning, when Ruth hit a towering drive over the right field roof. Facing the slugger again in the seventh, Sherdel worked the count to 0–2. As the Babe was busy talking to Cardinals catcher Earl Smith, Sherdel resorted to one of his favorite tricks, delivering a quick pitch that caught the slugger completely off guard. It landed in the strike zone, but umpire Cy Pfirman disallowed it, prompting a heated debate involving several St. Louis players. From a rules standpoint, a quick pitch is an illegal offering that takes place before the batter is set and is thrown with the deliberate intention of surprising the hitter. With runners on base, it counts as a balk. With the bases empty, it is considered a ball. Pfirman did the right thing and stuck by his call. According to Ruth, the rest of the at-bat played out as follows:

When the argument was concluded, the Babe applauded sarcastically and taunted Sherdel. Fans were still booing and tossing assorted bits of trash onto the field. The hurler—perhaps a bit rattled—missed the plate with his next two offerings.

"The National League is a hell of a league!" Ruth shouted.

"It sure is," Sherdel barked back at him.

The slugger gestured toward home plate.

"Put one here and I'll knock it over the fence for you," he said.[94]

The following pitch was a strike that Ruth crushed for a game-tying homer—his second of the afternoon. He laughed all the way around the bases, waving mockingly to fans.

If the Babe's colorful narrative is accurate (and it may not be, given his tendency to embellish and fabricate), then the celebrated home run he hit in Game 3 of the 1932 World Series was not the first "called shot" of his post-season career. Gehrig followed Ruth's blast with another long homer, giving the Yankees a 3–2 lead. A single by Bob Meusel ended Sherdel's luckless day on the mound. Summoned from the bullpen, Pete Alexander allowed two more runs to score before retiring the side.

Ruth added to the Cardinals' misery in the eighth inning with another bomb to deep right field. Securing his status as a World Series hero, he made a fine running grab in foul territory for the final out of the game. In order to make the catch, he had to reach into the stands while fans swatted him with newspapers and programs. He carried the ball all the way to the clubhouse, where the championship celebration commenced. One sportswriter gushed, "Of all the baseball memories, that shall be the clearest-etched and most unforgettable. Ruth, indomitable, unconquerable, triumphant."[95]

On an interesting final note, Ruth became an author in 1928, though it was obvious he didn't write the book that bore his name. When it was reissued in 1992, a reviewer from the *Baltimore Sun* pointed out that "the prose includes no profanity, not even a 'gosh,' and in general makes the Bambino sound like a boy scout. There are no references, or even hints of, George Herman's gargantuan appetites for beer, women and hot dogs. The voice in this quaint relic of a book sounds to me like the voice of an Edwardian or maybe Victorian gentleman trying to sound sporty."[96] A popular theory holds that the project, entitled *Babe Ruth's Own Book of Baseball*, was written by Ford Frick—an esteemed journalist who later became president of the National League. The book does contain some memorable quotes (even if they didn't actually come from Ruth himself) and was met with mostly positive reviews at the time of its original release.

A Wedding and Two Funerals

The New Year began on a depressing note for Ruth, who was left with the unenviable task of burying his estranged wife. He absorbed the cost of the funeral arrangements, which included preinterment services at the Woodward family home in South Boston. The grieving slugger paid his respects to Helen shortly after midnight on January 17. It took more than twenty Boston policemen to control a crowd of roughly 5,000 that had gathered to witness the Babe's appearance. An army of photographers greeted the Yankee icon with a blinding volley of flashbulbs when he arrived.

Kneeling beside Helen's coffin, Ruth began to cry as he clutched a chain of rosary beads. When he finally rose to his feet, he collapsed and was unable to walk to his car without an escort. In the morning, he returned for a brief service at the Woodward home and final goodbye at Cavalry Cemetery. To those who witnessed the events, he appeared to be in deep emotional distress—a man on the verge of a breakdown.

Newspapers reported that the Babe traveled back to New York with his daughter, Dorothy, but this was not accurate. She had been placed in a Catholic boarding school long before her mother's death and virtually forgotten by both parents. A week after the tragic house fire, she was awoken from a sound sleep by two nuns and instructed to pack her belongings. She ended up at New York Foundling Hospital, where she learned that she would be staying in Brooklyn with a woman named Miss Dooley until her father came to get her. The sizeable inheritance she received from Helen's estate did nothing to lift her spirits. Confused, angry, and despondent, she lived under the pseudonym "Marie Harrington" for five months until Ruth finally rescued her.

It was a busy time for the slugger. To avoid reporters and photographers, he left for Florida early and laid low. While spring training was in session, he ran up an exorbitant phone bill (said to be in excess of $1,600) talking to his longtime mistress. Though the public already knew a thing or two about her from assorted blurbs in gossip columns, they would soon learn the entire story.

A stunning beauty with sleek brown hair, soulful eyes, and a shapely figure, Claire Merritt had grown up in Georgia. Her father—a successful

trial lawyer in Gainesville—sometimes sat her in the front row of his courtroom to distract members of all-male juries. At the age of 15, she dated
Tigers superstar Ty Cobb. At 16, she married a man twice her age—Frank
Hodgson of Athens. When Hodgson died, she moved to New York with
her daughter, Julia.

In the Big Apple, Claire landed some modeling jobs and also pursued a
career as an actress. She was introduced to Ruth while playing a small role
in a stage production. After seeing the show, the Babe asked the director (a
friend of his) to bring Claire to a game between the Yankees and Senators so
he could meet her. She later wrote in her memoirs that "he was very much in
need of a sympathetic ear."[97]

Claire and the Babe hit it off instantly and continued their affair for the
next five years. Though Ruth told people that they were just friends, various members of the press speculated that they were romantically involved.
According to the slugger's daughter, he spent more time at Claire's apartment
than he did at his own home. And Claire sometimes accompanied him to the
farm in Sudbury. She would stay in a hotel while the Babe attended to his
floundering relationship with Helen. Because of his strict Catholic upbring-
ing, he refused to get a divorce.

With Helen a little more than three months in her grave, Claire and the
Babe decided to get married. The ceremony was held on Opening Day of the
1929 campaign. Though Ruth was scheduled to play that day, the game ended
up being rained out and the two were able to celebrate together. The following afternoon, he hit a homer off Red Sox hurler Red Ruffing. He tipped his
cap to Claire as he rounded the bases and blew kisses in her direction.

Wives of players were not in the habit of traveling with the club, but
Claire was an exception to the rule. Jacob Ruppert felt that she was a positive
influence on Ruth and welcomed her presence. The couple shared a private
compartment on the team's train, where they were sheltered from reporters.
Claire answered the phone in the hotels they stayed at and was surprised by
the number of women who called. She took great pleasure in telling them
that her husband was no longer available. "The Babe brought out the beast in
a lot of women the world over," she wrote, "and I enjoyed very much setting
them straight on the problem."[98]

There were other problems to be straightened out. Though Claire made
a conscious effort to tolerate some of her husband's unpleasant habits, she
saw fit to make some changes as well. Seizing control of the slugger's check-
book, she doled out money to him in $50 increments, drastically reducing

his spending. While she permitted him to consume alcohol, she steered him away from hard liquor. She also convinced him to make better culinary choices while cutting down on his massive food intake. The result was a (somewhat) healthier and wealthier Bambino.

The couple took up residence in a sprawling luxury suite on Manhattan's Upper West Side. In the hope of fostering a healthy family environment, Claire adopted Ruth's daughter and he adopted hers. In later years, Julia had many fond memories of the Babe, but Dorothy was not as enamored with Claire. "I was excess baggage," she wrote in her 1988 memoir. "Raising me was a burdensome job, like a stack of unexpected paperwork."[99]

With his personal affairs in order for the first time in years, Ruth enjoyed another fine season in 1929. He hit .345 with 46 homers—more than any other player in the majors. Unfortunately, many of his teammates didn't fare as well. After three consecutive pennant runs, the Yankees were finally slowing down. Gehrig looked more ordinary at the plate, hitting at an even .300 clip with diminished power numbers. Bob Meusel sat out 54 games and slumped to .261—the lowest batting average of his career. The Yankee pitching staff was eminently hittable, compiling a collective 4.19 ERA. Pennock was the biggest disappointment of all, losing 11 of 20 decisions while allowing close to five runs per nine innings. His career continued on a downward spiral after that.

There were a few bright spots in 1929. Catcher Bill Dickey—playing in his first full season—hit .324. Tony Lazzeri finished fourth in the AL batting race with a .354 mark. And Earle Combs accrued a handsome .414 on-base percentage at the top of the order. With an 88–66 record, the Yankees weren't bad. They just weren't as good as the Philadelphia A's.

After suffering a World Series sweep at the hands of the Braves in 1914, Athletics owner-manager Connie Mack dismantled the Philly roster, which included four eventual Hall of Famers. Speaking to members of the press about his decision to break up the club, Mack stood by his convictions and predicted he would have an even better team within two years.

He was wrong.

The A's floundered at the bottom of the standings for a decade, finishing dead last in seven consecutive seasons. But Mack remained patient, importing a steady mix of talent. By 1929, he had assembled a powerhouse with Al Simmons in left field, Jimmie Foxx at first base, and Mickey Cochrane behind the plate. Simmons won consecutive batting titles in 1930 and 1931. Foxx was among the most consistent run producers in either league. And

Cochrane was arguably the best offensive catcher of the Lively Ball Era. The Philadelphia pitching staff was anchored by ornery southpaw Lefty Grove. An intense competitor who made batters uncomfortable at the plate with brushbacks and menacing glares, he won nine ERA titles while leading the AL in strikeouts for seven straight campaigns.

The 1929 A's climbed into first place on May 13 and never let go. By season's end, they had pulled 18 games ahead of New York. Though the Yankees were never seriously in the running anyway, a tragic turn of events in September profoundly affected team morale.

Describing his passion for the game, Miller Huggins once said, "Baseball is my life. I'd be lost without it. Maybe, as you say, it will get me some day, but as long as I die in harness, I'll be happy."[100] Huggins had no idea when he spoke those words that he would be dead sooner rather than later.

Huggins grew up in Cincinnati during the early days of the National League. His father was a strict Methodist who disapproved of most leisurely pursuits—baseball included. To avoid his father's wrath, Huggins played under the pseudonym "Proctor." His tremendous height disadvantage inspired him to work harder and use his head to devise clever strategies. He assumed an exaggerated crouch at the plate to make his strike zone even smaller. In the field, he successfully executed the hidden ball trick a number of times. A switch-hitter with good speed on the bases, he received multiple nicknames pertaining to his size, including "Rabbit," "Mighty Mite," and "Little Everywhere."

In 1910, Huggins was traded from Cincinnati to St Louis, where he was installed as manager. Giants skipper John McGraw was among the many insiders who strongly endorsed the promotion. "There's no smarter man in baseball today than Miller Huggins," he said.[101] Huggins's remarkable eye for talent became legendary. Not only did he help build the powerful Yankee squads of the 1920s, but he had convinced the Cardinals to sign an untested teenager named Rogers Hornsby, who went on to compile the second-highest batting average of all time behind Ty Cobb.

In spite of his many good qualities, Huggins could be combative, brusque, and borderline antisocial. Jacob Ruppert once referred to him as a "grouch." Renowned sportswriter Damon Runyon remarked, "If there is any streak of humor in him, it does not make itself manifest."[102] Huggins had his hands full with all the egos in New York and took a lion's share of the blame for the team's failures. Unbeknownst to many, he suffered a nervous breakdown after the 1920 season. His recurring anxiety was accompanied by a host of other medical conditions.

When the A's ran away with the 1929 pennant, Huggins began losing sleep and looking extremely run-down. Though he was only 51, he could easily have passed for a man in his seventies. In early September, he came to the ballpark with an angry red boil under his left eye. Coaches and players were concerned, suggesting he get it checked out, but he ignored their advice. On September 15, Waite Hoyt got hammered by the Indians in a 10–0 loss. It was his fourth consecutive lackluster start. Huggins shut the veteran right-hander down for the rest of the season, but the decision weighed heavily upon him. When his skin condition had not cleared up by the third week of September, he checked himself into St. Vincent's Hospital. It was discovered that he was suffering from erysipelas, a serious infection known as St. Anthony's Fire for the intense rash associated with it. Blood transfusions were of no use. The bacteria spread throughout his body and he died in the hospital on September 25.

The Yankees were playing in Boston when they received the news. Players from both teams gathered at home plate to observe a moment of silence. Several members of the Yankees cried in the clubhouse afterward. When sportswriter Tom Meany relayed this to his New York newspaper via telephone, a member of the editorial staff allegedly said to him, "C'mon kid, stop over-writing."[103]

The funeral was held at the Church of the Transfiguration in Manhattan. Ruth served as a pallbearer along with several other players and coaches. The body was later transported to Cincinnati for burial. Pennock and coach Charlie O'Leary made the trip to represent the players. In a poignant statement that may actually have had some truth to it, Huggins's sister told a reporter, "Babe Ruth took five years off my brother's life."[104]

DISASTER IN RUTHVILLE

Incredibly, the passing of Helen Ruth and Miller Huggins were not the only tragedies of the 1929 campaign. Things turned ugly at Yankee Stadium on May 19, when a heavy rainstorm sent fans in the right field bleachers rushing for cover. Two people were killed and many more were injured in the resulting stampede.

A Sunday crowd of more than 50,000 had gathered to watch the Yankees take on the struggling Red Sox. Ruth and Gehrig gave fans something to cheer about in the bottom of the third with back-to-back homers off right-hander Jack Russell. Rain had begun to fall in the fourth inning, but many fans stuck around hoping to see the dynamic duo bat again in the fifth. By then, the Yankees were leading, 3–0, and the game could be counted as official. Russell retired Ruth on a groundout just before disaster struck.

The right field section of Yankee Stadium was known as "Ruthville" on account of the Babe's tendency to deposit home runs there. When the skies let loose with a drenching downpour, thousands of Ruthville patrons scrambled to get out of the rain. Most of the exits were located down a long flight of steps beneath the seats. Newspapers reported that several of them were closed that day for unknown reasons. A 17-year-old college student named Eleanor Price, who had taken her brother to the game, was among the first to reach the stairs. The surging crowd sent her tumbling to the bottom along with several young boys. An on-duty policeman drew his gun in an attempt to stop the rush, but he was knocked to the ground.

A writer from the Associated Press described the horrific scene as follows, "In a few seconds, the stairway was a mass of screaming, fighting, panic-stricken humanity while those in the rear, unaware of the crush in the stairway, pressed forward to push others into the human heap."[105]

When Ruth saw an injured boy being carried onto the field, he bolted from the dugout toward the right field stands to find out what was going on. He immediately began calling for medical assistance. According to multiple reports, he fought his way through the crowd to where Eleanor Price lay unconscious. She reportedly died in his arms before help arrived. A 60-year-old teamster named Joseph Carter was also crushed in the stampede.

Estimates of how many fans were injured vary from source to source. The five ambulances that responded were not sufficient to carry all the wounded to local hospitals. Two large buses were dispatched to the bleacher entrance for additional support. Ruth visited the victims at Lincoln Hospital, shaking hands, passing out souvenir baseballs, and promising home runs.

A negligence lawsuit was later filed on behalf of multiple parties, including the families of the deceased. The case dragged on for quite some time with a trial, an appeal, and an order for a second trial. Eventually, the Yankees settled for a sum in excess of $40,000. In the wake of the disaster, Jacob Ruppert promised not to oversell any games at the stadium.

Ruth's Biggest Payday

Throughout the 1920s, the US economy expanded at an exponential rate, causing the nation's overall wealth to double. Hoping to strike it rich, investors funneled their savings into the stock market. By the end of the decade, production had slowed significantly, causing unemployment to rise. As consumer spending declined and unsold goods began to pile up, the value of stocks continued to increase. This led to an epic crash that triggered the Great Depression.

By 1930, four million Americans were out of work and many of the nation's banks had failed. People found themselves standing in breadlines, eating at soup kitchens, and living in shanty towns. Amid all this hardship, Ruth landed the most lucrative contract of his career as a Yankee.

On January 7, 1930, the Babe sat down with Jacob Ruppert and Ed Barrow to discuss his salary for the coming season. In spite of the nation's economic downturn, he felt justified in seeking a raise. Not only did he finish among the league leaders in every major slugging category during the 1929 slate, but he was baseball's biggest drawing card. When he joined the Yankees in 1920, attendance figures doubled. The numbers hovered around a million per year, with the exception of the disastrous 1925 campaign, when he missed two months of action. From 1920 to 1930, the Yankees made more money than any team in baseball. Even spring training games generated substantial revenue with Ruth in the lineup.

Ruppert was eminently aware of the Babe's value to the club. And he worried that it might be difficult to sign other players if negotiations with his prized slugger dragged on for too long. Looking to close the deal quickly, he agreed to match Ruth's wages from the previous three campaigns. When the outfielder shrugged off the proposal, Ruppert increased his bid to $75,000, which was equivalent to President Herbert Hoover's annual salary. Incredibly, the Babe balked at the offer, countering with a figure of his own—$85,000 per year over three seasons.

Ruppert and Barrow were astounded. There was no doubt Ruth was immensely popular and abundantly talented. But the average major-league salary was around $7,000 at the time. And the slugger's asking price was more than the combined earnings of every other positional player in the starting lineup. The Yankee executives had no choice but to draw a line in the sand. The session ended on a friendly note without a contract in place.

After hearing about the failed negotiations, humorist Will Rogers joked in his syndicated column, "They offered Babe Ruth the same salary that [President] Hoover gets. Babe claims he should have more. He can't appoint a commission to go up and knock the home runs. He has to do it all himself."[106]

A few days later, Ruth departed for Florida to relax with his wife before spring training began. Following standard protocol, the Yankees mailed him the $75,000 contract he had rejected. By the time camp opened, he was the last unsigned player. A second meeting with Ruppert yielded positive results but no accord. Ruth agreed to a two-year term on his contract. The Yankees owner raised his offer to $80,000. Talks broke down from there.

Later that evening, the Babe had dinner with friends. One of them was Associated Press writer Alan Gould. Ruth was scheduled to play in an exhibition game against the Braves the following day, but Gould advised him not to, explaining that he could get hurt and lose all his bargaining power. Heeding Gould's warning, the slugger announced that if Ruppert had not met his salary demands by the morning, he would turn in his uniform and go back to New York. When word of the discussion reached Dan Daniel of the *Evening Telegram,* he wrote it up as a story and submitted it to his editor.

Known for his fickle nature, Ruth changed his mind the following day. He was anxious to swing the bat and also felt that Emil Fuchs—owner of the long-suffering Braves—could use a little extra cash. Fearing that the Babe would undermine his credibility as a journalist if he played without a contract that afternoon, Daniel confronted the slugger, urging him to cut a deal with the Yankees. He told Ruth about a bread riot that had taken place in New York City the previous day. "They're broke," he said, ". . . and you're holding out for $85,000 a year while they're starving."[107]

The Babe was shocked and appalled by the news. Shortly after talking to Daniel, he requested a meeting with Ruppert. A brief discussion was all it took to finalize a deal worth $80,000 per season over two years. As a gesture of good faith, the Yankee owner refunded the $5,000 fine levied by Miller Huggins during the ill-fated 1925 campaign. Ruth entered the 1930 season as the highest-paid player in baseball history. Questioned about his enormous salary and how it rivaled the earnings of a US president, he allegedly quipped, "What's Hoover got to do with it? Besides, I had a better year than he did."[108]

The Brief and Unhappy Managerial Career of Bob Shawkey

Immediately following the death of Miller Huggins, coach Art Fletcher took the reins, steering the Yankees to a 6–5 finish. Looking for a permanent replacement, team executives extended offers to Eddie Collins and Donie Bush. Both men declined, making Fletcher the next logical choice. After four losing seasons at the helm of the woeful Phillies, Fletcher was not enthusiastic about returning to managing on a full-time basis. He politely refused, putting Jacob Ruppert and Ed Barrow in a tight spot. In the end, they appointed Bob Shawkey to the task.

During his pitching days, Shawkey's lively fastball and sharp-breaking curve were well-respected by opponents. He won 168 games for the Yankees over portions of 13 seasons, collecting 20 or more victories four times. But managing the Yankees was an experience he was not prepared for. The club had slumped to second place in 1929. The pitching staff was in a state of disarray and reporters were skeptical about the road that lay ahead for the fledgling skipper. "If Huggins couldn't lead this team to a pennant, then how is Shawkey going to do it in 1930?" one writer remarked frankly.[109]

Prior to Shawkey's hiring, Ruth had expressed interest in the position. Half a dozen Yankees had served as player-managers over the years, leading the slugger to believe he could handle the additional responsibility. Given his volatile temperament and inability to manage his own personal affairs, Ruppert and Barrow convinced the Babe that he was more valuable to the club in a singular role. A bit wounded initially, Ruth put it behind him, pledging his support to Shawkey, who he considered a friend.

Others were not as enthralled with the new Yankees pilot. Waite Hoyt—a roommate of Shawkey's on multiple occasions—had grown to dislike him. Lingering tensions between the two led to a clash that set the stage for Hoyt's eventual release. On May 22, Hoyt served up a hittable fastball to future Hall of Famer Al Simmons, who drove it into the upper deck at Shibe Park. Between innings, Shawkey offered instructions on how to handle the dangerous Philly slugger. Hoyt rejected the input, prompting Shawkey to issue an ultimatum: "You'll pitch the way I tell you to or you won't pitch at all."[110] Two weeks later, Hoyt was traded to the Tigers along with infielder Mark Koenig.

Shawkey made Lou Gehrig cry, but it wasn't really his fault. Gehrig desperately wanted to please his managers and was known to become extremely emotional about his shortcomings. Shawkey had cautioned the ultratalented first baseman multiple times about taking his foot off the bag too early while receiving infield throws. When Gehrig's bad habit cost the Yankees a critical run one afternoon, the Iron Horse sobbed in the dugout. He later apologized and promised not to repeat the mistake. "Lou was that type of person," Shawkey recalled years later, "very sensitive."[111]

Interestingly, attendance at major-league games increased by 5 percent in 1930 despite the abysmal state of the US economy. Those who could afford to go to the ballpark witnessed an unprecedented offensive surge. American League teams hit at a collective .288 clip while averaging close to 11 combined runs per game. NL batsmen were even more productive, compiling a cumulative .303 average. Six players had at least 150 RBIs as Hack Wilson set a single-season record that still stands with 191.

Though Ruth was gaining weight and slowing down in the outfield, he was still a terror at the plate. He hit 15 home runs in June—a record for the month that remained unbroken for nearly 60 years. He finished the season with 49 but should have had more. Two of his blasts hit a loudspeaker at Shibe Park and bounced back onto the field. Under existing ground rules, they were counted as doubles. There was no doubt about the homer he blasted off Lefty Grove on May 21 in Philadelphia. It left the ballpark, sailed over a neighboring house, and cleared two backyards.

While the Yankees poured on the offense, averaging 6.9 runs per game, the pitching staff ran up a collective 4.88 ERA—among the worst marks in the majors. Just two games out of first place at the beginning of July, Shawkey's crew gradually fell out of contention, finishing a distant third behind the A's and Senators.

Ruppert and Barrow allowed Shawkey to finish out the season but neglected to tell him they were looking for a replacement. When Cubs manager Joe McCarthy was released with four games still remaining on the Chicago schedule, the Yankees offered him a contract. Shawkey didn't learn that he had been fired until he went to the team offices to discuss his options for the coming year. "It was a dirty deal," he commented bitterly.[112] Though he went on to a successful career as a minor-league manager and coach at Dartmouth College, he held a long-standing grudge against his former club. In spite of his bitterness toward team executives, he attended a number of special events at Yankee Stadium, including Gehrig's farewell speech and Ruth's final appearance. During the 1970s, he threw out the ceremonial first pitch at the stadium's 50th anniversary celebration and grand reopening.

During his only season at the Yankee helm, Shawkey created a lasting legacy. In May of 1930, he convinced the Yankees to sign right-hander Red Ruffing, who had led the AL in losses during the previous two seasons.

Shawkey worked with Ruffing on his mechanics, prompting a remarkable career revival. With only one toe on his left foot—the result of an unfortunate mining accident—Ruffing won 231 games for the Yankees and ended up in the Hall of Fame.

The Girl Who Struck out Ruth and Gehrig

While most teams were cutting down on exhibitions to save money in 1931, the Yankees made more than 30 stops on their annual spring tour. All of the games pitted them against minor-league clubs. A visit to Chattanooga at the beginning of April produced one of the most unforgettable moments in baseball history.

Women's teams began competing against each other during the 1860s. The earliest rosters were composed of actresses recruited (and often exploited) by male owners. In her book *Bloomer Girls: Women Baseball Pioneers*, researcher Debra Shattuck described these early exhibitions as "a burlesque of the game."[113] But by the dawn of the 20th century, women of genuine talent had begun to emerge.

The first female to appear in the minors was a Pennsylvania native named Lizzie Arlington. She got her start with a woman's barnstorming team at the age of thirteen. In 1898, she signed a minor-league contract with the Philadelphia Nationals, pitching and playing second base for the club's reserve squad. She made her official debut in July of that year with the Reading Coal Heavers. More than a thousand fans saw her enter the field in a fancy carriage drawn by a pair of white horses. Wearing stockings, bloomers and a knee-length skirt, she surrendered a pair of hits and a walk before retiring the next three batters to preserve a 5–0 victory over the Allentown Peanuts. Though she was later scheduled to pitch against a team from Hartford, the appearance was cancelled when her opponents expressed concerns about losing to a girl. She was subsequently released.

In 1931, a teenager named Jackie Mitchell became an overnight sensation when she struck out two of the most fearsome hitters of all time. Born in Chattanooga, Tennessee, Mitchell learned the rudiments of the game from her father during her formative years. She was taught how to throw a drop ball (which behaves like a sinker) by her neighbor—Hall of Famer Dazzy Vance. While pitching for a team known as the Engelettes, she attended a training camp in Atlanta. It was there that she drew the attention of Chattanooga Lookouts owner Joe Engel.

Engel was known for employing wild publicity stunts to lure fans to the ballpark. He once traded a player for a turkey that was cooked and fed to sportswriters. On another occasion, he gave away a horse to a random ticket holder. Recognizing a golden opportunity, he signed Mitchell to a minor-league contract and booked a pair of games against the New York Yankees.

On the heels of a rainout, the Yankees faced the Lookouts at Engel Stadium in front of 4,000 fans. Clyde Barfoot got the start for Chattanooga. When he gave up successive hits to Earle Combs and Lyn Lary, manager Bert Niehoff made a call to the bullpen. Mitchell was summoned to pitch. There had been a lot of hype prior to her appearance. One newspaper reported facetiously, "The curves won't be all on the ball when pretty Jackie Mitchell takes the mound." Another writer joked that "she has a swell change of pace and swings a mean lipstick."[114] Before the game, Mitchell—tall, slim, and passably cute—had posed for cameras while powdering her nose and gazing into a pocket mirror.

Fans were cheering wildly as Ruth stepped up to the plate with a wry smile on his face and tipped his cap to the 17-year-old southpaw. He appeared very relaxed in the batter's box. Mitchell's windup included a dramatic windmill motion followed by a sidearm delivery. The Babe swung through two of her first three offerings. After failing to connect a second time, he asked the umpire to inspect the ball. Finding nothing out of place, the arbiter indicated that play should continue. Mitchell's next pitch caught the outside corner for a called strike three. Though many have insisted that Ruth was a willing conspirator in the drama, he looked genuinely irritated when he flung his bat in the dirt and yelled at the official. The crowd was in an uproar as he stalked back to the dugout.

Gehrig's plate appearance was anticlimactic in comparison. The Yankee first-sacker, who would belt 46 homers and drive in 185 runs that year, swung through three straight pitches and returned quietly to the bench. Mitchell, nursing a little tenderness in her arm from weeks of arduous preparation, walked Tony Lazzeri before being removed from the game.

The debate over whether Mitchell's strikeouts were legitimate continues to the present day. After the game, Ruth remarked churlishly to reporters, "I don't know what's going to happen if they let women into baseball. Of course, they will never make good. Why? Because they are too delicate. It would kill them to play ball every day."[115]

A writer from the New York Times speculated that Mitchell's appearance had been a convincing bit of vaudeville, remarking that "[Ruth] performed his role very ably."[116] Since the game was originally scheduled for April Fool's Day, many sportswriters assumed that the strikeouts had been staged as a prank. Ben Chapman, who was waiting on deck when Mitchell was pulled from the mound, agreed that Ruth and Gehrig were probably in on the ruse. If they were, they never admitted it publicly. Lefty Gomez—a 21-game winner for the Yankees in 1931—expressed a different view, insisting that manager Joe McCarthy was far too competitive to have allowed his best hitters to lay down for a girl, even in an exhibition game.

Ruth's statement about women being too fragile to play professional baseball resonated with Commissioner Landis, who voided Mitchell's contract on the grounds that the game was "too strenuous" for her.[117] Mitchell continued to play for various barnstorming teams, including the House of David squads, until the latter half of the 1930s. When the All-American Girls Professional Baseball League (immortalized in the classic comedy film *A League of Their Own*) was formed in 1943, she refused to come out of retirement.

Years later, Joe Engel claimed that Mitchell's appearance had been an elaborate hoax. In a letter to a newspaper, he stated explicitly, "Between you and me, [Mitchell] couldn't pitch hay to a cow. But she looked mighty pretty in the regulation league uniform I had made for her, and I had a record attendance that day."[118] Mitchell insisted until the time of her death in 1987 that she had struck out the Yankees duo fair and square. "Hell, better hitters than them couldn't hit me," she said boldly. "Why should they have been any different?"[119]

Major League Baseball imposed a ban on signing women to contracts in 1952. It remained in place until the Chicago White Sox drafted an 18-year-old pitcher named Carey Schueler in 1993.

McCarthy in Charge

With the departure of Bob Shawkey, players were forced to adapt to the managerial style of Joe McCarthy. Described by multiple sources as "strict but fair,"[120] he seized immediate control of the club, imposing restrictions on card playing and shaving in the clubhouse. He also scheduled mandatory breakfasts at the team's hotel when the Yankees were on the road.

Unlike his predecessors, McCarthy never reached the majors as a player. He had grown up in Philadelphia and attended Niagara University on a baseball scholarship. Though he played for some of the top minor-league teams of the Deadball Era, a childhood mishap had left him with damaged cartilage in his knee. His career ended at the Double-A level in 1921. Finished as a player, he managed in the American Association for several seasons before taking over the Chicago Cubs.

McCarthy became popular in Chicago, receiving the nickname "Marse Joe." In 1929, he led the Cubs to a World Series appearance. It was the team's first pennant in more than a decade. But after burying the Yankees during the regular season, the A's continued their winning ways, eliminating Chicago in five games. The low point for McCarthy came in Game 4, when his pitching staff coughed up 10 runs in the seventh inning, squandering an 8–0 lead.

The Cubs failed to repeat as NL champions in 1930. Though the club spent most of August in first place, a September swoon cost McCarthy his job. He was replaced by Rogers Hornsby with four games still left to play. When the deal was finalized, owner William Wrigley Jr. remarked sourly, "I have always wanted a world championship and I am not sure that Joe McCarthy is the man to give me that kind of team."[121]

Ruth's relationship with his new boss was strained from the onset. Having been passed over for the manager's position, he grumbled behind the scenes, questioning McCarthy's ability to lead the Yankees without any big-league playing experience. Very much aware of the Babe's troubled history with authority figures, McCarthy chose not to confront the slugger on any major issues. His laissez-faire attitude achieved the desired effect, as Ruth behaved himself for the most part and performed commendably on the field. Author Leigh Montville described the arrangement as follows: "It was an efficient situation, a truce, but [it] lacked a certain joy."[122]

The pieces of a championship puzzle were already present in the Bronx. It was just a matter of making them all fit. McCarthy moved third baseman Ben Chapman to the outfield. He filled the hole with former Indians great Joe Sewell, who was in the late stages of a Hall of Fame career. Lefty Gomez and Red Ruffing became McCarthy's top pitchers as Herb Pennock and George Pipgras were gradually phased out.

Success did not happen overnight for Marse Joe. The Yankees increased their win total to 94 in his debut, but they lagged significantly behind the A's, who ran away with the pennant for the third straight year. Ruth had one of his best seasons ever, hitting .373 with 46 homers. It was the last time he would lead the league in that category.

Though the Yankees had placed numbers on their uniforms in 1929, McCarthy refused to wear one. He also refused to argue with umpires unless his disagreement pertained directly to the rulebook. Elaborating on his conservative approach to the game, *New York Times* correspondent Arthur Daley wrote, "Few men in baseball were as single-minded as [McCarthy]. That was his strength and weakness. Baseball was his entire life and it never was lightened by laughter because he was a grim, humorless man with a brooding introspection which ate his heart out."[123]

McCarthy's managerial philosophy was summarized in an article entitled "Ten Commandments for Success in Baseball," which first appeared in a 1949 edition of the *Boston Herald*. Highlights are as follows:

"Nobody became a ballplayer by walking after a ball."

"You will never become a .300 hitter unless you take the bat off your shoulder."

"Keep your head up and you may not have to keep it down."

"A pitcher who hasn't control, hasn't anything."

"Don't fight too much with the umpires. You cannot expect them to be as perfect as you are."[124]

Although he got off to a lukewarm start in New York, McCarthy would eventually become one of the most successful managers in Yankees history. In his first 13 seasons, the team finished in first or second place 12 times. This included six seasons with at least 100 wins. By the time he left New York in May of 1946 due to an ongoing drinking problem, he had led the team to seven World Series titles—a record later tied by Casey Stengel. He was the first manager to capture a pennant in both leagues.

RUTH'S LAST SPECTACULAR SEASON

On August 21, 1931, Ruth hit his 600th career homer. There were plenty of other fence-busters around by then, but the Babe was light years ahead of them all. His chief competitors were Jimmie Foxx, Lou Gehrig, and Rogers Hornsby. None had accumulated more than 295 homers by the end of the 1931 slate, and none would hit 600 during their careers.

As of 2021, there were only nine players in the elite 600 home run club. The Babe got there quicker than any slugger in history, reaching the milestone in just 6,821 at-bats. Though his lifetime totals were surpassed by Barry

Bonds and Hank Aaron, Ruth compiled the lowest at-bat per home run ratio among the three (as illustrated below):

Lifetime At-Bats Per Home Run
Hank Aaron   16.37
Barry Bonds   12.92
Babe Ruth   11.76

With the Great Depression in full swing, attendance at major-league ballgames dropped by 17 percent in 1931. Responding to this distressing trend, owners decided to reduce the size of their rosters before the 1932 campaign. Ruth haggled with Yankees executives for two months before accepting a $5,000 pay cut. He didn't deserve it. Attendance at the stadium remained robust throughout his career in pinstripes. And his presence on the field was a boon to opposing teams. "They would be drawing 1,500 per game in St. Louis," said former Yankee captain Roger Peckinpaugh. "We'd go in there with the Babe and they'd be all over the ballpark—thousands and thousands of people coming out to see that one guy. Whatever the owners paid him, it wasn't enough. It couldn't be."[125]

Joe McCarthy tinkered with the Yankees lineup again in 1932, promoting Frankie Crosetti and Johnny Allen from the minors. Crosetti, a mainstay at shortstop until the arrival of Phil Rizzuto, remained with the organization for almost 40 years as a player and coach. He won so many World Series rings that the Yankees eventually started giving him engraved shotguns instead. Allen, a right-handed pitcher who employed a variety of arm angles, posted a 17–4 record in his debut. His volatile temper and brooding nature led to an eventual trade in 1935.

For George Pipgras, the 1932 campaign was the beginning of the end. It was the last season in which he worked more than 200 innings and won at least 15 games. Herb Pennock was on the way out as well, making just 22 appearances—his lowest total in over a decade. Meanwhile, Lefty Gomez and Red Ruffing emerged as one of the most effective pitching duos in the majors, piling up 42 wins and 366 strikeouts. Their combined ERA was nearly a full point below the league average.

The A's remained the team to beat in 1932. Though Jimmie Foxx and Al Simmons jointly surpassed the power numbers of Ruth and Gehrig, the Yankees won 14 of 22 head-to-head matchups between the two clubs. It made all the difference as Philly slumped to second place for the first time since 1928. McCarthy's crew piled up 107 wins—the highest total since the Murderer's Row days.

While the Yankees were busy wrapping up the pennant, the Babe returned to the silver screen in a series of movie shorts, which were released through Universal Pictures. Shooting had taken place in Los Angeles during the fall of 1931. The most entertaining of the bunch was a comedy entitled *Fancy Curves*, which included a cameo appearance by the slugger's wife. In the nine-minute single-reel film, Ruth coaches a group of college girls in a game against a rival fraternity. In the final sequence, he disguises himself as a woman and hits a walk-off grand slam. As he tips his hat to the crowd, his wig comes off, revealing his true identity. He is promptly chased out of the stadium by his opponents, who realize they have been duped.

Before the 1932 campaign, a rumor surfaced that Ruth intended to buy the Red Sox and become a player-manager. As the story began to spread, the slugger felt obligated to negate its validity. "Right now, I haven't the dough," he told a writer from the Associated Press.[126] The Babe was in his late 30s at the start of the season and his knees were bothering him on a daily basis. To give him some rest, McCarthy got in the habit of inserting Sammy Byrd or Myril Hoag as late-inning replacements.

It was an excellent year for Ruth overall. He cracked 41 homers and drove in 137 runs. He also led the league with 130 walks and a .489 on-base percentage. He could have generated even better stats had he not been forced out of the lineup on two separate occasions. In mid-July, he injured his leg while chasing a fly ball and had to be carried off the field. He spent two days in the hospital recuperating. In early September, he experienced shooting pains in his right side after a game in Philadelphia. Convinced it was appendicitis, he sought medical attention in New York. No surgery was necessary, but he was sidelined for over two weeks. In his absence, the Yankees clinched the pennant.

On September 17, Ruth took batting practice against an amateur pitcher at Yankee Stadium. When he failed to hit a single ball into the stands, reporters expressed concern. "They had me packed in ice," he explained. "And I don't feel thawed out yet."[127] Any lingering doubts about his health were laid to rest a week later when he homered off of Red Sox reliever John Michaels. He finished the season with a .341 batting average—the fifth highest mark in the American League. When the World Series opened, he was back in top form.

THE CALLED SHOT

The 1932 Cubs had some excellent hitters in their lineup (including future Hall of Famers Gabby Hartnett and Kiki Cuyler), but the key to their success was strong pitching. Chicago hurlers collectively posted the lowest ERA in the majors while allowing fewer hits than any NL club. Lon Warneke—nicknamed "The Arkansas Hummingbird" on account of his darting fastball—became the ace of the staff with a league-high 22 wins. Three other starters gathered at least 15 victories as the Cubs returned to the postseason after a two-year absence.

The World Series was a grudge match. Chicago executives had abruptly dismissed Joe McCarthy near the end of the 1930 campaign. Now he was returning with the Yankees to crush their championship hopes. Heightening existing antipathy between the two teams, the Cubs offended the sensibilities of many with their excessive frugality. After being dismissed from his managerial duties in August, Rogers Hornsby was denied a World Series share. Several other staff members were allotted half or quarter shares. Mark Koenig—a former Yankee—was among those who were short-changed.

The story of Koenig's arrival in Chicago is like a chapter from a pulp crime novel. In July of 1932, a disturbed young woman named Violet Popovich booked a room at the Hotel Carlos, where many Cubs players stayed during the regular season. The 21-year-old showgirl had an axe to grind with infielder Billy Jurges. She had met the slick-fielding shortstop at a party the previous year and fallen head over heels for him. Jurges, who wasn't much of a ladies' man, was not as enchanted. When he tried to break off the relationship, Popovich made plans to kill him and end her own life. In a letter to her brother, she wrote: "To me, life without Billy isn't worth living, but why should I leave this earth alone? I'm going to take Billy with me."[128] Before a July 6 game against the Phillies, she went to Jurges's hotel room and pulled out a .25 caliber pistol. Three shots went off as the couple wrestled for possession of the gun. Two of them hit Jurges and one hit Popovich. Though the resulting injuries were not life-threatening, the Cubs found themselves in need of a shortstop.

Koenig had been a regular on two of the greatest Yankee squads of all time, but he was struggling to return to form. Traded to Detroit in 1930, he accrued a paltry .247 batting average over portions of two seasons. A subpar fielder with curiously small hands, he was equipped with a powerful arm. Taking note of this, the Tigers experimented with him as a pitcher. He failed miserably, posting an 8.44 ERA in five appearances. Demoted to the Pacific Coast League in 1932, he found his swing again. Called to Chicago, he assembled an 18-game hitting streak, finishing the season at .353. When his new teammates voted to give him a half share of the postseason proceeds, several members of the Yankees took exception.

According to Koenig, it would have cost Chicago players just $50 more per man to award him a full share. This didn't sit well with Ruth, who had been a friend to Koenig in New York. Ruth usually resorted to verbal sparring as a form of self-defense, but when the Cubs arrived at Yankee Stadium for the series opener, he went on the offensive.

"Hiya, Mark," he said to Koenig. "Who are those cheapskate, nickel-nursing sonsabitches you're with?"[129]

Inspired by the Babe's invective, other players joined in and didn't let up until the series was over. Naturally, the Cubs didn't take it lying down. They needled Ruth on a wide variety of topics from his failed managerial bid to the extra pounds he had added to his considerable frame. Their barbs failed to impair the slugger's usefulness at the plate. In the first two games—both of which were won by the Yankees—the Babe gathered a pair of hits and three walks, scoring four runs. His performance in Game 3 cemented his legacy as a World Series idol.

When the Yankees arrived at their hotel in Chicago before the third meeting, they were peppered with insults from a hostile crowd. The abuse continued at Wrigley Field, where more than 50,000 people showed up early to watch batting practice. Whenever a ball was hit to Ruth during warm-ups, fans tossed a few scattered lemons onto the field. The Babe picked them up each time and lobbed them back into the crowd. When it was his turn in the cage, he lifted more than half a dozen pitches into the seats. A strong wind was blowing toward right field—an ideal scenario for the Ruth/Gehrig tandem. Finished taking his practice swings, the Babe reportedly commented, "I'd play for half my salary if I could hit in this dump all the time."[130]

Chicago's Game 3 starter was Charlie Root. Among the most reliable members of the Cubs staff, he helped the club to four World Series appearances in a 10-year span. His 201 career victories are still a franchise record. Equipped with an explosive fastball and knee-buckling curve, he was not shy about throwing inside—a habit that earned him the nickname "Chinski."

The game got off to a rough start for the Cubs as Earle Combs reached base on an error by shortstop Billy Jurges (who had returned to the lineup when Koenig hurt his wrist in Game 1). Joe Sewell followed with a walk. As Ruth strolled to the batting circle, more lemons were thrown in his direction. One of Root's pitches caught a little too much of the plate and the Babe planted it in the seats for a three-run homer. It was the 14th postseason blast of his career.

Banter between the Cubs and Yankees continued throughout the game. Fans in the right field bleachers harassed Ruth relentlessly—especially in the fourth inning, when he was slow retrieving a weak liner hit by Jurges. Taking advantage of the aging outfielder's sluggishness, Jurges ended up on second base. Ruth, in response to the deafening shouts of bleacherites, tipped his cap and hollered back at them.

After being retired on a fly ball in the third, the Babe came to bat again in the fifth inning. There are so many conflicting accounts of the plate appearance, it is difficult to determine precisely what took place. Sticking to established facts, another lemon was thrown at the slugger as he approached home plate. He gestured toward the stands and settled into the batter's box with one out and nobody on. The first pitch from Charlie Root was a strike. Several Cubs players were out on the dugout steps shouting. Ruth gazed in their direction and defiantly held up one finger. Working carefully, Root missed the plate with his next two offerings, pushing the count to 2–1. His fourth pitch was another called strike, prompting more catcalls from the Chicago bench jockeys. The Babe held up two fingers, perhaps to remind his antagonists that he still had one strike coming to him. Catcher Gabby Hartnett swore he heard Ruth say, "It only takes one to hit it." Root barked at the slugger then, prompting a threat in return. According to Lou Gehrig, who was stationed in the on-deck circle, Ruth snarled something to the effect of, "I'm going to knock the next one down your goddamn throat."[131]

Then came the ambiguous gesture . . .

Did Ruth point to center field or did he motion toward the Cubs bench? No one seems to know for certain. A 16mm home movie that surfaced many years later (though shaky and somewhat out of focus) suggests that the latter scenario was likely. Whatever the case, the events that followed have never been up for debate. Root delivered a slow curve that the Babe positively destroyed. Aided by the prevailing winds, the ball sailed clear out of the park, giving the Yankees a 5–4 lead. Ruth appeared joyous as he jogged around the bases, waving his arms and talking trash to Chicago infielders. In a box seat behind home plate, presidential candidate Franklin Delano Roosevelt threw his head back and laughed as the Babe crossed the plate.

The idea of a "called shot" was championed by Tribune Syndicate reporter Westbrook Pegler. In the days, months, and years that followed, the story was debunked, confirmed, and then held in question all over again. Ruth verified and denied the details on multiple occasions. "He called shots all the time," researcher Leigh Montville wrote. "He loved to create situations. It was for the other people to determine what they meant."[132] Weighing in on the topic, Charlie Root told a journalist unequivocally, "Ruth most certainly did not call his home run in that game. . . . I'd have put one in his ear and knocked him on his ass."[133]

While Ruth's memorable at-bat has been discussed exhaustively over the years, Gehrig's performance has been virtually forgotten. The Iron Horse hit .529 in the series sweep with three homers—one of them immediately following Ruth's "called shot." He gathered eight RBIs and scored nine runs. But all anyone could talk about was the Babe's disputed home run. Commenting on this glaring injustice, biographer Jonathan Eig remarked, "Gehrig must have been used to it by then. Somehow, the spotlight always seemed to miss him. He had all the talent in the world but little of the luck. Yet he never grumbled and never cried for attention."[134]

That attention would come soon enough. Past his prime as a player, Ruth would fade rapidly over the next three seasons, leaving Gehrig to carry the club until the arrival of Joe DiMaggio.

THE RIFT BETWEEN RUTH AND GEHRIG

When the Yankees placed numbers on their uniforms in 1929, Ruth and Gehrig became indelibly connected to one another. In a way, Ruth's number 3 and Gehrig's number 4 were a symbolic representation of their complex relationship. The Babe always came first in order of importance. And Gehrig was content to remain out of the limelight.

Ruth's public image as a mentor to Gehrig was manufactured to a great extent by agent Christy Walsh. If Walsh hadn't brought the two together, it seems doubtful they would have forged a bond beyond the confines of the ball field. They were polar opposites. Gehrig was humble, reserved, and respectful of authority figures. Ruth was none of those things. Yet Gehrig appreciated the opportunity to get to know the Babe on a personal level. He was in awe of Ruth. And he learned a lot while barnstorming with baseball's most colorful character. "It was an education to travel around with the Big Bam," Gehrig once said. "Not a book education I mean, but for a boy like me getting his first long-distance close-up of these United States, it was an education in meeting people and seeing things."[135]

In spite of their differences, Ruth and Gehrig got along famously—for a while anyway. During the offseason, they played cards, fished, and interacted regularly with one another's families. Author Jane Leavy wrote that at the height of the friendship, "their admiration and affection were reciprocal."[136]

The disparity between the two personalities was readily apparent whenever they got together for a round of bridge. Ruth always drank during the games while Gehrig—an extremely cautious player—preferred to remain sober. The Babe invariably made outrageous bids, knowing it drove Gehrig crazy. Many of the sessions ended with the Iron Horse abruptly throwing his cards on the table in frustration and asking Ruth to tally up the final score.

Reporters often wondered if Gehrig was jealous of the Babe. An article published in *Liberty* magazine after the 1932 World Series dismissed that notion to an extent. Gehrig reported that he had no inferiority complex when it came to his more celebrated teammate. He made it clear that he considered Ruth a friend and equal as well as a rival. Though he didn't mind losing the annual home run races, he admitted that he took great pride in gathering more RBIs (which became a regular occurrence after the 1926 campaign).

Even when things were going well, the two remained at odds on a wide assortment of subjects. They were of completely opposite mindsets when it came to Miller Huggins, whom Gehrig adored and Ruth habitually abused. Gehrig also got along well with Joe McCarthy, a man the Babe had deemed unfit for major-league service. Another point of contention: Gehrig didn't approve of Ruth's philandering. Conversely, the Bambino found the Yankee first baseman a bit too prudish for his tastes.

At some point in 1932, a major schism occurred. Ruth had always liked Gehrig's mother, Christina, and the meals she prepared. He sometimes brought his daughter, Dorothy, along with him when he visited her home. But after he married Claire, he was not as warmly received.

Though images of Ruth's seemingly happy family often graced the pages of newspapers and magazines, there was trouble in paradise. Dorothy had never felt that her father was attentive enough. And she never forgave him for leaving her in the hands of a caretaker after the death of Helen. In her memoirs, Dorothy described Claire as a raging alcoholic who assigned her to the maid's quarters, dressed her in secondhand clothing, and sent her off to deficient schools. In Claire's defense, Dorothy was a sullen child who regularly defied the input of adults. An incorrigible tomboy, she was better suited to hand-me-down clothes. Sadly, it was Dorothy's wardrobe that indirectly drove a wedge between Ruth and Gehrig.

When Dorothy showed up at the Gehrig home one day looking particularly disheveled, Christina commented that Claire's daughter, Julia, often appeared in public wearing "silks and satins" while Dorothy was given "nothing but rags to wear." The remark got back to Claire, who issued a direct order to the Babe: "Tell Lou to muzzle his mother." Ruth was none too happy himself and, during a clubhouse confrontation, he barked at Gehrig, "Your mother should mind her own goddamn business."[137] Gehrig—a mama's boy since early childhood—was highly offended by the remark. The two men had to be separated by teammates. It was the end of their friendship. Though they posed for group photos and traveled together with the team, they stopped speaking to one another. Gehrig even refused to shake Ruth's hand after his home runs.

In spite of his matinee idol looks, Gehrig was awkward around women. He had met his future bride, Eleanor Twitchell, at a party in Chicago during the 1920s, but was too shy to ask her out on a formal date. In 1932, he ran into her again. They began exchanging letters and talking regularly on the phone. After months of avoiding the topic, Gehrig finally admitted to Eleanor that he was in love with her. Things moved rather quickly after that and the couple was married in 1933. To avoid interference from Gehrig's meddling mother, a private ceremony was held at the infielder's apartment in New Rochelle. The Ruths were conspicuously absent from the reception.

In 1934, Ruth and Gehrig traveled to Japan for an exhibition tour. Gehrig had injured his hand on a previous visit to the Far East and Jacob Ruppert advised him not to go. When Gehrig explained that he intended to use the trip as a honeymoon of sorts, Ruppert reluctantly offered his blessing. During the voyage across the North Pacific, Eleanor ran into Ruth's wife. They got to talking about how silly the feud between their husbands had become. Claire extended an invitation to join her for a few cocktails and Eleanor accepted. Unable to locate his spouse, Gehrig became frantic, enlisting the help of staff to search the ship. When he found the two women drinking in the Ruth's cabin, he was infuriated. The Babe showed up later in an attempt to make amends, but his offer of friendship was coldly rejected by Gehrig.

Hostility between the two men was rekindled in 1937, when Ruth made some disparaging remarks to reporters. By then, the Babe had retired as a player while Gehrig was padding his "Iron Man" record. Gehrig's streak of consecutive games stood at 1,808 at the end of the 1936 campaign. Offering his unabashed opinion to reporters, Ruth commented, "I think Lou's making one of the biggest mistakes a ballplayer can make by keeping up that 'Iron Man' stuff. He's already cut three years off his baseball life with it. He ought to learn how to sit on the bench and rest because the Yankees aren't going to pay off on how many games in a row he's played."[138] Ruth's words (though they actually had merit) really got under Gehrig's skin. The Yankees first-sacker told writers that he felt great and knew how much his body could handle. He assured them that he would bench himself if he felt he was a detriment to the club. Most reasonably informed baseball fans know how that turned out. The feud continued until the day of Gehrig's famous "Luckiest Man" speech, when the Iron Horse finally accepted a public gesture of affection from the Babe.

BIRTH OF THE MIDSUMMER CLASSIC

Before the start of the 1933 campaign, Jacob Ruppert made it known that he had refunded a small fortune to ticket holders for the World Series games that weren't played. With 15 million Americans out of work and half of the nation's banks unable to meet their financial obligations, it was obvious to everyone that pay cuts were on the way. Ruth took a tremendous hit when he signed for $52,000—a loss of more than 30 percent. He grumbled about it, but not very loudly and not for very long. Commissioner Landis had set the tone the previous year when he shaved a large chunk off of his own salary. He took another 20 percent cut in 1933.

Ruth was optimistic about his physical health during spring training. He told reporters that he intended to play every day. But as usual, this turned out to be a gross overstatement. Though he appeared in 137 games, he was pulled for a defensive replacement in more than half of them. Thick in the middle and slow afoot, he stopped running out ground balls. His limited range made him a liability in the outfield. He also experienced the longest home run drought of his career to that point—a ponderous streak spanning more than three weeks. When rumors surfaced that his eyesight was failing, he adamantly denied the claims.

Though the Babe was clearly fading, he generated plenty of highlights. In a doubleheader against the Tigers on July 9, he went 5-for-7 at the plate with three home runs, six RBIs, and five runs scored. He cleared the fence twice in the opener—one of four multihomer games that year. At season's end, his numbers weren't exactly Ruthian, but they weren't bad at all. He finished second in the annual home run race to Jimmie Foxx. And he led the majors with 114 walks. His most exciting performance came during a ground-breaking event at Comiskey Park on July 6.

When *Chicago Tribune* sportswriter Arch Ward unveiled his plan for an All-Star Game, he knew he would face multiple obstacles. For starters, he had to convince baseball executives that it was a good idea. With the Great Depression wreaking havoc on America, team owners needed all the paid admissions they could get. The idea of shutting down the season for two or three days to stage an exhibition—no matter how grand—was not supported by all 16 clubs. But Ward was determined to make it happen.

With the help of league presidents William Harridge (AL) and John Heydler (NL), the pieces began to fall into place. The World's Fair was being held in Chicago, and given its rich baseball tradition, the city seemed an ideal setting. Comiskey Park was chosen as a venue on account of its large seating capacity and proximity to the fair's "Century of Progress" exhibition, which featured the first appearance of central air conditioning and dishwashers (along with a host of other new technologies). Organizers announced that the proceeds would go to a charity benefiting disabled and retired major leaguers.

Selling the concept to the general public, Ward wrote in a May 19 edition of the *Tribune*, "Never has the maximum strength of one major league been pitted against the maximum strength of the other. For years, baseball fans the country over have been arguing the relative class of the two leagues. National League fans, for instance, had to admit after the 1932 World Series that the American League had at least one team that was far superior to any in the National. But they were insistent that the league as whole was a match for the American. Player talent, they said, was more evenly distributed in the National League. The game in Chicago July 6 will help clear up this controversy."[139]

Fans were asked to mail their votes for the starting lineups to the *Tribune* offices. Within a few weeks, more than 50 other newspapers had joined in the balloting process, including the *New York Daily News*, *Boston Herald*, and *Cincinnati Post*. League presidents were assigned the task of selecting two umpires apiece. They were also put in charge of choosing the managers. Two of the all-time greatest were recruited: Connie Mack for the Americans and John McGraw for the Nationals. By early June, the idea of a clash between the rival leagues had caught fire. Reporter Westbrook Pegler referred to Ward's brainchild as "the only constructive original idea which has been introduced into the baseball industry since the invention of the recording turnstile."[140]

More than 49,000 tickets were sold, generating more than $45,000 for charity. On an interesting side note, box seats for the game cost just $1.65 while grandstand tickets sold for $1. Only five players received more votes than Ruth and, not surprisingly, two of them were from the host city—Al Simmons of the White Sox and Gabby Hartnett of the Cubs. The starting lineups featured 11 future Hall of Famers with nine Cooperstown greats landing among the reserves. In addition to Ruth, four other Yankees were selected. Gehrig was a starter along with pitcher Lefty Gomez, but Bill Dickey and Tony Lazzeri ended up as spectators. There was no convention requiring managers to use every player on the roster, and in an almost comical oversight, Connie Mack left Jimmie Foxx—a Triple Crown winner that year—on the bench. "I made no changes in the team because I did not believe in breaking up a winning combination," Mack later said.[141] The *Sporting News* reported, "Most of the 49,000 fans at Comiskey Park were disappointed because Jimmie Foxx didn't get into the game and they gave Lou Gehrig the razzberry in the fifth inning when he dropped Dick Bartell's easy foul."[142]

Though the game served as a who's who in baseball, Ruth was still the main attraction. NL starter Bill Hallahan remarked: "We wanted to see the Babe. Sure, he was old and had a big waistline, but that didn't make any difference. We were on the same field as Babe Ruth."[143] As he had done so many times before, the Yankees idol rose to the occasion. Associated Press writer William Weekes summarized Ruth's big moment: "The typical Ruthian gesture came in the third inning with Charlie Gehringer of Detroit on first base. Wild Bill Hallahan of the St. Louis Cardinals, who was Wild Bill at his wildest while he was in there, was the victim. With the count one ball and a strike, Hallahan served the next one up about knee-high and outside. A mighty swing by the 39-year-old Ruth and the ball sailed on a line into the lower deck of the right field stands."[144]

Ruth's big homer held up as the deciding blow in a 4–2 AL victory. He made the defensive play of the game as well. With Lefty Grove on the mound in the eighth, the Nationals sent the tying run to the plate. Reds outfielder Chick Hafey lifted a towering drive to deep right field. In spite of his ongoing knee problems, Ruth tracked it all the way to the wall, where he hauled it in for the final out of the inning. "He was marvelous," McGraw commented after the game. "That old boy certainly came through when they needed him."[145] Writing for the *New York Times*, John Kieran wholeheartedly agreed: "Give him a crowd, a gallery worth his best effort, and the old warrior will put on his show. . . . He isn't what he used to be. But pack the stands, set the stage, turn up the lights and who is it brings down the house with his act? The Babe."[146]

The season held at least one more remarkable moment for Ruth. With the Yankees out of pennant contention on October 1, Joe McCarthy allowed him to take the mound against the Red Sox. Though he was known to pitch in exhibition and barnstorming games from time to time, he hadn't logged any official regular season work in more than three years. His last outing had ended well—a 9–3 win over Boston. And so, in an attempt to pump up attendance at Yankee Stadium, the veteran southpaw returned to the hill.

The game had been widely advertised beforehand. Ruth had thrown several rounds of batting practice in preparation. A crowd of 25,000 turned out—more than four times the single-game average of any American League club that year. Creating a picnic-like atmosphere, there were pregame festivities that included a fungo-hitting contest and races on the basepaths. When the game started, Ruth looked a lot like his former self. He turned in five solid innings before fatigue set in. In the bottom of the fifth, he helped his own cause with his 34th homer of the season. It gave the Yankees a 4–0 lead. The sixth inning was a disaster as he yielded 4 runs on 5 hits and a walk. Most managers would have pulled the Babe at that point, but with the Yankees ahead, 6–4, McCarthy let the wilting star finish what he had begun. After coughing up another run in the eighth, he retired the side in order in the ninth. It was the 107th complete game of his career. The victory pushed his lifetime won-loss record to 94–46. The runs he surrendered raised his ERA slightly, from 2.25 to 2.28. When it was over, his arm hurt so badly he swore he would never pitch again. By his own report, he was unable to comb his hair or feed himself for a week.

THE DOWNWARD SPIRAL

Ruth told reporters multiple times that he would retire after his 20th season. As the new year approached, he changed his mind. He still wanted to manage the Yankees. The fact that Joe McCarthy was signed through the 1935 campaign was not the only thing standing in his way. Though Yankees executives kept up a cordial front, they were not-so-secretly looking for an end to their long association with the Babe. His skills were in decline. His relationship with Gehrig was in ruins. And he was harboring ongoing feelings of resentment toward McCarthy. The negatives were beginning to outweigh the positives. Ed Barrow told the slugger that if an offer to manage elsewhere surfaced, he ought to take it.

When Tom Yawkey purchased the Red Sox in 1932, he considered hiring Ruth as manager. It was GM Eddie Collins who ultimately talked him out of it. Reports later surfaced that the White Sox might be interested. Vague overtures were made by the Reds as well, but nothing substantial ever materialized from either source. The Babe assured writers that he wouldn't be picky about his choice of clubs. He figured he might fare better with a noncontender since any improvement would be credited to him.

At the end of the 1933 campaign, a tangible gesture was made by Tigers owner Frank Navin. Attendance in Detroit had been declining for years and Navin thought that putting Ruth in charge might help. While the 1933 World Series was underway, Yankee executives indicated that they might be able to orchestrate a deal. With the preliminaries out of the way, the onus was on the Babe, who had been booked by Christy Walsh to participate in a series of barnstorming games in Hawaii. Navin invited the Yankee outfielder to speak with him in Detroit, but for some reason, Ruth chose to delay the meeting. Barrow knew he was making a mistake and said so.

The Babe spent a few days at the World's Fair in Chicago with his wife and daughter Julia. He then traveled to California, where a cruise ship was waiting to take him and the other all-stars to Honolulu. When he arrived in Los Angeles, he telephoned Navin explaining that he would be leaving soon and wanted an answer regarding the manager's position. According to one source, it was 3:00 a.m. in Detroit when the conversation took place. Irritated by Ruth's arrogance, Navin responded with a firm "no." Numerous writers criticized the slugger's poor handling of the situation.

After learning of Navin's rejection, Barrow launched a clever subterfuge, offering the Babe a position with the Newark Bears of the International League. He was positive that Ruth would screw it up somehow or grow tired of the job altogether and quit. The gambit failed. Viewing it as a demotion of sorts, baseball's reigning home run king flat out rejected the proposal.

On January 15, the Yankees resigned themselves to tolerating their fading star for at least one more season. Ruth signed a contract for $35,000—another major reduction from the previous year. He was still the highest-paid player in baseball, but his best days were clearly behind him. His performance in 1934 dramatically illustrated that fact.

Though the Babe hit .429 in spring training games, the regular season was full of lowlights. About a month into the campaign, he caught a bad cold and was out for several days. In June, he was struck by a pitch on the wrist and fell into a horrendous slump, going eight straight games without a hit. A couple of weeks later, he was lumbering from first to second when a grounder off the bat of Gehrig hit him in the leg. He went down hard and had to be carried off the field. While waiting for an ambulance to transport him to the hospital for X-rays, he talked about quitting.

Throughout the 1934 slate, Ruth was more vocal than ever in his criticism of Joe McCarthy. The Yankees weren't doing terribly, but Ruth's conspicuous decline left a gaping hole in the lineup. Bill Dickey led first-string catchers in both leagues with a .322 batting average. And Gehrig had another phenomenal season, capturing a Triple Crown. But the rest of the Yankee hitters were just okay. When centerfielder Earle Combs incurred serious injuries after crashing into the outfield wall at Sportsman's Park in St. Louis, Myril Hoag was inserted as a replacement. Proving he was half the player Combs was, he batted .267 with 13 extra-base hits in 97 appearances.

Originally intended as a one-and-done affair, the All-Star Game became an annual custom. The 1934 edition was held at the Polo Grounds in New York. Ruth was inserted as a starter again, but he was not as spectacular this time around, going 0-for-2 at the plate with a pair of walks. Carl Hubbell of the Giants stole the show when he struck out five Hall of Famers in a row. The Babe was among them. After allowing Charlie Gehringer and Heinie Manush to reach base in the first inning, Hubbell followed with punch-outs of Ruth, Gehrig, and Jimmie Foxx. His victims in the second inning were Al Simmons and Joe Cronin. Hubbell, who was elected to Cooperstown in 1947, was taken off guard by his performance. "I never was a strikeout pitcher like Bob Feller or Dizzy Dean or Dazzy Vance," he later said. "My style of pitching was to make the other team hit the ball, but on the ground. It was a big surprise to me to strike out all those fellows as it probably was to them."[147]

On July 13, Ruth hit his 700th career homer off Tommy Bridges of the Tigers. As he was rounding third, he told coach Art Fletcher that he wanted the ball as a souvenir. A 16-year-old kid named Lennie Bielski, who had snatched it from underneath a car parked outside Navin Field, got the surprise of his life when he was escorted into the stadium by ushers and policemen. In exchange for Ruth's home run ball, he received another baseball autographed by the Big Fellow himself, along with a box seat and $20.

Ruth had his own radio show, which aired three times per week throughout the season. Each installment featured a re-creation of the greatest moments of his career. Sadly, his biggest achievements were behind him now.

His 700th homer was not even the game-winning hit. Bill Dickey earned that distinction with a two-run double.

Ruth's season wasn't poor by any standards, but it paled in comparison to his past efforts. In 125 games, he gathered 43 extra-base hits (including 22 homers) and drove in 84 runs. His contributions failed to help the Yankees capture the pennant. They finished second behind the Tigers—the team that Ruth had blown a chance at managing!

Some would say it was poetic justice.

THE 1934 TOUR OF JAPAN

Baseball was introduced to Japan during the 19th century by Horace Wilson and Hiraoka Hiroshi. Wilson was an American professor teaching in Tokyo. Hiroshi—a Japanese engineer—studied in the United States and assembled a team with coworkers during the 1870s. The game quickly grew in popularity, especially on college campuses. Established in 1925, the Tokyo Big6 League featured teams from prominent universities. Prior to the birth of the Japanese Baseball League (the nation's first professional circuit), the Big6 was considered the highest level of competition.

American all-star teams began touring Japan during the early 1900s. A number of exhibitions were organized in the years that followed. Though the games were almost always won by visiting clubs, they never failed to draw legions of fans.

In 1934, media mogul Matsutaro Shoriki (universally known as the father of Japanese professional baseball) invited A's owner-manager Connie Mack to bring a team to Japan for an exhibition series. Though the National League prohibited players from participating, Mack assembled a team for the ages. In addition to Ruth, the roster included AL superstars Jimmie Foxx, Earl Averill, and Charlie Gehringer. Lou Gehrig and Lefty Gomez were also recruited. The team was dubbed the "All Americans."

Players traveled aboard the *Empress of Japan*—a state-of-the-art ocean liner reputed to be the fastest in the Pacific. On their way to Japan, the All Americans stopped in Honolulu to play a warm-up game against a team composed of Hawaiian all-stars. The Hawaiian squad was diverse, featuring Chinese, Portuguese, and Japanese players in addition to a number of native islanders. The game was held at Honolulu Stadium, which offered a spectacular view of the Diamond Head volcano beyond the center field fence. An indicator of things to come, the All Americans won easily by a score of 8–1.

Upon arriving in Japan, Mack's all-star squad was welcomed by half a million people, who jammed the streets of Tokyo. Proving that Ruth had admirers in the far corners of the world, enthusiastic fans shouted out his name as he rode through the streets waving flags from the United States and Japan. One ambitious admirer went as far as to knock on the door of his suite at the Imperial Hotel in search of autographs. Ruth cordially honored the man's request.

The Americans won every game, most of them by a wide margin. The combined score of three contests held in Tokyo between November 10 and November 13 was 37–2. But on November 20, at Kusangi Stadium in Shizuoka, the Americans met their match. A 17-year-old high school pitcher named Eiji Sawamura struck out Gehringer, Ruth, Gehrig, and Foxx in succession. He held the visitors to just five hits that day. Gehrig's seventh-inning homer proved to be the deciding blow in a hard-fought 1–0 victory. Sawamura went on to a distinguished professional career that included three no-hitters and a Triple Crown. But his participation in the 1934 barnstorming tour came at a tremendous price. Expelled from high school, he missed an opportunity to attend college. He was killed in action during World War II. An award bearing his name is given to the top starting pitcher in the Nippon Professional Baseball League every year.

Ruth played like a much younger man throughout the tour, hitting .408 with 13 homers. This served to enhance his folk hero status in Japan. When the games were finished, he traveled to other parts of Asia, the Middle East, and Europe with his wife and daughter Julia. Their trip lasted a total of four months.

The Japanese all-stars stayed together after the tour was over and became the country's first professional team. Initially named the Great Japan Tokyo Baseball Club, they later became known as the Yomiuri Giants—the nation's most storied franchise. The Babe remained so popular after his 1934 appearance that Japanese soldiers were known to shout, "To hell with Babe Ruth!" during World War II battles in an effort to discourage their US enemies. At one point, the US Department of Defense actually considered sending Ruth to Guam to deliver radio messages aimed at facilitating a Japanese surrender.

At least one member of the 1934 All American squad had a direct connection to the war effort against Japan. Moe Berg—a journeyman catcher who batted .243 for five teams during his major-league career—later joined the Office of Strategic Services during World War II. A graduate of Princeton and Columbia Law School, he spoke multiple languages and was said to read at least ten newspapers per day. Before the 1934 all-star tour, he signed a contract with *MovieToneNews* to film highlights of the trip. Using a 16mm camera, he generated extensive footage of Tokyo.

On one particular afternoon, he showed up at St. Luke's Hospital with a bouquet of flowers he said were for the daughter of an American ambassador. Instead of visiting the woman's room, he proceeded to the roof of the building, which was one of the tallest in the city. The film he took was said to have later been used by US forces in the planning of bombing raids. In spite of his own idiosyncrasies, Casey Stengel once referred to Berg as "the strangest man ever to play baseball."[148] Berg's 1994 biography was later made into a movie. A 2014 novel entitled *The Bridgeport Hammer* is very loosely based on his career as a US spy. The Office of Strategic Services became known as the Central Intelligence Agency in 1947.

RUTH'S NOT-SO-TRIUMPHANT RETURN TO BOSTON

Braves owner Emil Fuchs was a man of influence. He had a penchant for making things happen—sometimes good and sometimes not so good. An NYU law graduate, he aspired to the position of New York City magistrate. While handling a series of legal matters for the New York Giants, he established a number of connections within the baseball industry. Determined to make a go of it in the National League, he purchased the Braves and abandoned his legal pursuits.

The Braves had won a World Series in 1914, but their glory years were long behind them by the time Fuchs arrived. After a 50–103 showing in 1928, the former lawyer turned baseball magnate installed himself as manager. It was an unmitigated disaster as the club lost 98 games and finished 43 games out of first place.

In 1930, Fuchs hired former infielder Bill McKechnie to manage the club. McKechnie was known for getting the most out of marginally talented players—especially pitchers. He would later become the first manager to lead three different NL teams (the Pirates, Cardinals, and Reds) to pennants. Though improvement was evident on McKechnie's watch, the Braves placed no higher than fourth during his eight-year tenure in Boston.

To keep attendance up during the Depression, Fuchs increased the number of cheap seats, sponsored weekly Ladies' Day promotions and worked with organizations such as the YMCA to issue Knot Hole Gang cards, which entitled inner-city youths to sit in the third base pavilion at a discounted rate. Despite his exhaustive efforts, the team did not perform well enough to maintain a substantial following.

Before the 1934 winter meetings, Fuchs hatched a plan to bring dog racing to Braves Field. The proposal was shot down by Commissioner Landis and NL president Ford Frick, both of whom were fundamentally opposed to gambling on major-league premises. Unable to meet the demands of their stadium lease, the Braves were teetering on the brink of bankruptcy as the 1935 season approached. The NL Board of Directors was forced to extend a loan to keep the club afloat. In a desperate attempt to boost revenue, Fuchs approached Ruth with an offer.

Author Leigh Montville bluntly wrote of Fuchs's proposal: "The deal had a stench to it from the beginning. The Babe was the only pure heart in the entire proceeding. He had said he wanted to be a manager. Period. That was his goal. The other parties in the transaction took that desire and bent it to fit their needs. The Babe never knew what hit him."[149]

Fuchs was quite satisfied with McKechnie as manager. Ruth had said he didn't want to sign another player contract, but the shrewd Braves owner knew he might be able to lure the slugger back to Boston by granting him a position of perceived authority. During a late-February press conference held at Jacob Ruppert's brewery, Fuchs spoke of Ruth's contributions to the sport and the love that New England fans still held for him. He outlined the particulars of a deal that sounded magnificent on the surface. Ruppert, who couldn't wait to get rid of the washed-up outfielder, remarked that he considered it unethical to prevent the Babe from accepting this once-in-a-lifetime offer.

It was all smoke and mirrors. The only valid piece of the proposal was the $25,000 salary. Even that was a substantial pay cut for Ruth, who had made $35K with the Yankees in 1934. The rest of the contract was little more than window dressing. Stock options and profit-sharing were virtually worthless since the team was financially insolvent. The title of assistant manager was equally useless considering the fact that McKechnie had absolutely no intention of soliciting the Babe's input on any matter, public or private. And finally, the position of vice president carried no weight beyond an obligation to make public appearances and sign autographs. Ruth was being swindled—plain and simple.

Yet he bought it hook, line, and sinker.

Fans did too. When the Babe arrived at Back Bay Station in Boston on February 28 to sign the contract, he required a police escort to make his way through the enormous crowd that had gathered to wish him well. Braves VP Charles C. Adams (also owner of the Boston Bruins) exposed the reality of the situation when he commented to reporters that Ruth was clearly not managerial material. If the slugger heard about the remark, he gave no indication that he was offended by it.

McKechnie didn't particularly enjoy seeing his training camp transformed into a three-ring circus. There were more reporters and fans than the team was accustomed to. In a game against the Yankees, a crowd of nearly 5,000 showed up, breaking a Florida attendance record. By the end of the first eight exhibition games, the Braves had already drawn more than 20,000—enough to pay for spring training costs and potentially show a small profit. Even so, Ruth kept chattering about how he was going to be the next manager and McKechnie didn't like it one bit.

Ruth had not worked out with Artie McGovern before camp opened. He was grossly overweight and in poor physical condition. Though the big crowds flattered him, he wasn't having any fun. Baseball had once been a joyful experience for him, but now he described it as a laborious exercise. The Japanese tour had been an unrealistic measure of his abilities. American pitchers were striking him out routinely and making him look bad in the process.

The first day of the regular season was counterindicative of what was to come. With over 20,000 fans in attendance at Braves Field (more than five times the single-game average from the previous year), Ruth went 2-for-3 against Carl Hubbell of the Giants. This included a homer and three RBIs. He also went without an error in the outfield, a major accomplishment considering his abominable defensive performances during spring training.

Through the first several games, Ruth had 6 hits in 18 at-bats with 4 runs scored and 4 RBIs. But he couldn't keep it up. His annual spring cold arrived. As he struggled to regain his health, he gathered just one hit in his next 13 appearances. He began making derogatory remarks about himself and threatening to quit.

The Braves slipped in the standings. Attendance plummeted, and some of the fans who showed up at the ballpark took to booing the Babe. As the losses piled up, it began to dawn on Ruth that there would be no profits to share by season's end. Ordered by Fuchs to appear at the opening of a clothing store in Boston, he refused. When the unhappy merchant returned hundreds of unsold tickets, Fuchs confronted Ruth. The Babe angrily advised him to attend to business matters while he attended to matters on the field.

By the second week of May, Ruth had suffered enough. He asked to be put on the voluntarily retired list, which would technically make him property of the Braves though not a member of the active roster. Fuchs persuaded him to remain with the club through a western road trip, which was scheduled to begin in St. Louis on May 17. Appealing to the Babe's charitable nature, Fuchs told him that advance ticket sales for those games had been excellent and that there were special events planned for him in multiple cities.

Ruth played poorly in St. Louis and Chicago. His batting average was down to .157 when the Braves arrived in Pittsburgh on May 23. Two days later, he delivered one last glorious performance. Before the game, a sportswriter told Pirate manager Pie Traynor that Ruth had been out all night on a bender and would be useless at the plate. That report was greatly exaggerated. With one out and one on in the first, the Babe smashed a homer to deep right field off right-hander Red Lucas. In the third, he went deep against reliever Guy Bush, who had heckled him unremittingly during the 1932 World Series and hit him with a pitch. In the seventh, he drilled another one of Bush's offerings over the double-decked grandstand in right field—a feat no one had accomplished before. Estimates of the shot vary widely from 540 to 600 feet. It was the last of Ruth's career. As he rounded third base, Bush tipped his cap. Hobbling along, the Babe smiled and waved back. Years later, the hurler remarked, "It was the longest cockeyed ball I ever saw in my life."[150] With nothing left to prove, the slugger removed himself from the game.

Keeping his promise to Fuchs, Ruth played out the string. It was far from eventful. On Babe Ruth Day in Cincinnati, he struck out several times and left the game with a pulled muscle. In the third game of the series, he had an embarrassing experience in the outfield as Cincinnati batters deliberately lofted balls in his direction. Dead on his feet, the Babe failed to snare three of the five flies hit to him in the fifth inning. Several runs scored as a result of his immobility. Fans hooted as he bypassed the dugout and headed directly to the clubhouse. As the story goes, a small boy approached him on the way. He picked up the kid and hugged him before completing the walk of shame.

Ruth's last career appearance came in Philadelphia on Memorial Day. He grounded out in his only at-bat of the afternoon. In the bottom of the frame, he hurt his knee going after a ball and ended up on the bench. On June 1, the *New York Times* reported, "He fears he has a touch of water on the knee and, likewise, that he will be unable to get into the series."[151] On June 2, the most storied career in the history of sports came to an end. Whether Ruth quit or was released remains undetermined. But there were definitely parting shots fired from both sides. Ruth called Fuchs a "dirty double-crosser." The conniving Braves executive referred to the Babe as an "imbecile."[152]

Ruth's numbers during his final season are largely forgettable. He hit .181 with 6 homers and 12 RBIs in 72 at-bats. The Braves went 8–20 during his appearances and 38–115 on the year. No one could have saved them. In August, VP Adams took over Fuchs's stock and appointed McKechnie as temporary president. The NL declared the franchise forfeited. New owners were located and the team was renamed the Bees before the 1936 campaign. Following suit, Braves Field became known as The Beehive.

An Invitation to Brooklyn

Now that he had reached the end of his playing career, managerial opportunities for Ruth were scarce. In the wake of the Babe's perceived snub, Frank Navin hired Mickey Cochrane to run the Tigers. Cochrane, nicknamed "Black Mike" for his fiery personality, led the club to its first World Series title. All of Ruth's prior suitors—the Red Sox, White Sox, and Reds—were no longer interested. Had he swallowed his pride and accepted one of the minor-league offers extended to him, things might have turned out differently. The Palatka Azaleas—a Florida State League club with ties to Detroit—wanted him. He was also said to have turned down an offer from the Albany Senators of the International League. Jacob Ruppert and Ed Barrow had helped spread the belief that the Babe was unfit to run a major-league ball club, but that wasn't necessarily a valid opinion. He had played in portions of 22 seasons as a pitcher and outfielder. He had established himself as the greatest power hitter in the game's history. He was confident, likeable, and fundamentally good-natured. If Rogers Hornsby and Ty Cobb—both universally despised by teammates and opponents—could manage in the majors, then why not Ruth? Sadly, that question would never be answered.

At the end of the 1936 campaign, the struggling Dodgers replaced manager Casey Stengel with Burleigh Grimes. A Hall of Fame pitcher, Grimes had earned a well-deserved reputation as a curmudgeon. He threw at batters regularly and he was once accused of punching an autograph seeker in the stomach. The Dodgers finished with a losing record in Grimes's first season at the helm. They were off to a rough start the following year when Ruth suddenly entered the picture.

On June 15, 1938, Johnny Vander Meer of the Reds made history by tossing a second consecutive no-hitter against Brooklyn at Ebbets Field. Aside from slugger Dolph Camilli and aging future Hall of Famer Kiki Cuyler, there wasn't much punch in the Dodger lineup. The Babe, who was in attendance during Vander Meer's historic game, found himself surrounded by swarms of admiring Flatbush fans. This drew the attention of Dodgers executive Larry MacPhail. Though Grimes was in charge of the team on the field, it was generally accepted that Brooklyn's light-hitting shortstop, Leo Durocher, was next in line for the manager's position. After talking it over with Grimes and Durocher, MacPhail decided that it couldn't hurt to have Ruth around. He still drew crowds wherever he went. And his presence might help motivate players.

After signing a $15,000 contract to join the Brooklyn coaching staff, Ruth told reporters, "It's great to be back. I would have been back long before if I had the chance to hook on with some major-league club. But what could I do? I didn't get any offers. You can't make a guy give you a job. When I was offered one, I grabbed it quick."[153]

Ruth made his debut on June 19 in a Sunday doubleheader against the Cubs. Attendance was close to 30,000—well above average for the season. The Dodgers won the opener, 6–2, and nearly staged a remarkable comeback in the finale. When Ruth took his position in the coach's box at the start of the first game, he received a rousing ovation. He was an instant hit with players as well. He assigned new nicknames to several and regaled them with stories in the dugout. Even Cuyler, a 39-year-old veteran, admitted to being enthralled with the Babe. Everyone seemed enormously pleased, with the exception of Durocher, who clearly felt threatened.

Rumors had surfaced that Ruth might take over as manager in 1939. Though the Babe denied that this was true, it wasn't Durocher's only grievance. As teammates in New York, the two had started off as friends. But Durocher's poor hitting had prompted Ruth to jokingly refer to him as "The All-American Out." Durocher resented it immensely. Things deteriorated from there when the Babe accused the spirited infielder of stealing a watch from him. There was a brief scuffle in the clubhouse and the two remained at odds after that. Durocher won a World Series with the Cardinals before joining the Dodgers in 1938. He was anything but ecstatic about being reunited with Ruth.

The Bambino's brief career as a coach was an adventure. On August 5, he received a police escort from Ebbets Field to the Manhattan Eye, Ear and

Throat Hospital, where his daughter Julia had been admitted after falling ill. He made a sizeable blood donation to help nurse her back to health. Two days later, he was thrown out of a game for arguing a call on the basepaths. It was his first ejection as coach. Shortly after that, AL president William Harridge made a disparaging remark about Ruth's value to the Dodgers. This prompted a rebuttal from MacPhail, who referred to the Babe as "an inspiration to the younger players"[154]

Inspirational or not, Ruth had difficulty mastering the finer points of his new job. He couldn't remember all the signals. Since Grimes was often in the coaching box himself at third base, the Babe would clap, wave his arms, and shout encouragement instead. On August 19, Ruth supposedly called for a hit-and-run play while Durocher was at bat. Though "Leo the Lip" ended up delivering the game-winning hit, he was irritated with the Babe for invoking such a dangerous strategy. There was an argument in the clubhouse and the two had to be separated. According to some accounts, Durocher got a punch in, but Grimes, who had no vested interest in protecting his rookie coach, denied that this was true.

The incident damaged any chance that Ruth had at managing the ball club. He was let go at season's end. Though the Dodgers played close to .500 during the Babe's brief tenure, they finished 17½ games out of first place. From an attendance standpoint, Ruth's presence had been a triumph. More than 650,000 fans streamed through the turnstiles at Ebbets Field—an increase of nearly 30 percent from the previous year. Durocher took over as manager in 1939, gradually guiding the club back into contention. Ruth would never hold another job in the majors.

Election to Cooperstown

The Babe seemed lost without baseball. Describing what life was like for him after retirement, *Sports Illustrated* writer Robert Creamer remarked colorfully, "He was like an ex-President, famous but useless, creating a stir whenever he appeared in public but curiously neutered, no longer a factor."[155]

Ruth played golf often. He was good at it, in fact. He competed in an amateur tournament in Westchester County and placed among the top 20 out of a field of more than 200. In the fall of 1937, he played in a charity tournament that paired him with female multisport star Babe Didrikson. Held in Long Island, the event attracted 10,000 fans—one of the largest crowds ever assembled on an American golf course. At one point, Ruth was knocked to the ground by a surging mass of spectators. He compared the chaotic atmosphere to that of the World Series.

Ruth's favorite golf course was located in St. Albans on Long Island. He was said to drink scotch heavily and still shoot in the 70s, which is excellent for an amateur (especially a mildly intoxicated one). One night, on his way home from the course, he slammed into the back of another vehicle and drove away. The other motorist took down his license plate number and reported the incident. While sitting at a traffic light in Manhattan, a policeman ordered Ruth to step out of his car. He was taken to the station. When the other driver arrived to formally lodge a complaint, he had no idea who the Babe was and started shouting angrily. A heated argument ensued before officers negotiated an amicable agreement between the two men.

In February of 1936, Ruth learned that he had been elected to the Baseball Hall of Fame along with Ty Cobb, Honus Wagner, Walter Johnson, and Christy Mathewson. The ballots had been cast by members of the Baseball Writers' Association of America. They had been asked to choose candidates whose careers began during the 20th century. *New York Times* reporter John Kieran was surprised by the results. "The amazement in this corner is not the ballots that these leaders received, but the gap where 'X' failed to mark the spot," Kieran wrote. "It remains a mystery that any observer of modern diamond activities could list his version of the ten outstanding baseball figures and have Ty Cobb nowhere at all in the group. Four voters accomplished that amazing feat."[156]

Cobb was not alone. Ruth and Wagner were each left off 11 ballots. Mathewson was overlooked by 21 writers, while Johnson was snubbed by 37. It was an almost shocking turn of events.

Members of the inaugural Hall of Fame class waited until 1939 to be enshrined—the year the museum in Cooperstown officially opened. By then, the original members had been joined by several others, including seven executives and two managers. The Babe, who showed up looking very dapper in a cream-colored suit, kept his induction speech short. It was less than two minutes long. The ceremony was a celebration of baseball's centennial, though the date was actually based on a fictitious story involving a Civil War hero named Abner Doubleday, who had nothing to do with the game and was nowhere near Cooperstown at the time he was said to have invented it. At any rate, Ruth borrowed the words of Cy Young in his speech, commenting, "I hope it goes another hundred years and the next hundred years will be the greatest."[157]

A famous photo was taken of the living Hall of Fame members that day. Ruth is seated prominently in front between Eddie Collins and Connie Mack. Ty Cobb, who showed up late, is conspicuously absent. For years, writers speculated that his tardiness was a deliberate snub—a reaction to having been left off four ballots or perhaps a reluctance to engage in small talk with his former rivals (Ruth especially). But those assumptions are incorrect.

Known for being extremely thrifty, the Georgia Peach refused to pay for a room in a Cooperstown hotel. Instead, he booked an overnight train and rented a car in the morning to drive the remaining 40 miles with his son. It was frugality and poor planning that kept him out of the photo—not spitefulness. On the contrary, Cobb was proud of having been elected to the Hall and made a point of reminding people that he had received more votes than any member of the inaugural class. Upon arriving at the ceremony, he was quite congenial, making an official statement and signing autographs for fans before taking a tour of the museum. He was sufficiently impressed, telling Hall of Fame officials that he would donate some of his personal memorabilia to put on display. As for his reunion with Ruth—it went splendidly. The two struck up a casual friendship that lasted for several years.

FAREWELL TO GEHRIG

At the end of the 1938 campaign, Lou Gehrig's record of consecutive appearances stood at 2,122. Sportswriters were beginning to wonder if he would play forever. During the streak, he had taken the field with a broken toe, a torn muscle in his right leg, bone chips in his elbow, and multiple fractures of his pinky finger. He was also hit in the head with pitches on multiple occasions. Though his offensive production had declined somewhat in 1938, he was still one of the best hitters in the American League. It came as a surprise to many when he benched himself less than two weeks into the 1939 campaign.

During the offseason, the Iron Horse had been misdiagnosed with a gallbladder problem and placed on a special diet. As spring training progressed, it became fairly obvious that something was not quite right. In an exhibition game against the Dodgers, he hit a ball into the right-center field gap. Pete Reiser chased it down, and as his throw reached the infield, one of Gehrig's teammates said out loud, "Where's Lou?" Infielder Babe Dahlgren recalled, "He was still midway between first and second. He just made it in time, but as he got to second, his legs started to bow out."[158] It was not the only alarming incident of the spring. According to Dahlgren, Gehrig had trouble fielding a routine bunt during an exhibition game in St. Petersburg. "He juggled the ball, bent over to get it and couldn't straighten up," said Dahlgren, who was Gehrig's eventual replacement at first base.[159]

After hitting .143 in eight regular-season games, the Iron Horse decided to sit out for the good of the team. Interestingly, the Yankees beat the Tigers, 22–2, on the first day of his voluntary hiatus. Though the move was expected to be temporary, his condition worsened in the weeks that followed. He underwent testing at the Mayo Clinic and received bad news. He was suffering from a rare disorder known as amyotrophic lateral sclerosis, a disease of the nervous system that causes progressive loss of muscle control.

Given Gehrig's modest, private nature, teammates considered giving him a small send-off in the clubhouse. They took up a collection to get him a fishing rod and asked John Kieran of the *New York Times* to write a poem that would be engraved on the base of a trophy. But a handful of writers lobbied for a more public ceremony. Lou Gehrig Appreciation Day was officially scheduled for July 4 at Yankee Stadium with a ceremony to be held between games of a doubleheader.

Bunting was hung on the stadium's facade—a practice normally reserved only for the postseason. Members of the 1927 Yankees were invited to show up for a reunion. Ruth was one of several former teammates who agreed to be there. The stadium opened earlier than usual that day in an attempt to avoid a pressing crowd. A hazy morning gave way to a hot, muggy afternoon. Gehrig was visited in the clubhouse by a throng of old friends, including Joe Dugan, Waite Hoyt, and Herb Pennock. Everett Scott, owner of the "Iron Man" record before Gehrig, was also there along with Wally Pipp—the Iron Horse's predecessor.

Near the end of the first game, Gehrig begged manager Joe McCarthy to excuse him from the ceremony. McCarthy was having none of it. After a 3–2 loss to the Senators, the contemporary Yankees stood on the third base side of the infield with Washington players facing them. Ruth had arrived by then and was among the dignitaries assembled on the field. Gehrig stepped out of the dugout, helped along by Ed Barrow. When they were close enough to home plate, Barrow let the Yankee icon take the last few steps alone. Gehrig kept his head down and avoided eye contact as the crowd gave him a roaring ovation. He was clearly overwhelmed.

New York City mayor Fiorello La Guardia spoke first, followed by Postmaster General James Farley and Joe McCarthy. Gehrig kept dabbing at his eyes with a handkerchief throughout. After McCarthy, it was Ruth's turn. Though the Babe could be uncouth and thoughtless, he never held a grudge for long. He spoke affectionately about how Gehrig had carried the ball club. He wished his old friend luck as a fisherman in the days to come.

Gehrig had never promised to address the crowd himself, though he had worked on the rudiments of a speech beforehand. When he made no move to approach the microphones, the master of ceremonies (sportswriter Sam Mercer) announced that he was too emotional to speak. He might have returned to the dugout without a word had McCarthy not placed a hand on his back and encouraged him to say something. More than 60,000 attendees heard him declare, "Fans, for the past two weeks you have been reading about the bad break I got. Yet today I consider myself the luckiest man on the face of this earth."[160] It remains one of the most stirring moments in baseball history.

When Gehrig was finished, a band hired for the occasion broke into a German folk song. Caught up in the emotion, Ruth approached his former teammate for a handshake and wrapped him in a bear hug instead. "Damn it, I went over there because I had to," the Babe later said. "I wanted to laugh and cheer him up. I wound up crying like a baby."[161] Though no one is certain exactly what Ruth whispered into Gehrig's ear, they were the first words of friendship to pass between the two men in nearly five years. For a fleeting instant, Gehrig appeared genuinely happy.

Appearance in *The Pride of the Yankees*

Ruth had always been very generous with his time when it came to sick children. As World War II unfolded, he used his star power to raise money for the war effort. He was heavily involved with the Red Cross, even going so far as to participate in door-to-door activities. Additionally, he sold war bonds, umpired benefit softball games, and refereed charity wrestling matches. His last actual ballgame took place at Yankee Stadium—a fundraiser for the Army-Navy Relief Fund. Walter Johnson tossed over a dozen pitches to him, and after hitting a long drive that hooked just foul, he broke into a home run trot anyway.

In late 1941, Ruth was asked to appear in a Lou Gehrig biopic entitled *The Pride of the Yankees*. The film was being directed by Sam Wood, who had gained acclaim for a pair of Marx Brothers movies during the 1930s. Wood accumulated more than a hundred film credits over the course of his long career. Eight of his projects received Oscar nominations for Best Picture.

In addition to Ruth, three other former Yankee stars were recruited to play themselves—Bill Dickey, Bob Meusel, and Mark Koenig. Dickey was not enthusiastic about the project at first. When he found out that Gary Cooper had been hired to play Gehrig, he complained about having to refer to the actor as "Lou." A performer was recruited to play Dickey, but the all-star catcher eventually changed his mind.

While Cooper was a respected actor who would later win an Oscar for his performance in the popular Western *High Noon*, he was not a baseball fan. In fact, he had never played in a game or attended one prior to joining the cast. Consequently, he required a lot of coaching to prepare for the simulated live-action sequences. Lefty O'Doul, a two-time batting champion and Pacific Coast League managerial legend, was hired to instruct Cooper on the finer points of batting and fielding. To condition him for the role, O'Doul encouraged Cooper to practice his swing by chopping trees. The actor's throwing was another issue entirely. "You throw a ball like an old woman tossing a biscuit!" the former outfielder groused after watching Cooper demonstrate his abilities (or lack thereof).[162]

Wood was not initially pleased with Cooper's on-screen performance. It wasn't until he saw the final product that he enthusiastically endorsed the actor's efforts. "You're positive he's going to ruin your picture," Wood said comically to a reporter. "I froze in my tracks the first time I directed him. I thought something was wrong with him, saw a million-dollar production go glimmering. I was amazed at the result on the screen. What I thought was under-playing turned out to be just the right approach. On the screen he's perfect, yet on the set you'd swear it's the worst job of acting in the history of motion pictures."[163]

Regarding Cooper's baseball skills, a bit of movie magic had to be employed. Since the actor was right-handed, he had an extremely difficult time emulating Gehrig's southpaw style. In some of the action sequences, a former Dodgers star named Babe Herman was used as a stand-in. The images were flipped in postproduction to mask Herman's presence. A popular legend holds that Cooper—wearing a mirror-image uniform—was instructed to bat right-handed and run to third base instead of first during batting clips. But no one is precisely sure if this trick was actually employed. The topic has been a source of debate for several years.

When Ruth was hired to appear in the film, he weighed more than 270 pounds. Realizing that he was too heavy to play his former self, he went on a massive diet, losing more than 40 pounds in a span of two months. He ended up in the hospital. Later, while shooting in California, he contracted pneumonia and was hospitalized again. A publicity photo was taken of actress Teresa Wright (who played Gehrig's wife, Eleanor, in the film) holding a stethoscope to Ruth's chest. He looks dreadful in the picture.

Having appeared in a number of prior films, Ruth did a passable job of acting. He delivered his lines with enthusiasm. And he added some realism to a pennant-celebration scene by smashing his hand through the window of a Pullman train car.

Released in 1942, the movie received wide critical acclaim. It was nominated for several Academy Awards. It was also the seventh-highest-grossing film of the year. In spite of its popularity with audiences and critics, there are a handful of minor historical inaccuracies. In the movie's climax, the words of Gehrig's "Luckiest Man" speech are altered. In another scene, first baseman Wally Pipp complains of a headache and asks to be taken out of the lineup. Inserted as a replacement, Gehrig's "Iron Man" streak begins onscreen. In reality, the streak began the day before, when Gehrig appeared as a pinch hitter. Furthermore, Pipp's removal from the lineup was due to the fact that he was in a slump, along with the rest of the team. The headache, if there was one, is irrelevant. The scene in which Gehrig receives his ALS diagnosis is another point of contention. In the movie, the doctor is very honest about the Yankees first-sacker's grim prognosis. This is not the way things played out in real life. Gehrig was given a 50 percent chance at remaining stable for an extended period of time. One Mayo Clinic representative actually told him he might need a cane in 10 or 15 years. As most people know, he died roughly two years after receiving the diagnosis.

END OF THE ROAD

At the conclusion of World War II, the Babe made one last effort to land a job as manager. Jacob Ruppert had passed away by then and his estate had been sold to a syndicate headed by Larry MacPhail. Barrow was no longer running the club and McCarthy was on his way out. In January of 1946, Ruth contacted MacPhail and asked him point-blank if he could manage the team in Newark. The Yankee executive said he would think it over.

Several weeks passed without a response. Ruth followed up with multiple phone calls but received the brush-off each time. Finally, an answer arrived in the mail—a polite "no." As an alternative, MacPhail strongly suggested that the Babe get involved with a youth sandlot program run by the City of New York. Given Ruth's outstanding track record with children, it was an excellent idea. But it was also the end of his managerial dream. Humiliated and hurt by the response, he buried his head in his hands and cried.

The Babe turned to golf as a consolation, playing as often as possible. Over the next few months, it became apparent that he was in poor health. His voice grew increasingly hoarse. He complained of headaches and pain over his left eye. In late-November, he entered French Hospital in Manhattan for observation. The left side of his face was swollen and his eye was closed. As if that wasn't bad enough, he could hardly swallow. In a story told by his daughter, Dorothy, the pain had gotten so intense that he had threatened to jump out of his bedroom window, which was located on the fifteenth floor.

The diagnosis was bleak. A malignant tumor had developed in his nasal passages and was pressing against nerves involved in the motor functioning of his throat and pharynx. It was in an area that was not easily accessible to doctors. Stated plainly, he was going to die. In an effort to keep his spirits up, the word "cancer" was never directly used by doctors. His prognosis was kept out of the newspapers as well.

Ruth kept himself busy in spite of his affliction, traveling and playing golf. In January of 1947, he underwent a surgical procedure to relieve the pressure of the tumor. By then, he had lost more than 50 pounds and looked truly awful. He wept as a crowd of onlookers wished him well on his way out of the hospital.

In April of 1947, Babe Ruth Day was held at Yankee Stadium. The Bambino—a shadow of his former self—addressed a crowd of more than 58,000. He had not prepared a formal speech, so he improvised. Reacting to the roar of the crowd, he got choked up and went into a coughing fit. When he recovered, he assured fans that his voice felt just as bad as it sounded. He closed with the following heartfelt words: "There's been so many lovely things said about me, and I'm glad that I've had the opportunity to thank everyone. Thank you."[164]

Ruth refused to give up hope. He underwent radiation. He also tried an experimental drug called teropterin, which had never been used on human subjects before. Initially, it seemed to help, prompting a subsequent medical report citing it as a possible cure.

A ghostwriter named Bob Considine began working on Ruth's autobiography. Since the Babe was too ill to focus on telling his story, historian Fred Lieb was brought in to help save the project. Together, they finished the book, entitled *The Babe Ruth Story*, and the rights were sold to Hollywood. William Bendix, known for his work on the radio and television sitcom *The Life of Riley*, was cast in the lead role. Hired as a technical adviser, Ruth traveled to California and posed for publicity photos with Bendix and costar Claire Trevor. By then, the cancer had eaten a hole in his throat.

On June 13, 1948, Ruth attended a 25th anniversary celebration at Yankee Stadium, where his number 3 was officially retired. Before the scheduled showdown against the Indians, an old-timers' game between the 1923 Yankees and a slightly younger platoon took place. Ruth served as honorary manager of the 1923 squad. The crowd gave him a nice ovation when he was introduced. A microphone had been set up and he told fans how happy he was to be there.

Less than two weeks later, Ruth was hospitalized again. The cancer had spread throughout his body. In spite of his rapidly deteriorating health, Claire arranged for him to be taken to the Astor Theater for the premiere of *The Babe Ruth Story*. The Yankee icon was so sick, he didn't make it through the entire film. He had to be transported back to the hospital about halfway through. Some would say that this was a small blessing. Hackneyed and unrealistic, the movie was universally panned by critics. Years later, a modern reviewer referred to it as "The *Plan 9 From Outer Space* of baseball biopics" and remarked that it had "an almost perverse disregard for the facts."[165]

On August 16, 1948, the man who had touched so many lives in so many ways passed away in his sleep at the age of 53. A number of extra telephone operators were put on duty at Memorial Hospital to deliver the news to countless callers. Roughly 80,000 people came to pay their respects as his body lay in state at Yankee Stadium. Around 75,000 more watched the funeral procession as it left St. Patrick's Cathedral on August 19. Explaining the strong connection that Ruth maintained with people throughout his career, a writer from *Time* magazine remarked, "His emotions were always out on the surface, which was one reason all the fans thought they knew and understood him."[166] Infielder Joe Dugan had a unique way of describing his former teammate and friend: "To understand [the Babe], you had to understand this: He wasn't human."[167]

A chronic rule-breaker, Ruth was suspended multiple times during his career. He looks miserable in this photo watching from the stands.

Ruth's bat was too powerful to be kept out of the lineup between pitching assignments. In 1919, he appeared in over 100 games for the first time, setting a new single-season home run record.

Growing up as a disadvantaged youth, Ruth had a soft spot for kids. Here he poses with a youngster named Ray Kelly, whom he selected to be his personal mascot.

Yankee uniforms had a different look during their World Series year of 1921. The caps were pinstriped and the jerseys were without the trademark interlocking "NY." Ruth is all business in this photo.

This is Ruth's iconic 1933 baseball card. Manufactured by the Goudey Gum Company, it is worth more than $20,000 today in medium-grade condition.

Ruth had adequate speed but was not the most graceful base runner. He looks a little awkward here sliding into third base against Ossie Bleuge of the Senators. He was out on the play.

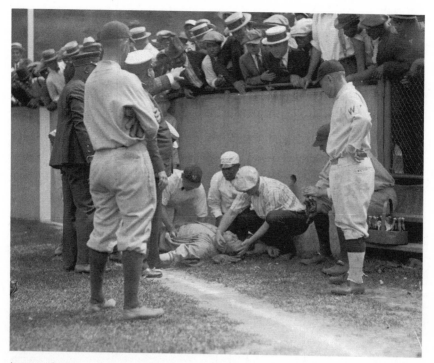

In one of the scariest moments of Ruth's career, he was knocked unconscious while chasing a fly ball at Griffith Stadium in Washington. He was revived and stayed in the game.

Though she is smiling in this photo, Ruth's first wife, Helen, was rarely pleased with her husband's behavior. The couple separated in the mid-'20s after years of infidelity on Ruth's part.

One of the many things that endeared Ruth to reporters and photographers was his fun-loving nature. Here he clowns around with a chimpanzee at the St. Louis Zoological Park.

Here is The Babe in action with the Yankees in 1920. Notice that the iconic #3 is missing from the back of his uniform. The Yankees didn't put permanent numbers on their jerseys until 1929.

Ruth poses with Giants manager John McGraw in 1923. The two were actually bitter rivals. Envious of Ruth's star power, McGraw spearheaded a movement to have the Yankees evicted from the Polo Grounds.

Ruth is pictured here during his pitching days with the Red Sox. He is seated next to Ernie Shore. Rube Foster and Del Gainer are on the right. In 1917, Ruth and Shore combined for a no-hitter. Ruth threw only four pitches in the game before being kicked out by umpire Brick Owens.

During his Red Sox days, Ruth rented a rustic New England cabin in the off-season. He later purchased a farm (which he named "Home Plate Farm") in Sudbury, Massachusetts. He is gathering wood for the stove in this photo.

Ruth poses with two of the era's biggest stars—George Sisler (left) and Ty Cobb (right). Cobb despised Ruth during his playing days and the two almost came to blows more than once.

Ruth had his own brand of nickel cigars during the early '20s. Here he is rolling some himself. Sadly, Ruth's habitual smoking eventually led to fatal cancer.

This photo shows Ruth in his prime with the Yankees, before he added excess weight to his frame. In spite of his broad shoulders and muscular build, his legs were actually quite thin.

PART 2:
ASSORTED ANECDOTES

Righting the Wrongs of History

The life of Babe Ruth is well documented. In fact, few players in baseball history have generated as much literature. But Ruth's mother remains an enigma. In both of the Babe's ghostwritten autobiographies, he got the basic facts about her wrong. Until fairly recently, no one even knew where her grave was located.

Information about Catherine "Kate" Schamberger is scarce and vague. She was born in Maryland, presumably in 1873. The daughter of German immigrants, she was small in stature at 4-foot-10. She gave birth to her famous son seven months after being wed to George Herman Ruth Sr.

The family struggled to make ends meet. George Sr. found work wherever he could get it. He was employed as a horse driver, streetcar gripman, and lightning rod salesman before settling into a career as a saloon owner. Kate gave birth to seven children after George Jr., but only one survived to adulthood. The Ruth household was a chaotic place. Kate had little control over young George, who frequently got into trouble on the streets of Baltimore. George Sr. accused Kate of drunkenness and infidelity, which reportedly led to their divorce.

By some accounts, Kate continued to visit her son once a month after he was sent to St. Mary's Industrial School for Boys. She grew increasingly unhealthy over the years. On August 1, 1912, she was admitted to the Municipal Tuberculosis Hospital. She died less than two weeks later. The official cause of death was listed as exhaustion and lung disease. Interestingly, her death note does not mention a husband or children. She was listed as a widow in spite of the fact that George Sr. outlived her by six years.

More than nine decades after Kate Schamberger's death, a Catonsville attorney named Paul Harris Sr. searched through public records in an attempt to find the missing pieces of Kate's life story. When he learned that she had been buried in an unmarked grave, he was determined to honor her memory. "It's the saddest thing I can imagine," he told a writer from the *Baltimore Sun*. "I had never seen or heard of a woman more neglected—and she was the mother of a world-famous man."[1]

Harris sent correspondences to various sources asking for donations. Michael Gibbons—executive director of the Babe Ruth Birthplace and Museum—rallied to the cause. In 2008, the museum raised enough money to have a headstone installed in Lot no. 126, Sec. G of Baltimore's Most Holy Redeemer Cemetery. It reads simply: "RUTH, Catherine. 1873–1912. Mother of George Herman 'Babe' Ruth Jr."

ON THE LAM

In addition to St. Mary's, the Xaverian Brothers ran an all-men's college known as Mount St. Joseph's. There was an ongoing rivalry between the two schools. St. Joseph's players saw the boys of St. Mary's as delinquents, while the collegians were viewed as elitist snobs by their younger counterparts.

While Ruth was earning a reputation as a top-notch hurler for St. Mary's, the St. Joe's team had its own star moundsman—a right-hander named Bill Morrisette (who forged a brief career in the majors). In order to make the 1913 Commencement Day ceremonies more festive, the Brothers scheduled an exhibition game pitting the two aces against each other. According to multiple sources, Ruth grew increasingly anxious about the impending showdown and went AWOL.

It was extremely unlike Ruth to behave in such a manner, and his peers were shaken by the development. As wild rumors began to spread regarding the cause of his disappearance, the Brothers canceled classes to develop a plan of action. They sent the school's probation officer and night watchman to comb the city in search of their star pitcher. They found him roaming the streets of his old neighborhood. He returned without much prompting and was punished for his transgression. For several days, he was forced to spend all of his free time "standing guard" on the road that separated the Big Yard from the Little Yard on campus. He was forbidden to play ball until shortly before his scheduled start against St. Joseph's.

On the afternoon of the big game, Ruth rose to the occasion as he would so many times in later years. A school newspaper reported that he pitched a one-hitter and struck out 22 opponents (though that number was likely exaggerated). St. Mary's won, 6–0. Ruth was promoted to the minor leagues shortly afterward.

BECOMING THE BABE

In his 1948 autobiography, Ruth shared an interesting (and possibly apocryphal) story about the origin of his most enduring nickname. While training for the 1914 season in Fayetteville, North Carolina, Orioles players stayed at the Lafayette Hotel. Ruth became obsessed with the hotel's elevator, riding it up and down constantly just for fun. He watched the lift attendant closely to see how the machine worked, wishing he could run it himself. Elevators were not automatic in those days and it was up to the operators to bring them to level stops between floors. Attendants were also charged with the task of opening and closing the doors.

One day, Ruth paid the operator at the Lafayette Hotel to let him take over the controls. It almost cost him his life. He left the door open and was gazing absently down the corridor while the elevator was in motion. Had one of his teammates not shouted at him to pull his head back inside, he could have been seriously injured or even killed.

As word of the incident spread, Ruth got yelled at by owner Jack Dunn and ridiculed by teammates. One of the older players, feeling sorry for the club's new pitching prospect, told the others to lay off because Ruth was just a "babe in the woods." As the story goes, everyone called him "Babe" from that point on.

ROUGH AROUND THE EDGES

When he signed with the Orioles, Ruth was as green as they come. He had never traveled by train or stayed in a hotel prior to leaving St. Mary's. Because he had spent most of his life in the company of delinquent boys, he frequently used vulgar language and was lacking in social graces. Even after many years in the limelight, he never fully learned how to edit himself. Stories of his boorish behavior abound.

During spring training one year, the Babe was seated at a table with a number of Yankee teammates and their wives. At some point during the gathering, he stood up and announced, "I've got to take a piss." Herb Pennock followed him to the rest room, cautioning him about cursing in front of women. Upon returning to the table, Ruth issued a genuine apology to the ladies, "I'm sorry I said 'piss.'"[2]

On another occasion, a friend and his wife were visiting the Babe at his Manhattan apartment. When Ruth shared an off-color anecdote, his friend tried to redirect the conversation to the many trophies lined up on shelves along the walls. The Babe pointed to one of them and boasted: "Look at that one. I won first place in a farting contest. Boy, I had to down a lot of beer and limburger to win that one." By the end of the evening, Ruth's friend was sure that his wife had been offended by some of the slugger's remarks. He was relieved when she commented on the elevator ride down, "What a fascinating man."[3]

During the 1928 presidential campaign, the Babe announced his support for New York governor Al Smith. In an effort to generate votes for the Democratic candidate, he attended a radio interview and brought teammate Tony Lazzeri along. During the broadcast, he blurted out, "Hey Tony, tell everybody who all the wops are going to vote for."[4]

Ruth worked tirelessly to raise money for charity throughout his career. During one particular black-tie affair, he was approached by the event's organizer—a prominent New York socialite named Adler. After receiving an outpouring of gratitude for his appearance, he told the congenial host, "Oh shit, lady—I'd do it for anybody."[5]

How Ruth Almost Played for the Reds

In July of 1914, Red Sox owner Joseph Lannin purchased the Providence Grays of the International League. At the time of the transaction, the club was affiliated with the Tigers. As part of the deal, Lannin agreed to send a Grays pitcher to Detroit. Minor-league teams had significant fans bases in those days and the pennant races were actually meaningful. Realizing that Providence manager Bill Donovan would not be happy about losing one of his pitchers so late in the season, Lannin promised to send Ruth as a replacement. In order to make it work, he had to place Ruth on waivers.

Before the Babe ended up in Boston, Orioles owner Jack Dunn—completely strapped for cash—had offered Ruth and Ernie Shore to the

Reds. Cincinnati's team president, Garry Herrmann, wanted to close the deal, but manager Buck Herzog was interested in a different pair of players. Herrmann grudgingly conformed to Herzog's wishes, coughing up $15,000 for shortstop Claud Derrick and outfielder George Twombly. Neither helped the Reds escape a last-place finish.

When the Babe suddenly reappeared on the market, Herrmann swooped in and grabbed him off waivers. In a panic, Lannin penned a letter to the Reds executive explaining his rationale for releasing Ruth and cordially asking him to retract his claim. Herrmann, renowned for his generosity, honored Lannin's request. Ruth helped the Grays to an International League pennant. Had he joined the lowly Reds, he almost certainly would have become the ace of their pitching staff. His 1915 home run total (compiled in 42 appearances) was higher than all but one of Cincinnati's everyday players that year.

PICKING UP THE TAB

In July of 1918, Secretary of War Newton D. Baker issued a "work or fight" order, compelling all draft-eligible men in "nonessential" jobs to sign up for war-related work or risk being drafted. Baseball was considered exempt initially, but Baker soon changed his mind, stating publicly that ballplayers should channel their athleticism toward the war effort. Beginning in 1917, many major leaguers found work in the shipyards and factories that manufactured military supplies to avoid combat. Ruth officially registered for the draft but was never called to active duty.

Jack Barry, who had served as player-manager of the Red Sox in 1917, took a job in the Boston Navy Yard along with several other teammates. Prior to the 1918 campaign, he applied for a special furlough that would allow him to play, but his request was denied. In his absence, owner Harry Frazee hired future Yankee GM Ed Barrow as manager.

With a depleted roster, Barrow used Ruth as a first baseman in a few exhibitions. During a game against the Dodgers, the Babe slammed a pair of homers. The second shot landed in a neighboring alligator farm. During batting practice the next day, he knocked two more balls over the fence. Frazee, known for being tight with money, shouted at the BoSox pitching ace: "That's ten bucks in balls you've cost me!" Ruth responded with characteristic brashness. "I can't help it," he said. "They oughta make these fuckin' parks bigger."[6]

THE UNSINKABLE SLUGGER

In 1918, Ruth led the American League with 11 home runs. He won 13 games on the mound and set a World Series record for consecutive scoreless innings. In addition to his heroics on the field, he battled two serious ailments that year, successfully recovering both times.

The 1918 Spanish Flu pandemic sickened 500 million people worldwide—about one-third of the world's population. The final death toll was around 50 million. On the first warm day in May that year, the Babe took his wife, Helen, to Revere Beach. By the time he returned home, he was running a temperature of 104 degrees. He also had body aches, chills, and a sore throat. Unable to play the following day, Red Sox team physician, Dr. Oliver W. Barney, diagnosed him with the flu (sometimes referred to as "the grippe" in those days) and swabbed his ailing throat with a silver nitrate mixture. Unfortunately, the doctor was too liberal with the application and Ruth became gravely ill. He was rushed by ambulance to the hospital. A throat specialist at the Massachusetts Eye and Ear Infirmary determined that he was suffering from an extreme case of tonsillitis. Though his condition was very serious, he returned to the lineup less than two weeks later.

The pandemic, coupled with the outbreak of World War I, prompted major-league officials to shorten the season. The World Series opened on September 5 in spite of warnings from health experts that a second wave of the flu was imminent. The city of Boston played host to three World Series games, multiple war rallies, and a number of parades. As a result, the projected spike in flu cases arrived as predicted. The second wave was worse than the first. When the season was over, Ruth contracted the dreaded virus. Showing the resiliency that would come to characterize him throughout his career, he regained his health and had a monster year at the plate in 1919.

THE ABORTED WORLD SERIES STRIKE

With the United States embroiled in a war overseas, baseball didn't seem as important to many fans in 1918. The US government's "work or fight" order brought the regular season to a close on September 1. To cut down on travel expenses, the first three World Series games were scheduled in Chicago with the final four slated to take place in Boston. The National League Champion Cubs elected to play their games in Comiskey Park (home of the White Sox) on account of its larger seating capacity.

For years, players on World Series teams were awarded bonuses drawn from a pool that included a percentage of the gate receipts from the first four games. Prior to the 1918 season, the National Commission (baseball's three-man governing committee) announced that an additional portion of the postseason shares would go to the second-, third-, and fourth-place clubs from both leagues. When attendance sagged during the first few games, players realized that the winners would be lucky to receive $1,000 apiece, which was a fraction of the payout from the previous October.

Harry Hooper and Dave Shean of the Red Sox went before the National Commission along with Bill Killefer and Les Mann of the Cubs. Their request to return to the prior profit-sharing arrangement was denied on the grounds that altering the deal could result in legal action from the six other clubs that had been promised bonuses. Players decided to make a statement by threatening to boycott Game 5.

A crowd in excess of 22,000 at Fenway Park grew restless when neither club had taken the field by the scheduled start time. An emergency meeting took place in the umpire's dressing room. After being chastised by American League president Ban Johnson for letting fans down in a time of national crisis, the players reversed their stance. They took the field with a promise that no disciplinary action would follow.

Winning shares for the Red Sox were $1,103 per man while Cubs players received a mere pittance of $671 apiece. A few weeks later, the National Commission voted to deprive Boston players of their World Series emblems (the 1918 equivalent of a World Series ring). And so, in spite of his two victories on the mound during the series, the Babe was robbed of his just desserts. On the 75th anniversary of the championship 1918 season, the Red Sox finally got around to handing out emblems. Not a single member of the championship squad was alive to receive them.

THE LOST PIANO

During his time in New England, Ruth was drawn to the Sudbury area by several teammates who owned hunting and fishing camps on a secluded body of water known as Willis Pond. Ruth rented a cabin there with his wife, Helen, during the offseason in 1917 and 1918. The cabin had been named "IHateToQuitIt" by its owner. Ruth threw many wild parties there, but the one that is most widely remembered took place farther down the shore at a place known as the Point.

During the winter of 1918, a large crowd of revelers assembled in a rustic cabin at the Point for a booze-filled bash. There are two versions of what happened that night, both involving an upright piano. In one adaptation, the piano was rolled down an embankment onto the frozen pond for musical entertainment. Since moving it back up the hill was a back-breaking task, it was left stranded on the ice. When the spring thaw arrived, the piano sank into the depths. In an entirely different version, an intoxicated Ruth threw the piano off the porch of the cabin in defiance of a writer who said that he didn't look strong enough to do it. No one knows for certain what happened that night, but the location of the piano generated a great deal of interest in later years.

As the Red Sox failed to win a World Series for more than eight decades, desperate fans went to great extremes to break the so-called Babe Ruth Curse. A Sox fanatic named Kevin Kennedy came up with the idea of recovering the piano and playing it at a Red Sox game to ward off the evil spirits that had been bedeviling the club since 1918. An underwater researcher went out on the pond with an infrared camera but found nothing of substance. In February of 2002, an expert named John Fish (who had found pieces of TWA Flight 800 off Long Island) was recruited to search with more sophisticated equipment. It was a swing and a miss.

Years later, the truth about the piano was finally revealed. Its location was discovered in the 1960s by a pair of elementary school boys who were out hunting for berries. Exposure to the elements had taken a toll and the instrument was literally falling apart. The boys used the strings to make bows and arrows then hid the remaining pieces. They built a fort on the site, which they eventually outgrew. The surviving piano remnants were later tossed into the water during a clean-up effort.

When one of the boys (grown to manhood by then) heard about a search being conducted by the Sudbury Historical Society, he drew a map leading to the cove in which he had found the piano. A leg from the instrument was recovered in 2010, but the rest was unsalvageable. It wasn't an issue, since the Curse of the Bambino had been broken several years earlier.

THE CURIOUS TALE OF EDDIE BENNETT

Though most batboys remain anonymous during their years of service, Eddie Bennett became the most famous practitioner of his trade. While working for three different major-league teams in a 14-year span, his name and picture appeared in multiple newspapers. He also formed a personal bond with the game's most prominent star.

Bennett was born in the Flatbush neighborhood of Brooklyn. A spinal injury during his childhood stunted his growth and left him with a hunchbacked appearance. Adding to his misery, he lost both of his parents in the Spanish Flu pandemic of 1918. Baseball became a welcome escape for him after that. In 1919, he attended a game at the Polo Grounds, where he allegedly told White Sox centerfielder Happy Felsch that he had mystical powers and could serve as a good luck charm to all who used him. Superstitions were rampant among players of the era, and after a productive day at the plate, Felsch convinced Chicago manager Kid Gleason to hire Bennett as a batboy.

The 1919 World Series scandal brought Bennett's stint with the ChiSox to an abrupt end. He began frequenting Ebbets Field the following season. Looking to improve the team's fortunes, Hall of Fame skipper Wilbert Robinson welcomed Bennett aboard. The little man's presence may or may not have helped Brooklyn to a pennant that year. After winning two of the first three World Series games at home, the Robins left Bennett behind when the team traveled to Cleveland. In his absence, the New Yorkers dropped four straight, prompting rumors that Bennett had put a curse on the club.

In 1921, the Yankees enlisted Bennett's services. He performed his job devotedly for more than a decade. He was meticulous about the way he lined up the bats, and many players refused to let anyone else handle them. Swingman Wilcy Moore got in the peculiar habit of making Bennett catch his first warm-up toss whenever it was his turn to pitch.

During his days in the Bronx, Bennett struck up a friendship with Babe Ruth. The Yankee icon amused fans who arrived early to the ballpark by playing catch with Bennett. He deliberately threw balls over the smaller man's head and feigned innocence whenever Bennett barked at him for it. Bennett didn't mind being the brunt of Ruth's jokes. The two had a genuine affection for one another. Bennett was always eager to run errands for the Babe. And he routinely kneeled beside the slugger in the on-deck circle to bring him luck.

In May of 1932, Bennett was hit by a New York City taxi, sustaining a broken leg. He never recovered fully and was forced to give up his job. Yankees owner Jacob Ruppert continued to provide him with financial support after he left the team. Sadly, Bennett began drinking heavily to numb the chronic pain that plagued him in the wake of the accident. He died in 1935 from chronic alcoholism. His funeral was paid for by the Yankees and attended by the entire front office staff.

WEARING THE BROWN DERBY

The Yankees began the 1920 campaign with a shortage of outfielders. Chick Fewster had been hit by a pitch, sustaining a serious injury, and Ping Bodie had taken a leave of absence due to personal problems. The Babe asked Miller Huggins if he could play center field to avoid getting hurt while chasing flies in the tight corners of the Polo Grounds. Huggins agreed to test Ruth's aptitude, putting him in center field on Opening Day at Shibe Park in Philadelphia.

Wally Pipp put the Yankees on the board early with a first inning solo homer. Bob Shawkey pitched four scoreless innings for New York before surrendering a leadoff homer to Philly catcher Cy Perkins. The game remained tied until the bottom of the eighth. With two outs and a pair of runners on, Joe Dugan lifted a catchable fly to Ruth, who botched the play. Both runners scored, lifting the A's to a 3–1 win.

On the day after the Babe's costly error, Dugan (who joined the Yankees a couple of years later) arranged to have a messenger deliver a package to the slugger while he was at bat. Inside the package was a brown derby, which was a symbol of inadequacy in those days. Ruth had been known to lose his temper when the joke was on him, but he handled it well. After opening the parcel, he put the hat on with a smile and waved to fans. In spite of his good humor, it was another forgettable day as he went 0-for-5 at the plate with three strikeouts. Ruth finished the season with 54 homers and a .376 batting average but suffered through one of the slowest starts of his career. He hit .210 with a pair of homers in his first 18 games.

ROADHOUSE BLUES

In the spring of 1921, the Yankees trained in Shreveport, Louisiana. The discovery of oil at nearby Caddo Pine Island had brought unparalleled prosperity to the area, and the city was teeming with activity when the New Yorkers arrived. During a ballpark ceremony, Ruth received an Essex automobile to use while the team was preparing for the upcoming season. Instead of a license plate, the vehicle had a sign on the back that read: "Babe Ruth's Essex."

Looking for a taste of the Louisiana nightlife, Ruth began frequenting a roadhouse outside of town that served bootleg liquor and fried chicken. One evening, he and a handful of teammates were being excessively boisterous. A local patron took offense and got into a heated argument with the Babe. A round of fisticuffs was narrowly avoided.

The local man left the bar, followed shortly afterward by Ruth, who was known for his abrupt departures. As the Babe's Essex sped out of the parking lot, pitcher Harry Harper noticed another vehicle following it. Harper alerted his teammates that there was trouble afoot.

The players piled into Harper's sedan and took off in hot pursuit. Roughly a mile up the road, they saw Ruth's car parked on the shoulder. He was being held at gunpoint by the man from the bar. Taking decisive action, Harper laid on his horn and drove his vehicle directly toward the gunman. This afforded Ruth an opportunity to grab hold of his adversary. Harper bravely jumped out of the car and took possession of the weapon. Threatening words were exchanged, but in the end, the Yankees players released the man unharmed. No police report was ever filed. Years later, pitcher Waite Hoyt admitted that they were all afraid of what manager Miller Huggins would do if he found out about the incident.

Ruth's Little Pal

A chance encounter in 1921 allowed a youngster named Ray Kelly to become the envy of American schoolboys across the nation. One day, when Kelly was playing catch with his dad in a park on Manhattan's Upper West Side, Babe Ruth (who lived nearby) suddenly appeared and began chatting him up. Impressed with little Ray's abilities, Ruth asked permission to bring him to the Polo Grounds for a game the following day. The boy's father agreed.

Kelly, who was just three years old when he met Ruth, served as the slugger's personal mascot for a decade. He shared the dugout with a slew of Hall of Famers and got to witness firsthand some of the Babe's most epic career moments, including the first home run ever hit at Yankee Stadium. Sometimes he even accompanied the Yankees on road trips, sharing a hotel room with the team's adult batboy, Eddie Bennett. Asked if players toned down their language with a kid on the bench, Kelly responded comically, "Are you kidding? Where do you think I learned to swear?"[7] Multiple photos of him posing with Ruth exist.

Feeling that he needed to focus more on his schoolwork, Kelly left the Yankees at the age of 13. He was invited to attend a game during the 1932 World Series. It just happened to be the one in which Ruth allegedly called his shot off of Charlie Root. Kelly watched it happen from a box seat, and when the validity of the event came into question, he went on record saying: "He absolutely did it. I was right there. . . . Never in doubt."[8]

Kelly served as a sergeant in the US Army Air Forces during World War II. He graduated from Pace University and made a comfortable living as an accountant for the Mobil Oil Company. He passed away in 2001 at the age of 83.

The Babe Becomes a Guinea Pig

Ruth's 54 homers in 1920 were more than the collective total of most major-league teams. Looking to uncover the secret of his apparent superpowers, sportswriter Hugh Fullerton talked the slugger into undergoing a battery of tests at the Columbia University psychology lab. Though the equipment used was not as sophisticated as the machinery of today, the results were not at all surprising. The Babe was well ahead of the curve.

Various electrically wired devices were used to measure his coordination. He was asked to insert a stylus into holes in a triangular board and to tap a metal plate as fast as he could. To assess his perceptual abilities, letters were flashed quickly in groups and he was required to identify them afterward. Arrays of dots were also presented to him; he was asked to determine how many were in each set. Another experiment measured his reaction time to light and sound. In the only test directly resembling a game situation, a ball suspended at a height determined to be optimum for his home run swing was connected to a timer that recorded his bat speed and estimated his power.

Fullerton, who was known for his use of statistics in predicting game play, published his interpretation of the results in the *New York Times* and *Popular Science* magazine. He reported that Ruth's success as a hitter was due to the fact that his sensory abilities and fine motor skills were far superior to those of the average healthy man. Fullerton also pointed out that the Babe was tested on a hot day in which he had played a nine-inning game and may not have been operating at full capacity. Interestingly, slugger Albert Pujols (then with the Cardinals) was subjected to some of the same tests in 2006. Like Ruth, he scored well above average.

Mystery Child

The Yankees were on their way to clinching the American League pennant in September of 1922 when a major news story broke. A banner headline in the *New York American* proclaimed: "Ruth a Daddy for 16 Months and Has Hidden Facts from the World."[9] The Babe's daughter Dorothy soon became the most famous toddler in America as journalists scrambled to get the inside scoop.

In Cleveland, where the Yankees were taking on the Indians, Ruth was besieged by an army of inquisitive reporters. He acted very casual about Dorothy's sudden appearance in the spotlight, explaining that she had weighed just two pounds at birth and had to be placed in an incubator. Meanwhile, back in New York, the Babe's wife, Helen, found herself in an identical situation. Asked by the press if the baby had been adopted, she became extremely defensive and refused to allow pictures to be taken. Later in the interview, she revealed that Dorothy had been under the care of a nurse for more than a year due to a serious vitamin D deficiency.

A number of facts supplied by Helen and the Babe didn't match up. The slugger said that Dorothy had been born in Presbyterian Hospital on February 2. Helen insisted that she had been delivered at St. Vincent's on June 7. The plot thickened when reporters discovered that there was no official record of the birth at the Bureau of Vital Statistics or the Department of Health. Complicating matters even further, the priest at St. Catherine's, where Dorothy was said to have been baptized, had no recollection of the christening.

In late-September, Helen brought Dorothy to Fenway Park for a game. After parading the child around the field and introducing her as the Yankees' new mascot, the Babe and Helen faced the press together for the first time. Reporters demanded the details and pointed out holes in the couple's story. Helen grew increasingly agitated, snarling: "People have been very mean about making all the mystery about Dorothy. I won't give them the satisfaction of telling them anything."[10] The Babe supported her, abruptly ending the impromptu press conference.

The truth remained buried for many years. Dorothy's biological mother was a model named Juanita Grenandtz, who had changed her last name to Jennings. As the granddaughter of former Mexican president Francisco Madero, Jennings had lived a life of privilege. Strikingly attractive and incorrigibly flirtatious, she had caught the eye of the Babe during an exhibition tour in 1920. Dorothy was a product of their illicit affair. Jennings later married a wealthy accountant named Charles Ellias. She remained involved in her daughter's life for many years, though the biological connection was not revealed until shortly before her passing.

Senator Walker's Humiliating Speech

Ruth was suspended on multiple occasions during the 1922 slate. He played in just 110 games and yielded the AL home run crown to Ken Williams of the Browns. The Yankees won the pennant anyway, but Ruth had his worst World Series ever, hitting just .118 with one RBI. A few weeks after the disastrous season was over, the Babe's agent, Christy Walsh, organized a dinner at the midtown Elks Club in New York. A number of sportswriters and Broadway performers attended. What began as a lighthearted tribute turned ugly when New York state senator James J. Walker took the podium.

Walker, who would later become mayor of New York City, painted Ruth as a buffoon who had let down the sportswriters and officials of baseball. He also insisted that the Babe had disappointed the children of America with his carousing and overindulgence. "It is exactly as though Santa Claus himself suddenly were to take off his beard to reveal the features of a villain," said Walker. "The kids have seen their idol shattered and their dreams broken."[11]

According to multiple reports, the Babe was crying by the time Walker's rant was finished. He owned up to his excesses and vowed to get back in shape: "I want the New York fans and sports writers to know that I've had my last drink until next October. I mean it. Tomorrow, I'm going to my farm. I'm going to work my head off and maybe part of my stomach."[12] Though his promise to abstain from alcohol was overambitious, he returned to form on the ball field the following season.

The Rise and Fall of Home Plate Farm

By 1922, the Babe's wife, Helen, had become increasingly unhappy. Fed up with Ruth's extramarital affairs and a life of constant scrutiny, she threatened to leave him. In an attempt to patch up the floundering marriage, the slugger purchased a farm in Sudbury, Massachusetts. Located on two acres, the colonial farmhouse offered more than 5,000 square feet with five bedrooms and three and a half baths. There were a number of outbuildings, including a massive barn suitable for livestock.

Shortly after finalizing the deal, Ruth invited his Yankee teammates to come see the place, which he named Home Plate Farm. Future Hall of Famer Waite Hoyt was among the visitors. The previous owners had left most of their furniture behind and Hoyt, who knew a little bit about antiques, recognized it as being rare and extremely valuable. He told the Babe that it might be worth as much as the property itself. In the months that followed, Ruth had the place remodeled. When the renovations were complete, he invited his Yankee friends back to have a look. Hoyt noticed that all the antique furniture was gone and asked what had happened to it. Ruth told him that it was just "junk" cluttering up the place and that he had paid a man to get it out of his way.

Ruth actually tried his hand at farming, stocking the property with chickens, turkeys, horses, and cows. There was a large pond adjacent to the farm, and he invited pitcher Bullet Joe Bush to join him on a "hunting" excursion. They went out in a rowboat after dark and began shooting at bullfrogs by lantern light. One of Ruth's shotgun blasts reportedly tipped the boat, dumping both men into the water.

The Babe's farming experiment came to an end when one of his dogs (an ill-tempered bull terrier named Dot) wandered onto a neighboring farm and attacked a cow, killing it. The owner of the cow sued him for a reported sum of $5,000. He got rid of his livestock after that. By 1925, his marriage to Helen had completely deteriorated. She moved out of Home Plate Farm and Ruth sold the place the following year.

IN THE NICK OF TIME

Throughout his career, the Babe had a knack for hitting home runs at opportune moments. On May 22, 1923, a 22-year-old White Sox rookie was pitching the game of his life against the Yankees. "Little Mike" Cvengros, who stood just 5-foot-8 and weighed less than 160 pounds, had held the New Yorkers to just one run through 14 innings. The Yankees were scheduled to board a train back to the Bronx and team secretary Mark Roth was getting anxious. Roth checked his watch repeatedly and fidgeted behind the Yankee dugout. When the top of the 15th was underway, he expressed his concerns to manager Miller Huggins: "Hug, if the game doesn't end this inning, we'll miss our train. What'll I do?" Ruth, who was scheduled to bat, overheard Roth's comment and laughed about it. "All right, quit worrying," he told the frazzled secretary, "I'll get this over with right now."[13]

Through 14 innings, Cvengros had limited Ruth to a pair of walks in seven trips to the plate. With a runner on base and a tight schedule to keep, the Babe lifted the hurler's first offering into the outfield seats for a two-run homer. Herb Pennock shut down the White Sox in the bottom of the frame to claim a hard-fought 3–1 win. Ruth, who told his story to sportswriter John P. Carmichael, said that the Yankees caught their train in plenty of time that day.

THE SWITCH-HITTING EXPERIMENT

During the 1923 campaign, Ruth hit .393 and led the majors with 41 homers. He had become such a fearsome presence at the plate that teams refused to pitch to him. He walked 170 times that season—a record that stood for nearly 80 years. Fed up with intentional passes, he tried his luck as a switch-hitter.

On August 1, the Yankees were facing the Indians at home. The Tribe was leading, 5–1, when the Babe stepped into the box against southpaw Sherry Smith. He had already walked twice that afternoon. The *Pittsburgh Daily Press* offered the following description of his at-bat: "His last time up, Babe introduced a new one. He became a right-handed batter for a moment. He looked one over while standing on the left side of the plate—that one a strike. Then he switched back to the trances of his childhood and biffed the first one."[14] It was his 25th "biff" of the season.

A few days later, the Yankees were hosting the Browns. Ruth already had a pair of homers to his credit when he came to the plate against Elam Vangilder in the 11th inning. With third base open, he attempted to bait the reliever into facing him by batting right-handed. The ploy didn't work. Taking no chances, Vangilder issued an intentional walk. The Yankees failed to score and the game dragged on for two more innings. In the bottom of the 13th, Ruth faced Vangilder as a right-hander again. The end result was the same—an intentional pass. This time, the hurler's strategy backfired as Bob Meusel delivered a walk-off single. A writer from the *New York Daily News* joked afterward: "Babe is getting so weary of walking that he'll try anything to make the opposition pitch to him. Someday, we expect to see him go to bat with the stick in his teeth."[15]

DOG ACT

Though his hitting was quite extraordinary, Ruth was only slightly above average as an outfielder. On the plus side, he had a strong, accurate arm. On the negative side, he was a bit clumsy at times, finishing among the top five in errors during eight seasons. On August 20, 1923, he was forced to make one of the trickiest catches of his career.

During the ninth inning of a 16–5 Yankee blowout in Chicago, a dog somehow got loose and wandered into left field, where Ruth was stationed. With the game well in hand, the playful Yankee slugger began clowning around. He got down on all fours and followed the dog around. He then removed his glove and threw it, prompting the canine to fetch. As the Babe's new friend ran off with his mitt, rookie pitcher Paul Castner hit a fly ball to left field. Ruth caught the ball barehanded for the first out of the inning. The Chicago crowd roared with laughter and gave the Babe an appreciative round of applause.

Ruth's adventures in the outfield were numerous. He once got his finger caught in the right field screen at Yankee Stadium, tearing his nail off in the process. During a spring training game, he ran headfirst into a palm tree in pursuit of a fly ball. Even so, his lifetime fielding percentage was slightly above the league average at the time of his retirement.

THE BABE AND HIS CIGARS

Ruth was a habitual smoker. At one point during his career, he had his own brand of nickel cigars, which featured a picture of him on every wrapper. A man of enormous appetites, he lived his life to extremes—especially in regard to women. Cigars became the measure of his sexual prowess.

During his time with the Red Sox, the Babe roomed with pitcher Ernie Shore. It was not a good fit. The mild-mannered Shore complained about a number of Ruth's bad habits, which included bringing women back to the room after curfew. One night, as Shore was trying to sleep, the Babe engaged in multiple rounds of noisy coitus with a woman he had picked up. Shore finally drifted off as the sun was coming up. When he awoke, the woman was gone and his teammate was in a deep slumber. He noted that there were four or five cigars in an ashtray next to the bed. Ruth later explained that he was in the habit of smoking each time he had sex.

A similar story exists involving Yankee outfielder Bob Meusel. While sharing a suite with the Babe during a road trip, Meusel noticed a parade of women coming in and out of the room all night. True to his nickname, "Silent Bob" minded his own business and was eventually able to get to sleep. In the morning, he asked Ruth how many women he had been with. The Babe told him to count the number of cigars in the ashtray. Meusel was somewhat startled to see seven of them.

Somehow, Ruth's trysts rarely affected his on-field performances. In another tale recounted by infielder Joe Dugan, Ruth visited a notorious Philadelphia brothel owned by a woman named Rose Hicks in late April of 1924. He was spotted in an upstairs room seated in a chair with a prostitute on each knee. The women were pouring champagne over his head and massaging it into his hair. "Anybody who doesn't love this life is crazy!" he proclaimed. After partying all night and getting less than three hours of sleep, he hit a pair of homers and scored three runs against the A's. "That's the way he lived all the years I knew him," said Dugan.[16]

THE SHOW MUST GO ON

One of the most frightening moments of Ruth's career occurred at Griffith Stadium in 1924. In the first game of a July doubleheader against the Senators, the Babe was chasing a fly ball that was drifting into foul territory along the right field line. There was no warning track and he didn't see the outfield wall as he approached it on the run. He slammed into the concrete barrier at top speed and crumpled on the field in a heap. A famous photo shows him lying flat on his back with his eyes closed. Team physician Doc Woods rushed to the scene. Unable to revive Ruth, he poured water over the outfielder's head. Finally, after about five minutes, the Babe woke up.

During the early part of the 20th century, the effects of traumatic brain injuries were poorly understood. There were no protocols in place to protect players. Ruth was helped to his feet and asked if he wanted to come out of the game. Though he was most likely suffering from a concussion, he insisted on staying in. Incredibly, he had two more at-bats that afternoon. Facing Walter Johnson—one of the most dominant hurlers in history—he doubled and walked!

Having hurt his hip in the outfield collision, Ruth was noticeably limping. It didn't prevent him from playing in the second game. By then, he may have been feeling the effects as he went 0-for-3 at the plate. Any concerns about his physical status were laid to rest the following day, when he pounded out three hits, including his 22nd homer of the season.

MYTH BUSTING

Considering Ruth's extraordinary batting feats, it's hard to believe that any of his managers would ever have replaced him with a pinch-hitter. But according to numerous sources, it actually happened once. Due to the scarcity of play-by-play data from the early 1900s and the many legends surrounding Ruth's career, the identity of the Babe's alleged substitute remains uncertain. There are three players who have been singled out, though each account is dubious in its own right. In fact, the tale of the mysterious pinch hitter may be just another myth.

An outfielder by trade, Sammy Vick spent portions of five seasons in the majors, fashioning a .248 lifetime batting average. Many years after his retirement, he drafted a letter to Marshall Smelser (a Ruth biographer and Notre Dame professor) claiming that he had delivered a three-run triple while pinch hitting for the Babe one afternoon. Unfortunately, the story doesn't hold water. Ruth and Vick played together for the Yankees during the 1920 season. Vick subbed for Ruth in one game and didn't drive in any runs. Furthermore, he was inserted as a defensive replacement. There were three other games that the Babe didn't finish that year, but none of his surrogates were listed as pinch hitters.

In his only authorized autobiography, Ruth shared a story about Mike McNally, a former Red Sox teammate. According to the Babe, McNally used to carry around a box score clipped from a newspaper that gave him credit for batting in place of Ruth. The event allegedly occurred during a blowout loss when the Babe was still primarily a pitcher. Specifics such as the date, venue, and opponent were not provided, however, making it extremely difficult to verify. The story—though likely apocryphal—has an amusing twist. When McNally pulled out the box score for the umpteenth time and showed it to a group of sportswriters, Ruth allegedly told him that he would make him eat it if he ever did it again.

Other sources have proposed that it was Bobby Veach who pinch hit for Ruth. Veach was a major star for the Tigers during the Deadball Era. He played for the Red Sox briefly before joining the Yankees in 1925. According to an unattributed game recap that appeared in the *Chicago Tribune*, Veach's landmark plate appearance occurred on August 9, 1925. Researcher Robert Creamer alleged that Ruth had wrenched his back on the date in question and had been struggling at the plate. The official box score credits Ruth with a 1-for-3 performance that day, including an RBI. Veach, who is not listed as a pinch hitter in the official box score, went 1-for-2 as a substitute. Considering that Wally Pipp and Ben Paschal were both credited with pinch-hitting appearances, it's likely that Veach entered the game in the middle innings as a defensive replacement. But given the fact that the play-by-play is missing, there is some room for doubt.

Bombs Away!

Having missed out on military duty during World War I, Ruth joined the Army National Guard in 1924. Serving as a private in the 104th Field

Artillery Unit, he made numerous public appearances on behalf of the armed forces. In July of 1926, he participated in an unusual publicity stunt designed to generate interest in the Citizens' Military Training Camps.

The event took place at Mitchel Field in Garden City, Long Island. A plane piloted by Captain Harold McClelland circled the airport as the Babe—dressed in army garb—waited below. Traveling at 80 mph, McClelland dropped balls from an estimated height of 300 feet. The Yankee outfielder was unable to get his hands on the first two balls, which hit the ground untouched. But on the seventh try, he successfully caught one. The *New York Times* reported, "Ruth was darting about the field under the blistering sun, getting hotter and hotter. The only breeze was the twisters kicked up by the plane which sent tornadoes of dust about the baseball hero."[17] After receiving a nice round of applause from the small crowd in attendance, the Babe went directly to the officers' club to shower and change.

Newspapers claimed that Ruth's catch had been a world record, but that wasn't entirely true. In 1908, Washington Senators catcher Gabby Street had caught a ball dropped from the top of the Washington Monument, which is 550 feet tall. Cubs catcher Gabby Hartnett set a new record in 1930 when he snared a hurtling sphere released from a blimp over Wrigley Field in California. Estimates of that catch vary, but various sources have cited it at 800 feet. The quest to grab baseballs falling from perilous heights continued in 1938 as two members of the Indians turned the trick while standing at the bottom of Cleveland's Terminal Tower. Attempting to outperform them all, Pacific Coast League catcher Joe Sprinz was seriously injured the following year when a ball dropped from a blimp hovering over Seals Stadium in San Francisco shattered his jaw, broke several teeth, and knocked him senseless.

THE SULTAN OF STEROIDS

Performance-enhancing drugs have been pervasive in baseball for longer than most people realize. During the second Industrial Revolution, an eccentric French scientist named Charles Edouard Brown-Sequard set out to increase the size and strength of workers. To that end, he began injecting himself with an extract from the testosterone of dogs and guinea pigs. He claimed that the injections made him smarter and stronger while providing other health benefits.

In 1889, aging future Hall of Famer Pud Galvin experimented with the mixture, which came to be known as the "Brown-Sequard Elixir." After receiving an injection, he pitched a shutout and drove in three runs with a pair of extra-base hits. But his performance soon declined, along with empirical support for Brown-Sequard's research. The quest to build stronger humans continued nevertheless.

As baseball became a multimillion-dollar enterprise in the 1920s, team trainers saw vast potential in PED's. The use of sheep's testicles in injectible form gained some credibility, inspiring members of the Yankees staff to try it out on Babe Ruth. The slugger was receptive to the idea of improving his prowess on the field and in the bedroom. But after a single injection, he became severely ill. According to author David Zirin, the Yankees allegedly covered up the story with a claim that he was having one of his regular bouts of stomach upset.

THE VAUDEVILLE FIASCO

At the end of the 1926 campaign, Ruth signed up for a 12-week, 14-city vaudeville tour. His act included comedy skits, musical numbers, and baseball stories. At the conclusion of each performance, he invited a few children onto the stage to showcase their own talents. The routine eventually landed him in hot water.

On the day of his final shows at the State Theater in Long Beach, California, the Babe went to the San Bernardino Mountains to fish. The destination was located about three hours from the theater. After catching and eating over a dozen trout, he realized he would never make it back to the venue on time for a scheduled matinee. His handlers were forced to hire a stunt pilot named Roman Warren to fly him back to Long Beach. He made it to the venue on time—just barely. As he was preparing to go on stage, the theater manager informed him that he was about to be served with a warrant for violating child labor laws.

The charges stemmed from a January 14 show in San Diego, during which an eight-year-old girl named Baby Annette de Kirby had recited a poem on stage without a permit. Ruth was justifiably upset, commenting, "They forget how much I've done for kids. I've done nothing that would harm them. I've only tried to give them a little bit of sunshine."[18] He turned himself in at the Long Beach Police Station and posted bail, returning in time to complete his remaining performances.

A few weeks later, a San Diego judge acquitted Ruth on the grounds that the children who appeared with him onstage were not members of the cast nor were they technically reimbursed for their acts. Each had received an autographed baseball, which qualified as a "gift"—not an actual payment.

Unhappy with the decision, Deputy State Labor Commissioner Stanley M. Gue (who had filed the original complaint) pressed new charges against Ruth, asserting that some of the young performers had appeared after 10:00 p.m. in violation of existing statutes. During the second hearing, the presiding magistrate dismissed the case and lectured Gue for requiring work permits "to step up onto a stage and get a free baseball."[19] Ruth's tour received mostly positive reviews. A writer from the *New York Times* reported that "Ruth has a good stage presence, a winning smile and gets away with the singing part."[20] Not everyone agreed. The Babe's teammate and friend Mark Koenig said that the show was "boring as hell."[21]

A MAN OF MANY NAMES

By the time he slammed 60 homers in 1927 (a single-season record that stood for more than 30 years), Ruth was among the most renowned celebrities in the world. His daily exploits on and off the field took up more newspaper space than President Calvin Coolidge. Sportswriters competed with one another to get the latest scoop. And to make their stories more sensational, they tagged Ruth with a number of colorful nicknames. No player in history has been given as many aliases. Though the list is not all-inclusive, the cleverest ones are included below:

- The Big Bam
- The Behemoth of Bust
- The Bazoo of Bang
- The Bulky Monarch
- The Caliph of Clout
- Circuit Smasher
- The Colossus of Crash
- Diamond-Studded Ball-Buster
- Demon Swatter
- G. Herman Hercules
- The Hedjaz of Hit
- Homeric Herman

- The King of Crash
- The Mammoth of Maul
- The Monarch of Swatdom
- The Mauling Mastodon
- The Mandarin of Maul
- The Paladin of Punch
- The Potentate of Powders
- The Prince of Ash
- The Priest of Swat
- The Rajah of Rap
- The Sultan of Swat
- The Sheik of Slam
- The Sachem of Slug
- The Swattingest Swatter of Swatdom
- The Slambino
- The Terrible Titan
- The Titan of Thump
- The Wizard of Whack
- The Wali of Wallop

BABE AND LOU CHANNEL LAUREL AND HARDY

While Lou Gehrig was challenging the Babe for the 1927 home run crown, executives from Perfect Records (an imprint of the international Pathe Records label) thought it might be amusing to make an album featuring the duo performing a comedy sketch. Released as a 78 rpm disc, it remains the only commercial audio recording of both players together.

Stated bluntly, the Yankee icons were way better at baseball than comedy. Gehrig's timing is frequently off and Ruth fumbles his lines more than once. The jokes are neither sophisticated nor terribly amusing by modern standards. During an awkward dialogue spanning more than 10 minutes, the Babe slams his teammate for being stupid ("You're so dumb, you thought the St. Louis Cardinals were appointed by the church") and for having big feet ("Is there any truth in the story that you sell [your] shoes for bungalows?").

As the performance continues, Ruth becomes the butt of a few jokes, getting picked on for his eating habits along with his exorbitant salary and reckless driving. In one fairly humorous exchange, Gehrig points out how Ruth has not been arrested for speeding in a while. "I found a way out of it," the Babe explains. "When a policeman stops me, I autograph the car and give it to him as a souvenir."[22]

Despite its over-the-top corniness, the routine does have a kind of archaic charm. There aren't too many recordings of Gehrig's voice in existence. And the relationship between the two men eventually turned sour, making this early collaboration a cheerful reminder of better times.

ACCUSATIONS OF ASSAULT

On September 13, 1927, Ruth was arraigned in West Side Court after an alleged attack on a disabled man. According to the victim, a 49-year-old artist named Bernard Neimeyer, the incident had taken place on the evening of July 4 at the corner of Broadway and 74th Street in Manhattan. Neimeyer claimed that he had been accused of making a rude remark to the Babe's wife, prompting the slugger to punch him in the face.

At the time of the hearing on September 17, the Yankees had built an enormous lead in the standings and Ruth was threatening to break the single-season record for homers he had set several years earlier. The courtroom was jam-packed with reporters, police, and curious fans. Upon taking the stand, Neimeyer became extremely agitated. The *New York Times* reported that he "rose excitedly to his feet, waving a book of notes which he added to from time to time as the hearing proceeded. He was often cautioned by the clerk of the court not to talk so loudly."[23] By the time he was finished, it was evident to nearly everyone present that he was probably suffering from some kind of mental disorder.

Asked by the magistrate if he had ever seen Ruth before, Neimeyer said "no." The Babe had brought multiple witnesses to vouch for the fact that he was nowhere near the corner of Broadway and 74th Street at the time of the alleged assault. The charges were subsequently dropped. Interestingly, the Yankees had destroyed the Senators in a doubleheader on July 4 by a combined score of 33–2. Ruth gathered five hits that day and walked three times.

GETTING HIS LICKS IN

After the Yankees efficiently disposed of the Pirates in the 1927 World Series, Ruth and Gehrig appeared in a round of exhibitions arranged by their mutual agent, Christy Walsh. Walsh had expected the series to last longer than four games, and with an unanticipated opening in the schedule, he arranged for the Yankee superstars to play in Providence, Rhode Island, on October 10.

The game took place at Kinsley Field, which served as home to the Providence Grays—the club Ruth had helped to a first-place finish in 1914. Gehrig's team was composed of players from the Universal Winding Company, a leader in the yarn industry. The Babe batted cleanup for the Immaculate Conception Institute, popularly known as the ICI's.

Prior to the first pitch, the Yankees icons were greeted at home plate by a vaudeville troupe composed of dancers, jugglers, comedians, and musicians. A home run–hitting contest pitting Ruth against Gehrig followed. The actual game began shortly afterward. In an effort to give fans their money's worth, it was announced that pitchers would not be allowed to walk either of the Yankee sluggers.

In the seventh inning, Ruth decided he wanted to pitch. Facing Gehrig, he coughed up the only home run of the afternoon—a long shot to center field. In the eighth, Gehrig took to the mound for the Universals. There were two hitters scheduled to bat before Ruth, but he came to the plate out of turn, hoping for a chance at redemption against his teammate. Since it was only an exhibition, Ruth kept hacking away until the supply of baseballs was exhausted. A local newspaper reported that Gehrig struck out Ruth at least three times and walked him several more. To keep the game going, a prominent sandlot organizer named Tim O'Neill donated a ball that the Yankee icons had signed for him. Ruth made a show of it, waving the outfielders back before dropping a single into right field. A throng of children bolted out of the stands to scoop up O'Neill's autographed souvenir. The umpires penalized Ruth for batting out of order and declared the game finished due to an absence of baseballs.

RUTH AND INTEGRATION

Though baseball wouldn't be integrated until 1946, the Babe's barnstorming tours frequently included games against Negro League clubs. Ruth was no civil rights activist, but he had no qualms about playing against all-black teams even when many of his major-league peers did. Before the games, he would socialize with opponents and mingle in the segregated stands. He maintained friendships with African American sports figures such as boxing champion Joe Louis and Bill "Bojangles" Robinson, who was co-owner of the New York Black Yankees. At Ruth's request, Robinson was the first black man ever to visit the Yankee clubhouse. Given up by his parents as a child, the Babe knew what it was like to feel alienated. And his ethnicity had come into question at multiple points during his lifetime. He shared a mutual respect with black athletes, many of whom idolized him.

In 1920, Ruth's All-Stars played the Bacharach Giants of the Independent Negro League. The Giants top pitcher at the time was "Cannonball Dick" Redding—a big right-hander with a nasty fastball. He used a no-windup delivery and "hesitation pitch" long before Satchel Paige made both tactics famous. Over the course of his long career, Redding was said to have tossed 30 no-hitters. He was also one of the sturdiest pitchers in history, often throwing both games of a doubleheader on consecutive days. Ruth went 2-for-4 against Redding in the 1920 exhibition, which was held at Shibe Park in Philadelphia. One of those hits was a monstrous blast that left the park and reportedly landed on 20th Street.

In 1925, Ruth faced Redding again in Red Bank, New Jersey. By then, the durable flamethrower was playing for the Brooklyn Royal Giants of the Eastern Colored League. The Giants were leading by a run in the ninth when the Babe came to bat. Redding was instructed to walk the Yankees slugger, but refused. He paid the price as one of his fastballs ended up in the outfield seats for a homer.

The final confrontation between Ruth and Redding took place in Trenton, New Jersey, at the end of the 1927 campaign. Though Redding was 36 years old and no longer in his prime, he had tossed a no-hitter earlier that year. The event's organizer removed any semblance of real competition when he instructed the hurler to groove pitches to Ruth every time he came to bat. The Babe hit three "gift" homers that day. When Redding finally retired in the mid-1930s, Ruth told a reporter from the *Pittsburgh Courier* that he could have done well with any major-league team.

SPARRING WITH TEAMMATES

In spite of his amiable personality, Ruth did not mix well with all of his teammates and managers. He was often crude, boastful, and antagonistic in the clubhouse. This led to a number of confrontations over the years. Though the Babe engaged in bitter disputes with Miller Huggins, Carl Mays, and Leo Durocher during his time with the Yankees, none of those arguments amounted to much more than idle threats of physical harm. Ruth was unable to restrain himself with others, however.

In July of 1922, first baseman Wally Pipp—normally an excellent fielder—went through a brief defensive lapse. After making a boneheaded play during a game against the Browns, he skulked to the dugout when the inning was over and told teammates that he would pop Ruth in the nose if the slugger criticized him for his mistake. The scenario played out exactly as predicted. The Babe started in on Pipp as he headed down the dugout steps, prompting a punch that was right on target. Pipp was no lightweight at 6-foot-1, 180 pounds, but Ruth was an inch taller and much heavier. Still, the ensuing fight produced surprising results. While the Babe missed with several wild swings, Pipp landed a multitude of open-handed slaps to Ruth's face. Third baseman Frank Baker stepped between the two and paid the price, getting smacked in the eye and the back of his neck. Ruth vowed to settle the score after the game, but when Pipp confronted him later, the slugger had forgotten all about it and was in no mood to tussle.

During a 1927 exhibition game in Baltimore, Ruth tangled with infielder Mark Koenig. According to Koenig, Ruth swore at him and accused him of loafing after a throw that was well over his head. Taking offense, the error-prone Yankee shortstop responded with a stream of invective. The Babe grabbed him from behind and shoved him down the dugout steps. They wrestled briefly before teammates pried them apart. Hoping to avoid future hostilities, Miller Huggins separated their lockers, which were side-by-side. The two men, who had enjoyed a friendly relationship before then, refused to speak to one another until the Yankees clinched the pennant that year. They shook hands and agreed to put their differences aside.

NOT QUITE DEAD YET

There were a handful of pitchers who fared extremely well against the Babe in his prime. One of them was a left-hander named Ed Wells. Known for his changeups and agonizingly slow curves, the Bethany College graduate joined the Tigers in 1923. Over portions of five seasons, he held Ruth to a .204 batting average without any homers. The Yankee slugger continually joked that he was going to find a way to bring Wells to New York so he wouldn't have to face him anymore. It finally happened in 1929. Wells was struggling with his mechanics and had been sent to the minors. The Yankees purchased his contract from the Birmingham Barons.

The fun-loving Ruth was an incorrigible prankster. Though a majority of his practical jokes were crudely orchestrated (he once urinated on a teammate in the showers), he was known to stage some fairly elaborate gags from time to time. Looking to exact some long overdue "revenge," he allegedly conspired with teammates to put one over on the unsuspecting Wells.

After a game against the Tigers at Navin Field, Ruth invited Wells to accompany him on a double date at a private home in the Detroit suburbs. Ruth told the hurler that the girls they were meeting enjoyed drinking and instructed him to purchase some alcohol. Wells showed up with a fifth of gin. The house was dark when the Yankee duo arrived. Ruth rang the bell and a man opened the door, looking extremely agitated.

"So, you're the scum who have been after my wife," he growled. "I ought to kill you."

Standing by those convictions, the man pulled out a pistol and fired it at the Babe.

"I'm hit," the outfielder croaked, collapsing on the porch. "Run for your life, Ed!"

The terrified moundsman fled the scene in haste, making it safely back to the Book Cadillac Hotel, where the team was staying. He encountered a throng of Yankee players waiting for him in the lobby. Tony Lazzeri informed Wells that the Babe was in rough shape and had been asking for him. Lazzeri and his fellow conspirators escorted the hurler to a dimly lit room where Ruth lay sprawled out on the bed. They had covered his face with talcum powder to make it look ghostly pale and covered his shirt with ketchup to simulate a gunshot wound.

"He's dying, Ed," Earle Combs said as Wells entered the room.

Completely overwhelmed, the Yankee southpaw allegedly fainted at that point. The sound of roaring laughter brought him back to his senses. Utility infielder Billy Werber, who relayed this story to a freelance writer, said that Wells failed to see the humor in the situation when the prank was finally revealed.[24]

THE BABE IN PRISON

Founded in 1826, Sing Sing Correctional Facility in Ossining, New York, is among the oldest prisons in the United States. The maximum-security facility, which sits on the east bank of the Hudson River about 30 miles from New York City, became renowned for the high-profile executions that took place there in the 1950s and 1960s. The electric chair in residence was nicknamed "Old Sparky." It fell into disuse in the early 1970s and was eventually moved to the Greenhaven Correctional Facility (though it was never used again).

Sing Sing had developed a baseball program under Warden Thomas Mott Osbourne in 1914. Known as a great reformer, Osbourne helped form the Mutual Welfare League, which was composed entirely of amateur clubs. The idea of bringing big-league teams to the prison was championed by Warden Lewis E. Lawes during the 1920s. Lawes believed that inmates could be rehabilitated through morale boosting as opposed to strict discipline. He introduced many recreational and work activities to the facility while granting prisoners easy access to books and medical treatment.

During the 1920s, the New York Giants played against teams from Sing Sing on several occasions. On September 5, 1929, the Yankees followed suit. Tony Lazzeri, Bob Meusel, and manager Miller Huggins (who had fallen seriously ill) were all absent that day along with several pitchers. But Ruth and Gehrig made the trip. Upon arriving, the players were taken on an extensive tour of the grounds. Ruth exchanged friendly greetings with prisoners and even signed his name on one of the cell walls.

Sing Sing Stadium had no vendors or concession stands. The towering walls of the prison served as the outfield perimeter. Armed guards in towers kept watch over the field. Prior to the Yankees' arrival, no ball had ever cleared the center field wall. After doubling in his first at-bat, Ruth sent a monstrous drive to center field. It sailed past a watchtower and over the wall, prompting the other tower guards to set their machine guns aside so they could cheer. The ball was said to have traveled more than 600 feet.

Ruth added a pair of homers later in the game and pitched the last two innings. When one of the inmates slammed a shot over the left field wall, the Babe shouted, "Hey! Are you available to sign a contract?" Somebody sitting in the stands shouted back, 'He's got one now. He's a ten-year man, Babe!"[25]

TIT FOR TAT

Bill Dickey was the Yankees' first-string catcher for more than a decade. Among the premier defensive backstops of the era, he led the league in fielding percentage four times. When he first arrived in the Bronx, he admitted to being in awe of Ruth and Gehrig. He tried to match their power, and his batting average suffered as a result. Manager Miller Huggins realized what was going on and intervened, advising Dickey to get a lighter bat, choke up, and work on hitting the ball to all fields. It was good advice; he retired with a .313 lifetime batting average.

The hazing of younger players was common in baseball's early days. One afternoon, Dickey came into the clubhouse and found his shoes nailed to the floor. Tony Lazzeri, who was the only one present at the time, told him Ruth had done it. Looking to assert himself, Dickey hatched a devilish plan. He purchased an egg before the next day's game and placed it inside Ruth's shoe. The Babe was very stylish, priding himself on his fine clothing. When the egg broke inside his loafer, he looked around the room incredulously as if to say, "Oh no you didn't." He turned the shoe upside down and, as the yolk oozed out, his face turned bright red. During the subsequent interrogation, Dickey assumed responsibility for the prank. Ruth ran over to him looking positively furious. Just when it seemed as if a fight would break out, the Babe suddenly burst into hysterical laughter. All at once, the tension was relieved and other players joined in.

THE TROUBLE WITH HUB

During his 12 seasons in professional baseball, Hub Pruett was not an especially overpowering pitcher. He compiled a 92–103 record and spent significant stretches of time in the minors. But there was one thing that set him apart from the hurlers of his era: an uncanny ability to get Babe Ruth out.

A University of Missouri graduate, the left-handed Pruett joined the St. Louis Browns in 1922. Mild-mannered and gentlemanly, he earned the nickname "Shucks" because it was said to be the strongest word in his vocabulary. Working mostly in relief, he had the best season of his career in 1922, recording a 2.33 ERA in 39 appearances. Several of those appearances came against the Yankees. After striking out Ruth nine times in their first 13 encounters, newspapers began referring to Pruett as "the Babe's nemesis."[26]

No one is precisely sure why the Yankee icon was so ineffective against the middling southpaw, but many have suggested that Ruth found Pruett's fadeaway pitch especially troublesome. The fadeaway (a kind of reverse curve later known as the "screwball") had been famously used by Hall of Famer Christy Mathewson. Few if any left-handers employed it during Pruett's career. Though he was far less effective in his sophomore campaign, the Browns kept Pruett around for three full seasons on account of his ability to neutralize Ruth. By the time Pruett left baseball in 1932, the Babe had compiled a 42 percent strikeout rate against him.

Pruett's father, a practicing physician, had died tragically in a horse-and-buggy accident on his way to a house call. Following in his dad's footsteps, Pruett used the money he made from baseball to attain a doctorate degree from the St. Louis School of Medicine. Though he never actually spoke to Ruth during his playing days, he felt strangely indebted to the Yankees hero. He got a chance to thank the Babe in person at a 1948 baseball dinner. Flattered by Pruett's gratitude, Ruth responded kindly, "If there would have been more like you, no one would have ever heard of me."[27]

The Shot He Didn't Call

Ruth's life story is inundated with legends and myths. Nearly everyone who saw him play had a memory to share. Because he was a larger-than-life character, many anecdotes were transformed into fables over time. The Babe did very little to dispel his fairytale image. He enjoyed spinning yarns and often got his facts mixed up. But there is a grain of truth in almost every fish story.

In 2008, former Yankees infielder Billy Werber shared an astonishing anecdote with a writer from Duke University's literary magazine. The story, which allegedly came straight from the Babe's mouth, was somehow kept out of the mainstream. During spring training one year, the Yankee superstar had an affair with a woman from Ybor City—a primarily Hispanic neighborhood in Tampa, Florida. He eventually grew tired of the relationship and broke it off. When the slugger's jilted lover found him at a country club sharing a meal with another woman, she pulled a revolver from her purse and approached him with it. Fearing for his life, Ruth fled through the doors of the dining hall onto the golf course. A shot rang out behind him. The bullet allegedly passed cleanly through his calf, leaving him with a noticeable scar, which he showed to Werber and teammate Tony Lazzeri.

It's difficult to believe that an episode of this nature could be concealed. Not only were there witnesses, but a gunshot wound would undoubtedly have required medical attention. Still, there are credible elements to the story. Ruth had hundreds—possibly thousands—of trysts over the years and was confronted by angry parties wielding weapons on multiple occasions. Since he was friendly with all the journalists who covered the Yankees, a majority of his squalid exploits were kept hidden from the public.

BROTHER MATTHIAS'S FALL FROM GRACE

Of all the men in Babe Ruth's life, Brother Matthias Boutlier probably had the most profound impact. During the 12 years Ruth spent at St. Mary's, the strict but kindly brother served as a teacher, coach, and confidant to the Babe. In his 1948 autobiography, Ruth recalled, "It was at St. Mary's that I met and learned to love the greatest man I have ever known. . . . He was the father I needed. He taught me to read and write, and the difference between right and wrong."[28]

In addition to being the school's disciplinarian, Brother Matthias served a dual role as assistant athletic director. He has been widely credited with teaching Ruth how to swing for the fences. During the Deadball Era, runs were manufactured one base at a time. Batters habitually chopped down on the ball and utilized their speed to get on base. Brother Matthias had a different philosophy. During his weekly hitting demonstrations, he used a fungo bat and swung at a sharp upward angle, generating towering flies that sailed to the deepest recesses of the schoolyard. Young George adopted the same approach to hitting.

After his departure from St. Mary's, Ruth maintained a strong personal bond with Brother Matthias, inviting him to Yankee Stadium regularly and showering him with lavish gifts that included a small fleet of Cadillac Touring Cars. By the time the 1930s arrived, the Babe's childhood mentor had faded from public view. The cause of his disappearance was a secret known only to a handful of insiders.

In June of 1931, Brother Matthias was accused of having carnal relations with a young woman named Helen Bownes, who lived a couple of miles from the school. Neighbors reported seeing Boutlier arriving and departing at assorted hours of the day and night. His frequent visits were reported to a local priest, who passed the information on to his superiors.

Brother Matthias initially denied any impropriety when confronted on the issue, but he was spotted soon afterward leaving the woman's house at 3:00 a.m. When the archbishop received word of the incident, he sent Boutlier to St. John's Preparatory School in Danvers, Massachusetts, with instructions to stay away from Baltimore. Incredibly, the incorrigible Brother defied the archbishop's orders and got caught visiting Miss Bownes again. Rather than leave the brotherhood, Boutlier decided it was best to admit his indiscretions and atone for his sins. He was allowed to hold a staff position in one the Xaverian schools, but he spent the latter part of his life in relative anonymity.

DOUBLE WHAMMY

During the ten full seasons in which Ruth and Gehrig played together, the Iron Horse matched the Babe's home run output twice, but only once when both players were in their prime. The year was 1931. Gehrig had been chasing the lead all season. Ruth pulled ahead on September 25 with a pair of blasts against the Senators, but Gehrig managed to tie him in the Yankees' final game. It shouldn't have ended that way.

On April 26, Gehrig was stripped of a home run at Griffith Stadium in Washington. With two outs in the top of the first, he drilled a Firpo Marberry pitch to center field. The ball cleared the wall and landed in the bleachers before bouncing back into the glove of Harry Rice. Shortstop Lyn Lary, believing that the ball had been caught and the inning was over, cut across the diamond toward the Yankee dugout. Gehrig started running with his head down and was called out for passing Lary on the basepaths. Though it seemed relatively unimportant at the time, it loomed large when the season was over.

Gehrig told a reporter he didn't mind sharing the home run lead with Ruth, but he couldn't have been entirely pleased with the loss of two RBIs. He ended up setting the American League record that year. Had Lary been paying closer attention on that fateful day, Gehrig's total could have been even higher.

TAPE MEASURE BLASTS

Babe Ruth hit some of the longest home runs in history. During a barnstorming tour in 1926, he allegedly drilled a 650-foot shot. Facing a prison-based team at Sing Sing Correctional Facility in 1929, he was said to have clubbed a 620-footer. But both of those drives came against amateurs. The Babe's most expansive homer against a major-league opponent occurred during spring training of 1934.

Ruth had several things working in his favor that year. His contract negotiations went smoothly for a change and he was able to join the team in St. Petersburg on the first day of camp. A new practice regimen afforded him extra time in the cage during batting practice. He made adjustments to his grip and swing while using a lighter bat. The results were remarkable.

Entering the 1934 slate, the Babe did not have a stellar record in spring training games. A writer from the *St. Petersburg Independent* remarked, "Usually Ruth starts slowly in the spring and has found it difficult to find the right field range with any degree of consistency in the exhibition games. . . . [H]is home runs at Waterfront Park in the ten years of training here can be counted on two hands."[29]

The Babe's first home run of the spring came on March 17 against Bob Smith of the Braves. A few days later, he drove an offering from Boston's Huck Betts into the great beyond. Covering the game that afternoon, Burt Whitman of the *Boston Herald* wrote, "The crowd of 1,200 got the customary home run treatment from Babe Ruth. He socked a Huck Betts pitch 10,000 leagues to right field . . . almost into the West Coast Inn."[30] The ball reportedly landed on the second-story porch of the inn (which served as a spring home to the Boston Braves), startling guests who were seated there. Like many things associated with Ruth, the incident attained mythical status over the years and came to be referred to as the longest home run ever hit in a big-league game.

In 2009, a national committee headed by cousins Bob Ward and Tim Reid was assembled to honor the memory of Babe Ruth. The committee appointed a four-man research team to investigate the legendary St. Petersburg home run. After an exhaustive examination of the facts, it was determined that Ruth's homer hit the hotel on the fly and that it traveled at least 611 feet (probably even farther).

TOUCHING THE UNTOUCHABLES

Occasionally referred to as Hansen's disease, leprosy is an infection caused by slow-growing bacteria. The tiny pathogens—known as mycobacterium leprae—affect nerves, skin, eyes, and the lining of the nose. Without the benefit of modern treatment, leprosy can cause hideous disfigurement. In Babe Ruth's day, the disease was incurable and said to be highly contagious. On the islands of Hawaii, individuals who contracted the illness were exiled to a remote peninsula. More than 8,000 victims were forcibly removed from their families and quarantined in the Kalaupapa colony over the span of a century. During the Babe's playing days, the area was off limits to the general public.

In October of 1933, Ruth went on a barnstorming tour of Hawaii. When he learned there were sick people on the Kalaupapa Peninsula who would not be able to come see him, he was determined to go to them. His handlers tried to discourage him by explaining that leprosy was contagious and that he might contract the disease, but the Babe would not be so easily deterred. He ignored their warnings, spending the better part of a day visiting with inhabitants. Though the language barrier made it somewhat difficult to communicate, his bright smile and cheerful manner endeared him to residents. He played ball with some of them and enjoyed a pleasant lunch. The excursion to the colony received no media attention.

WHAT'S MY AGE AGAIN?

In 1934, a team of American League all-stars managed by Connie Mack traveled to Japan for a barnstorming tour. Ruth was among several future Hall of Famers chosen to make the trip. In order to go, he needed a passport, and that necessitated a search for his birth certificate. This led to a surprising discovery. For years, he had been led to believe that his birthday was February 7, 1894. But the date on his birth certificate was listed as February 6, 1895, making him almost a full year younger than he thought he was!

Though it's hard to fathom how such a mistake could occur, it should be noted that record keeping wasn't as detailed or reliable in the 1800s. The Bureau of the Census was formed in 1902, but standardized birth registrations would not appear until the 1930s. Ruth's parents suffered through the death of six children. According to multiple sources, the Babe's mistaken birth date corresponded to an unnamed male child that never survived infancy.

With his true age finally revealed, Rut made no changes. He continued to celebrate his birthday on February 7. And he followed the previously established timeline, considering himself a year older.

BESTED BY OL' DIZ

Cardinals pitching sensation Dizzy Dean was a lot like Ruth in his prime—loud, boastful, and supremely confident. Dean burst upon the scene in 1932, capturing four consecutive strikeout titles. As Dean was emerging as one of baseball's most gifted hurlers, Ruth was fading away. During a 1935 confrontation, the cocky St. Louis ace helped demonstrate just how much the Babe's skills had deteriorated.

The two giants faced each other for the first time at Braves Field. A crowd of 30,000 gathered in anticipation of the showdown. Before the game, Ruth and Dean greeted each other warmly and posed for photographs. The hurler later remarked that "Babe was watching me pretty closely while I was warming up.... He had that eagle eye of his on every move I made."[31]

After drawing a walk in his first at-bat, Ruth returned to the plate in the fourth inning. "Ol' Diz" was cruising by then, having retired eight straight hitters. While the Babe was getting set in the batter's box, Dean turned toward his outfielders. He made a major production of waving them back toward the fences. He didn't stop motioning with his glove until Joe Medwick, Terry Moore, and Jack Rothrock were practically leaning against the outfield walls. Satisfied with the defensive alignment, Dean then stepped onto the rubber to face Ruth. After working the count to 1-and-2, he challenged the slugger with a straight fastball right down the middle. The Associated Press reported that "the Babe almost broke his back going for that steaming third fastball."[32] He came up empty, becoming Dean's second strikeout victim of the afternoon. It served as a dramatic illustration of Ruth's painful descent into mediocrity.

YET ANOTHER TRAGEDY

The Babe endured a fair share of heartache during his lifetime. Abandoned as a child, he lost nearly everyone who had meant something to him by the time he was in his mid-30s. This included both of his parents, his first wife, and the minor-league owner who had taken a special interest in him as a teenager. In 1936, as he was adjusting to life outside of baseball, tragedy struck again.

The Babe's second wife had two older brothers—Eugene and Hubert, both of whom lived with the Ruths in a palatial apartment on Riverside Drive in Manhattan. Born in 1890, Eugene was the oldest sibling. During active combat in World War I, he was exposed to toxic gas in the Argonne Forest of France. His lungs were ravaged and his condition deteriorated over time. Ruth's daughter, Dorothy, recalled in her memoirs, "He rarely complained, but I could tell that he was in constant pain. I watched as his spirit dwindled and the end approached."[33]

During the winter of 1936, the Babe and Claire went on a vacation to Florida, leaving Dorothy behind with Claire's mother, Carrie, who also shared the apartment. One morning, while the Babe and Claire were away, the doorman rang the bell and informed Carrie that Eugene was lying on the pavement, having fallen fifteen stories to his death. There was no evidence of foul play. It was presumed that he had jumped out the window while in the throes of a depressive episode.

Claire remained in Florida while the Babe rushed home to make funeral arrangements. He was assisted in the matter by Dorothy's biological mother and her husband, Charles, who were close friends of the family. Members of the press made a concerted effort to keep a respectful distance. Very little information appeared in newspapers.

THE MARTIANS ARE COMING!

On October 30, 1938, a Mercury Theater production of H. G. Wells's science-fiction classic *The War of the Worlds* panicked many Americans. The novel, originally published in 1898 and set in England, tells the story of an alien invasion of Earth. The radio dramatization was set in contemporary New Jersey. Orson Welles played multiple roles in the one-hour program, which began as a typical broadcast being interrupted by a series of fictional news bulletins. The performance prompted scores of listeners to flee their homes in search of safety from Martian invaders. At a Halloween press conference the following day, Welles said that he was extremely surprised by the public reaction, since the story had become familiar to children through comic books and many succeeding adventure stories.

Babe Ruth wasn't much of a reader, but he did love his radio programs. He religiously followed the adventures of the *The Lone Ranger* and *The Shadow*, often planning his activities around the broadcasts. During Welles's *War of the Worlds* performance, the Babe was among the many listeners who believed that extraterrestrials had landed in Grover's Mill, New Jersey, and were wreaking havoc there. As the crow flies, the distance between Manhattan and Grover's Mill is a little over 50 miles. Fearing that the invaders were within striking distance, the Babe began anxiously peering through the blinds of his Riverside Drive apartment. He reportedly instructed members of his household to hide under their beds.

RUTH AND COBB HIT THE LINKS

During their playing days, Ty Cobb and Babe Ruth were sworn enemies. Though they buried the hatchet in later years, promoter Fred Corcoran helped rekindle the rivalry by inviting the pair to compete in a best-of-three golf tournament. Though Cobb initially declined, Corcoran wouldn't take no for an answer. He put Ruth's name on a mocking telegram that read, "If you want to come here and get your brains knocked in, come on."[34] Upon reading the message, the Georgia Peach boldly declared, "I could always lick [Ruth] on a ballfield and I can lick him on the golf course now."[35]

The matches took place during the summer of 1941. Before the first meeting in Newton, Massachusetts, the two baseball icons clowned around for photographers. Cobb was all business once the game was underway. Ruth's attempts to engage in friendly banter were largely ignored. "In all my life, I never had to bear down as hard as I did in that match," said Cobb afterward.[36] He edged the Babe by a narrow margin and won a silver cup that had been donated by actress Bette Davis.

Ruth came out on top in the second match, which took place at Flushing, New York, and was somewhat sparsely attended. A large crowd saw both men play sloppily at the finale in Detroit. It ended on the 16th hole when Cobb was declared the winner at 15 strokes over par. The three-game playoff raised thousands of dollars for the USO. When it was over, the Georgia Peach gloated, "I beat Ruth, so I have something to tell my children. I have finally beaten the Babe at something."[37]

CALLED TO THE MAT

The world of professional wrestling has always been open to gimmicks of all kinds. In 1945, the Babe had not lost his star power and still derived great pleasure from connecting with fans. He agreed to referee a pair of wrestling matches set in Boston and Portland, Maine.

Ruth was no stranger to the job. He had served as a wrestling official several times during his years with the Yankees. Proving that he could still draw a crowd, the show in Portland was a near sellout. The main bout featured Manuel Cortez versus Leo Numa. Cortez won many titles during his long career, which included more than 1,400 matches. Numa was less successful, though he did claim an international championship in 1940. On the evening in question, Numa played the role of the "good guy." Cortez had established a reputation as a rogue. Ruth spent a lot of time separating the two combatants. At one point, Cortez threw a punch at the Babe, but he was able to avoid it. The match ended with Cortez being disqualified. It appeared as if he and Ruth might come to blows, but in the end, hostilities were avoided.

In Boston, the main attraction featured Steve "Crusher" Casey versus Sandor Szabo. A Hungarian immigrant, Szabo used his signature "Death Swing" to capture seven championships during his days in the ring. Casey was the second Irish wrestler to claim a world title. He also competed in rowing. The 50-year-old Ruth worked very hard during the match. He narrowly avoided being kicked in the face at one point and he ended up putting Szabo in a headlock to prevent him from using an illegal hold on Casey.

When the shows were over, the Babe was approached by several promoters who wanted him to continue as a referee. He had been reimbursed handsomely for his appearances and could have drawn a steady paycheck. But for undisclosed reasons, he declined.

To Papa, from the Babe

Ruth's final autobiography, *The Babe Ruth Story*, was released in 1948. *Washington Herald* columnist Bob Considine, who received partial writing credit, met with the former Yankee star on several occasions in an attempt to gather information. Unfortunately, Ruth was extremely ill at that time, having just completed an experimental round of cancer treatments. Considine didn't know enough about the Babe to complete the project on his own, so historian Fred Lieb was hired to help out. Lieb had covered Ruth for 15 years as a beat writer and was able to fill in the blanks for Considine. Not all the blanks ended up being filled, however. Since some of his unethical behaviors were considered unfit to print, the book offered a G-rated account of the former outfielder's life.

In spite of his deteriorating health, Ruth agreed to attend a book-signing party when the project was completed. It was held at the E. P. Dutton offices in New York City. Realizing that the Babe was approaching his final days, a number of publishers were there, including Bennett Cerf, cofounder of Random House. Ernest Hemingway was among the other luminaries waiting in line for an autographed copy. Though some of his most acclaimed works had already been released by then, *The Old Man and the Sea* (a Pulitzer Prize–winning novella) was still a few years off. Hemingway had grown up as a fan of the Cubs but later switched his allegiance to the Dodgers while living in Cuba. He built a makeshift ball field on his property outside of Havana so he and his sons could play with local boys.

A serialized version of *The Babe Ruth Story* appeared in the *Saturday Evening Post*. This helped the book make the *New York Times* bestseller list. Hemingway may or may not have realized the value of what he acquired that day. In 2008, a signed copy of the original hardcover edition sold for close to $6,500. One can only imagine what Hemingway's personal copy (if it still exists) might go for.

WORST BASEBALL MOVIE OF ALL TIME?

The film based on Ruth's 1948 autobiography was an unmitigated disaster. To begin with, William Bendix was miscast as the Babe. In order to make him look like the former Yankee hero, makeup artists dyed his hair and gave him a prosthetic nose. Attempts to coach him on the finer points of Ruth's swing were fruitless. John McCarten of the *New Yorker* wrote, "[Bendix] handles a bat as if it were as hard to manipulate as a barrel stave. Even with a putty nose, Mr. Bendix resembles Mr. Ruth not at all and he certainly does the hitter an injustice by representing him as a kind of Neanderthal fellow."[38] Physical disparities between the actor and baseball icon were the least of director Roy Del Ruth's problems. The script was an absolute mess. Bosley Crowther of the *New York Times* observed that "[the film] has much more the tone of low-grade fiction than it has of a biography."[39] He was spot-on with that remark. Historical inaccuracies are rampant throughout the film—some more preposterous than others:

- In one scene, the Babe's second wife, Claire, warns him that he is tipping his pitches by sticking out his tongue. While it's true that Ruth arrived in the majors with the bad habit of curling his tongue when he delivered curve balls, he had not yet met Claire during his time with the Red Sox. Another major oversight: Ruth's first wife, Helen, is never mentioned in the film.

- During the "called shot" sequence, Claire shouts at the Babe, "Don't forget Johnny!" in reference to Johnny Sylvester, the boy Ruth famously promised a home run to. But the homer Ruth is said to have hit for Sylvester happened during the 1926 World Series against the Cardinals, not the 1932 Fall Classic versus the Cubs.

- In two of the film's most ludicrous scenes, Ruth orders a glass of milk in a bar and heals a crippled boy by waving at him. In another laughable clip, the Babe hits a dog with a foul ball, severely wounding it. When he sees a little boy crying next to the fallen animal, he scoops it up and hurries out of the stadium in search of medical attention. Accompanied by the crying boy, he ends up at a local hospital, where a physician performs a successful operation, saving the dog's life.

Bendix himself once referred to the movie as the worst he ever made and said he was embarrassed by the audience's reaction at the premiere in Los

PART 2: ASSORTED ANECDOTES

Angeles. In particular, he alluded to a scene early in the film when the Babe is discovered by a scout while playing at St. Mary's. The kids in the scene are all actual teenagers, but Bendix (at 38 years of age) was forced by the director to appear wearing makeup. The final cut is unintentionally funny, and according to Bendix, LA moviegoers laughed when they saw it.

THE PHYSICS OF INSIDE-THE-PARK INFIELD HOMERS

A number of stories exist about the dizzying altitudes of Ruth's pop flies. According to many sources, he was sometimes able to almost completely circle the bases before they landed. Carrying this a step further, Yankee pitching great Waite Hoyt claimed that Ruth hit an inside-the-park infield homer during a game in Boston. Though it seems pretty far-fetched, it's actually not impossible from a scientific standpoint.

It takes a typical player anywhere between 17 and 22 seconds to navigate the bases. The average exit velocity generated by modern power hitters is around 92 mph, which translates to 135 feet per second. The highest fly ball ever recorded was 564 feet, hit by Ted Williams in 1941. We can confidently assume that Ruth was equal if not superior to both Williams and the sluggers of today. With an exit velocity of 92 mph, it would take a baseball about four seconds to reach an apogee of 564 feet. Since objects fall at 32 feet per second, the ball would return to earth in roughly 17.5 seconds. That's a total of 21.5 seconds—plenty of time for a runner of average speed to complete the circuit (in theory at least).

Hoyt alleged that Ruth's infield homer got hung up in a strong wind that was blowing toward home plate. The ball supposedly drifted into left field before landing untouched in front of the shortstop, who had completely lost track of it. But there's a glaring problem with Hoyt's narrative. Ruth was moderately fast in his prime—stealing more than 100 bases by the time he was in his mid-30s. And he did hit several inside-the-park homers during his career. However, none of them happened at Fenway Park. Though Hoyt's memory of the specific venue could have been faulty, it seems an unlikely scenario. Ruth lived his life in the spotlight. Nearly everything he did, on and off the field, was newsworthy. Had he actually accomplished such a rare (and seemingly impossible) feat, it would have generated a lot more hype. Aside from Hoyt's memoirs and the 1992 cinematic flop *The Babe* (starring John Goodman), there is little to no mention of an infield homer anywhere in the mainstream. So the chances are good that it never actually happened.

SAYING GOODBYE

Ruth's terminal cancer diagnosis was withheld from him for quite some time in fear that he would fall into a deep depression and do something drastic. Sick as he was, he attended the 25th anniversary of Yankee Stadium on June 13, 1948. Wearing his uniform for the last time, he posed with former teammates and addressed the crowd briefly. When the ceremonies concluded, he was helped to the clubhouse by his male nurse, who felt that the weather conditions were too damp and that he might catch a cold.

Joe Dugan, who played just one inning of the old-timers' game that day, came down to the clubhouse to visit with his old friend. He asked the Babe if he would like a beverage and Ruth said he would take a beer. As they sat side by side nursing their drinks, Dugan asked the fading slugger how he was doing.

"Joe, I'm gone," Ruth said sadly.[40]

Both men broke down crying.

The Babe spent his last days in the hospital. Connie Mack was among the final visitors. By then, Ruth had come to accept his fate. He joked to the legendary A's manager, "The termites have got me, Mr. Mack."[41]

DEATHBED DRAMA

The last two weeks of Ruth's life were marred by controversy. While the doctors at Memorial Sloan-Kettering Hospital did all they could to make him comfortable and keep him alive, a physician at Mount Sinai Hospital told the Babe's wife that an experimental treatment could add 10 years to his life. When Ruth's daughter Dorothy found out that Claire had made plans to have the Babe transferred to another facility, she consulted with the attending physician—Dr. Hayes Martin. Martin assured Dorothy that the Babe's internal organs were damaged beyond repair. This reportedly led to a confrontation between the two women, which ended with Dorothy threatening to have Claire arrested if she attempted to move her father.

A few days before Ruth died, a mysterious woman came to his room. She introduced herself as Loretta and claimed to be his girlfriend. "I certainly hope the Babe remembered me in his will," she said. "After all, I've given him ten years of my life."[42] As it turned out, last-minute changes to the will had been made by Claire, entitling her to a majority of Ruth's net worth. Dorothy chose not to contest it, but Loretta was prepared to make waves. When she learned that she had been cut out of the will, she threatened to go public with details of the Babe's alleged 10-year affair. According to Dorothy, she received a $25,000 settlement in exchange for her silence.

Interestingly, Dorothy favored the idea of the Babe having a mistress. She insisted that Claire had become cold, inattentive, and unsympathetic as the years wore on. "My father has always been accused of being a notorious womanizer," she wrote. "In the position he was in, women were literally throwing themselves at him all the time. But all my father ever wanted was a mate who could share his victories and console him in his defeats. Obviously, Loretta fit the bill."[43]

ROGER MARIS'S HARROWING ORDEAL

For decades, Ruth's single-season mark of 60 home runs seemed like an unassailable record. The Babe himself was so convinced that it would stand forever, he issued a bold statement: "Let's see some other son of a bitch match that!" The SOB arrived in the form of Roger Maris—a publicity-shy outfielder ill-equipped to handle the pressures of stardom. By the time he surpassed Ruth's feat in 1961, he was suffering from symptoms of acute anxiety. "As a ballplayer, I would be delighted to do it again," he told reporters. "As an individual, I doubt if I could possibly go through it again."[44]

Maris broke into the majors with the Indians in 1957. Though he was a highly touted prospect, he failed to live up to his potential until he joined the Yankees in 1960. After capturing MVP honors that year, he engaged in an epic home run duel with Mickey Mantle the following summer.

The 1961 home run race got off to a slow start. Maris managed just one clout in April to Mantle's seven. But by the end of June, both players (dubbed the "M &M Boys" by the New York media) were on pace to make history. Mantle had been a staple in the Bronx for more than a decade. His matinee idol looks and boyish charm made him baseball's golden child. In glaring contrast, Maris's serious nature and awkwardness in the spotlight were greatly misunderstood. He came to be viewed by many as a villainous figure out to steal Mantle's thunder and tarnish the Babe's accomplishment.

Ruth's widow was not terribly supportive of Maris's efforts. "Even if the record is broken, they'll always remember the Babe as the first to do it," she said to reporters.[45] Making matters worse, commissioner Ford Frick declared that the record would not be counted as official unless it was broken within a 154-game time frame (the length of a season in Ruth's era). The pressure on Maris was intense and he suffered greatly. Relentlessly interrogated by the press, he began experiencing debilitating headaches. He was losing sleep and his hair was falling out in clumps. Describing the club's reaction to Maris's plight, Pulitzer Prize–winning journalist David Halberstam wrote, "The Yankees, completely unprepared for the media circus, gave him no help, offered him no protection, and set no guidelines. They let him, stubborn, suspicious and without guile, hang out there alone, utterly ill-prepared for the ordeal."[46]

Mantle, who had helped draw some of the attention away from Maris, dropped out of the race in late September. Struggling with respiratory issues, he sought the assistance of a shady New York physician named Max Jacobson, who provided unorthodox treatments to a host of high-profile clients. Known to insiders as "Dr. Feelgood," Jacobson impaled Mantle's hipbone while administering an injection. The wound became abscessed, forcing the Yankee idol onto the disabled list. Maris suddenly found himself utterly abandoned.

Though he failed to meet Frick's 154-game deadline, Maris tied Ruth's record in fewer plate appearances (684 to the Babe's 687). Maris's historic 61st homer came on the final day of the season. Frick had threatened to put an asterisk next to his achievement, but it never actually appeared. Even so, the disillusioned outfielder remained bitter in later years. "They acted as if I was doing something wrong, poisoning the record books or something," he griped. "Do you know what I have to show for 61 homers? Nothing—absolutely nothing!"[47]

THE STOLEN HOMER

Some players remain statistically viable even after they have drawn their last breath. More than fifty years after his passing, Cubs outfielder Hack Wilson collected an RBI. In similar fashion, Babe Ruth was credited with a home run two decades after he was laid to rest. While Wilson's additional RBI still appears in record books, Ruth's has disappeared from existence. How that happened is a long, strange tale.

In 1918, the rules of baseball were a bit different. Balls bouncing over the fence into the stands were counted as home runs. Balls that caromed off the foul poles were considered doubles. And since a run could not be scored after the game was over, walk-off homers were downgraded depending on the final score and the number of runners on base. The latter rule deprived the Babe of a well-deserved homer.

On July 8, 1918, Ruth came to the plate in the 10th inning of a scoreless tie at Fenway Park. Facing Hall of Fame spitballer Stan Coveleski, he walloped a shot into the right field stands for a home run. But since outfielder Amos Strunk was on first base at the time, the game was technically over when he touched home plate. Ruth was therefore credited with a triple. It's important to note that this happened before Ruth (or anyone else in baseball) was hitting home runs in great numbers. Nobody realized how important it would be to count every long ball.

Ruth's lost homer was overlooked until the 1960s, when a baseball historian named David Neft assembled a team of researchers to create a reliable and accurate statistical database. Their research uncovered a total of 37 home runs by assorted players that should have been counted. This included the Babe's walk-off blast in 1918. Before the debut of Neft's landmark *Baseball Encyclopedia* in 1969, a special records committee was assembled by major-league baseball to figure out how to address the statistical errors uncovered by Neft's team. The committee voted unanimously to credit the 37 home runs to each player, thereby raising Ruth's lifetime total to 715. This created a bit of a stir.

Baseball columnist Joe Posnanski aptly described the situation in a 2018 article, "In 1969, there was no number in American sports more cherished than Ruth's 714. Every red-blooded American fan knew it by heart. In that year, the number seemed as unreachable as Mars. . . . Ruth was alone at the top, exactly where baseball fans wanted him."[48]

As multiple journalists railed against the idea of tampering with Ruth's record, a man named Joe Reichler rallied to the cause. Though he had been appointed to the special records committee, he was away on business when the vote took place. Looking to preserve the integrity of the sacred number "714," he demanded a revote and got one. By then, two other committee members—perhaps persuaded by the arguments of sportswriters—had changed their minds. The second vote was 3–2 in favor of leaving Ruth's lifetime total alone. And so, the Babe was stripped of a homer (again).

Thirty years later, baseball's official historian, Jerome Holtzman, discovered a missing RBI from a game played in 1930 and convinced officials to add it to Hack Wilson's long-standing single-season record. Since Wilson was a somewhat obscure figure, no one got terribly upset when his total was raised to 191. That number has not been challenged. As for Ruth, he remains stuck at 714 homers—though it's clear the number is incorrect.

ANOTHER RECORD FALLS

Hank Aaron didn't hit home runs in massive bunches. He pecked away at Babe Ruth's lifetime total steadily over time, averaging 36 blasts per year from 1954 through 1973. Entering the 1974 slate, he needed just one homer to tie the all-time mark. While Ruth was adored by fans the world over, Aaron had a very different experience. As he was closing in on the record during the 1973 slate, he received hate mail and death threats. Multiple kidnapping plots against his children were investigated by the FBI. And a bumper sticker appeared on cars in Atlanta reading, "Aaron is RUTH-less."[49]

Before the 1974 season was underway, a writer from *Sports Illustrated* remarked, "Is this to be the year in which Aaron, at the age of thirty-nine, takes a moonwalk above one of the most hallowed individual records in American sport? Or will it be remembered as the season in which Aaron, the most dignified of athletes, was besieged with hate mail and trapped by the cobwebs and goblins that lurk in baseball's attic."[50]

Ruth's widow was immensely proud and fiercely protective of her husband's major-league records, but she sympathized with Aaron. Taking a stand on the issue, she denounced racism and pledged her support for the Braves slugger: "The Babe loved baseball so very much and I know he [would have been] pulling for Hank Aaron to break his record."[51] In spite of her compassionate statements, controversy continued to swirl.

The Braves opened the 1974 slate in Cincinnati. Since the weather was cold and damp, manager Eddie Mathews announced that he would not be using Aaron during the series. Commissioner Bowie Kuhn undermined Mathews's authority, ordering him to put the slugger in the lineup. Mathews felt that Kuhn had overstepped his boundaries, but acquiesced. Aaron tied Ruth's record in his first at-bat of the season on April 4. Four days later, the Braves honored his accomplishments on Hank Aaron Night at Fulton County Stadium. Though many celebrities were in attendance, the commissioner was conspicuously absent. In his place, he sent Hall of Famer Monte Irvin, who served as assistant director of public relations. In his autobiography, *I Had a Hammer*, Aaron wrote, "I was deeply offended that the commissioner of baseball would not see fit to watch me break a record that was supposed to be the most sacred in baseball. It was almost as if he didn't want to dignify the record or didn't want to be part of the surpassing of Babe Ruth."[52]

While the commissioner was busy in Cleveland delivering a speech to the Indians' Wahoo Club, Aaron cracked his 715th circuit blast, becoming baseball's all-time home run king. President Richard Nixon telephoned the slugger to personally congratulate him. Years later, Aaron wrote, "I knew what the past twenty-five years of my life had been about. . . . I felt a deep sense of gratitude and a wonderful surge of liberation at the same time."[53]

DIFFERENT PERSPECTIVES

The Babe's daughter Julia Ruth Stevens released three books during her lifetime about the man she called "Daddy." Because she had received deferential treatment from both parents while growing up, memories of her childhood tended to be a bit sugarcoated. Dorothy Ruth Pirone, on the other hand, claimed to have been psychologically abused by the Babe's second wife as a child. Though she had a close relationship with her dad, she sometimes felt somewhat neglected by him. When her memoirs were released in 1988, she didn't shy away from sharing a few less-than-flattering stories. They included the following:

- Ruth threw parties for newspapermen every year at his Riverside Drive apartment. By the end of each gathering, the wastebaskets would be full of used flashbulbs, which had to be replaced between shots in those days. On the morning after these annual soirees, Ruth would gather the bulbs so he could drop them out of his apartment window. He enjoyed watching them explode on the sidewalk below.

- Glass bulbs were not the only thing the Babe threw out of his 15th-story window. When the Japanese attacked Pearl Harbor in 1941, he flew into a rage, cursing loudly and destroying items in his apartment that were of Japanese origin. The hand-embroidered, custom-framed flag he had received during his 1934 visit to the Far East was among several trinkets he tossed onto Riverside Drive that day. He also hurled a priceless Japanese urn against a doorjamb.

- Ruth frequently lied to his wife, Claire, about his whereabouts, habitually telling her he was hunting or fishing with friends. One time after returning from one of these excursions, he placed a bag of fish on the kitchen table, claiming he had caught them himself. He failed to notice that the vendor at the market where he purchased the fish had individually wrapped them in butcher's paper.

Appendix I

Records Held by Babe Ruth
at the Time of His Retirement

Major League Baseball Records, Regular Season
Slugging percentage, career: .690
Home runs, career: 714
Most times hitting multiple home runs in a game, career: 72
Longest home run: 575 feet (July 18, 1921)
Runs batted in, career: 2,213
Walks, career: 2,062
Lowest ratio of hits per nine innings pitched for a left-handed pitcher: 7.1774
Highest Winning Percentage for a left-handed pitcher, career: .671

American League Records, Regular Season
Slugging percentage, career: .692
Slugging percentage, season: .847 (1920)
Slugging percentage by a left-hander, season: .847 (1920)
Seasons leading the league in slugging percentage: 13 (1918–1924, 1926–1931)
Runs, season: 177 (1921)
Runs by left-hander, season: 177 (1921)
Seasons leading the league in runs: 8 (1919–1921, 1923, 1924, 1926–1928)
Consecutive seasons leading the league in runs: 3, (1919–1921) (1926–1928)
Seasons with 150 or more runs: 6 (1920, 1921, 1923, 1927, 1928, 1930)
Doubles by pitcher, game: 3, versus Washington Senators, May 9, 1918
Home runs, career: 714
Home runs with one club, career: 659, New York Yankees (1920–1934)
Home runs by left-hander, career: 714
Home runs in extra innings, career: 16
Home runs by outfielder, career: 686
Home runs, season: 60 (1927)

Seasons leading the league in home runs: 12 (1918–1921, 1923–1924, 1926–1931)

Consecutive seasons leading the league in home runs: 6 (1926–1931)

Home runs at home by left-hander, season: 32 (1921)

Home runs on road, season: 32 (1927)

Home runs on road by left-hander, season: 32 (1927)

Seasons hitting home runs in all parks, career: 11 (1919–1921, 1923, 1924, 1926–1931)

Seasons with 50 or more home runs: 4 (1920, 1921, 1927, 1928)

Consecutive seasons with 50 or more home runs: 2 (1920–1921) (1927–1928)

Seasons with 40 or more home runs: 11 (1920, 1921, 1923, 1924, 1926–1932)

Consecutive seasons with 40 or more home runs: 7 (1926–1932)

Seasons with 30 or more home runs: 13 (1920–1924, 1926–1933)

Seasons with 20 or more home runs: 16 (1919–1934)

Consecutive seasons with 20 or more home runs: 16 (1919–1934)

Home runs in two consecutive seasons: 114 (60 in 1927, 54 in 1928)

Home runs by left-hander, two consecutive seasons: 114 (60 in 1927, 54 in 1928)

Home runs by left-hander, one month: 17 (September 1927)

Home runs in June: 15 (1930)

Home runs through July 31: 41 (1928)

Home runs in September: 17 (1927)

Home runs through September 30: 60 (1927)

Most times hitting three home runs in a doubleheader, career (while homering in both games): 7 (1920, 1922, 1926, 1927, 1930, 1933, twice)

Most times hitting two or more home runs in a game, career: 71

Home runs, two consecutive days: 6, May 21, 1930—May 22, 1930

Grand slams, two consecutive games: 2 (Sept. 27 & 29, 1927) (Aug. 6 & Aug. 7, 1929)

Total bases, season: 457 (1921)

Total bases by left-hander, season: 457 (1921)

Seasons leading the league in total bases: 6 (1919, 1921, 1923, 1924, 1926, 1928)

Total bases by pitcher, game: 10, versus Washington Senators, May 9, 1918

Extra-base hits, career: 1,350

Extra-base hits, season: 119 (1921)

Extra-base hits by left-hander, season: 119 (1921)

Seasons leading the league in extra-base hits: 7 (1918–1921, 1923, 1924, 1928)

Consecutive seasons leading the league in extra-base hits: 4 (1918–1921)

Extra-base hits by pitcher, game: 4, versus Washington Senators, May 9, 1918,
Runs batted in, career: 2,202
Seasons leading the league in runs batted in: 6 (1919–1921, 1923, 1926, 1928)
Consecutive seasons leading the league in runs batted in: 3 (1919–1921)
Consecutive seasons with 150 or more runs batted in: 3 (1929–1931)
Seasons with 100 or more runs batted in: 13 (1919–1921, 1923, 1924,
    1926–1933)
Walks, career: 2,042
Walks, season: 170 (1923)
Walks by left-hander, season: 170 (1923)
Seasons leading the league in walks: 11 (1920, 1921, 1923, 1924, 1926–1928,
    1930–1933)
Consecutive seasons leading the league in walks: 4 (1930–1933)
Seasons with 100 or more walks: 13 (1919–1921, 1923, 1924, 1926–1928,
    1930–1934)
Two teammates with 40 or more home runs, season: *three times*
- 1927 (Ruth 60, Lou Gehrig 47)
- 1930 (Ruth 49, Gehrig 41)
- 1931 (Ruth 46, Gehrig 46)

Teams with three consecutive home runs in inning: *twice*
- YANKEES, 4th inning, versus Philadelphia Athletics, first game,
  September 10, 1925 (Bob Meusel, Babe Ruth, Lou Gehrig)
- YANKEES, 7th inning, versus Chicago White Sox, May 4, 1929
  (Babe Ruth, Lou Gehrig, Bob Meusel)

Shutouts won or tied by left-hander, season: 9 (1916)

ALL-STAR GAME RECORDS
Plate appearances, inning: 2, 5th inning, July 10, 1934
First home run in All-Star Game history: 1 on, off Wild Bill Hallahan, 3rd
    inning, July 6, 1933

WORLD SERIES RECORDS
Most World Series Played, career: 10 (1915, 1916, 1918, 1921, 1922, 1923,
    1926, 1927, 1928, 1932)
Home runs, career: 15
Runs scored, career: 37

Total bases, career: 96
Slugging percentage, career: .744
Extra-base hits, career: 22
Walks, career: 33
Strikeouts (as batter): 30
Earned Run Average, career: 0.87
Most positions played, career: 4 (pitcher, left field, right field, first base)
Series batting .300 or over: 6 (1921, 1923, 1926, 1927, 1928, 1932)
Runs, four-game series: 9 (1928)
Runs, game: 4, versus St. Louis Cardinals, October 6, 1926
Consecutive games scoring one or more runs, career: 9 (1927 (2), 1928 (4), 1932 (3))
Hits, four-game series: 10 (1928)
Most times reached first base safely, game (batting 1.000): 5, *twice*
- versus St. Louis Cardinals, October 6, 1926 (3 HR, 2 BB)
- versus St. Louis Cardinals, October 10, 1926 (1 HR, 4 BB)

Home runs, seven-game series: 4 (1926)
Series with three or more home runs: 3 (1923 [3], 1926 [4], 1928 [3])
Series with two or more home runs in a game: 4 (1923, 1926, 1928, 1932)
Most home runs, three consecutive series (three consecutive years): 9 (1926 [4], 1927 [2], 1928 [3])
Home runs, game: 3, *twice*
- versus St. Louis Cardinals, October 6, 1926 (2 consecutive)
- versus St. Louis Cardinals, October 9, 1928 (2 consecutive)

Home runs, two consecutive innings: 2, *twice*
- 2, 4th and 5th innings, versus New York Giants, October 11, 1923
- 2, 7th and 8th innings, versus St. Louis Cardinals, October 9, 1928

Total bases, four-game series: 22 (1928)
Total bases, game: 12, *twice*
- versus St. Louis Cardinals, October 6, 1926 (3 HR)
- versus St. Louis Cardinals, October 9, 1928 (3 HR)

Extra-base hits, four-game series: 6 (1928)
Walks, game: 4, versus St. Louis Cardinals, October 10, 1926
Stolen bases, inning: 2, 5th inning, versus New York Giants, October 6, 1921
Innings pitched, game: 14, versus Brooklyn Dodgers, October 9, 1916
Consecutive scoreless innings pitched: 29 2/3 innings

Appendix II

Pitching and Hitting Stats

Regular Season Pitching Stats (10 Seasons)

W	L	%	ERA	G	GS	GF	CG	SHO	SV	IP	H	R	ER	BB	SO
94	46	.671	2.28	163	147	12	107	17	4	1221.1	974	400	309	441	488

Regular Season Batting Stats (22 Seasons)

AB	R	H	2B	3B	HR	RBI	BB	AVG.	OBP	SLG%	SB
8,399	2,174	2,873	506	136	714	2,214	2,062	.342	.474	.690	123

World Series Pitching Stats (2 World Series)

G	GS	W	L	%	ERA	CG	SHO	IP	H	R	ER	BB	SO	WHIP
3	3	3	0	1.000	0.87	2	1	31	19	3	3	10	8	0.953

World Series Hitting Stats (10 World Series)

AB	R	H	2B	3B	HR	RBI	BB	AVG.	OBP	SLG%	SB
129	37	42	5	2	15	33	33	.326	.470	.744	4

Appendix III

Babe Ruth Movie Credits

Headin' Home (1920)
Produced by William Shea and Herbert H. Yudkin. Directed by Lawrence C. Windom. The Babe plays himself in this silent biopic film. The fictionalized script attempts to build a mythology around Ruth's personal story. *Running Time: 1 hour, 11 minutes*

Babe Comes Home (1927)
Produced by Wid Gunning. Directed by Ted Wilde. In this silent comedy, Ruth stars as Babe Dugan, a slovenly ballplayer who falls in love with the laundress who cleans his uniform weekly. Ruth's love interest is played by Anna Q. Nilsson, a Swedish actress who appeared in many silent films. *Running Time: 1 hour*

Speedy (1928)
Produced by Harold Lloyd. Directed by Ted Wilde. In his last silent film appearance, comedian Harold Lloyd stars as Harold "Speedy" Swift, a die-hard Yankees fan who saves New York City's last horse-drawn trolley from the evil railway magnates who want to take control of the route. Ruth has a cameo, appearing in a scene in which Speedy is working as a cab driver. Nominated for one Oscar: Best Director, Comedy Picture. *Running Time: 71 minutes*

Slide, Babe, Slide (1932)
Directed by Benjamin Stoloff. In the first of several 1932 movie shorts starring Ruth, the Babe gets off a train and plays ball with a group of kids who refuse to believe he is who he says he is. *Running Time: 10 minutes*

PERFECT CONTROL (1932)

Directed by Benjamin Stoloff. A small-town boy grows bored with his lessons in school and dreams that Ruth invites members of his class to play a round of sandlot ball. The Babe shows off his pitching skills. *Running Time: 10 minutes*

OVER THE FENCE (1932)

Directed by Lou Breslaw. The Babe saves a group of schoolboys from an arithmetic lesson by coercing their teacher to let them go outside and play ball. Ruth hits a long homer. *Running Time: 10 minutes*

JUST PALS (1932)

Directed by Benjamin Stoloff. In this longer short, the Babe visits an orphanage and is asked to umpire a game. After a young boy named Freddy strikes out with the bases loaded and is berated by schoolmates, Ruth offers him a hitting lesson. The next day, Freddy becomes a hero by hitting a clutch homer. *Running Time: 20 minutes*

FANCY CURVES (1932)

Directed by Lou Breslow. In this short comedy, Ruth agrees to coach a women's baseball team. During a big game against a men's team, Ruth sneaks to the plate disguised as one of the girls. He delivers the game-winning homer, but his identity is revealed when he tips his cap to the crowd and the wig he is wearing falls off. He is chased from the field and narrowly escapes. *Running Time: 9 minutes*

HOME RUN ON THE KEYS (1937)

Directed by Roy Mack. Released after Ruth's retirement as a player, this movie short features the Babe with musical composers Zez Confrey and Byron Gay. After regaling the musicians with his version of the famous "called shot" story, the Babe helps them write a song about baseball. *Running Time: 9 minutes*

THE PRIDE OF THE YANKEES (1942)

Produced by Sam Goldwyn. Directed by Sam Wood. In this Lou Gehrig biopic featuring Gary Cooper as the Iron Horse, Ruth played himself, appearing with former teammates Bill Dickey, Mark Koenig, and Bob Meusel. Nominated for ten Oscars; won for Best Film Editing. *Running Time: 2 hours, 8 minutes*

Appendix IV

Products Endorsed by Babe Ruth

From the time he arrived in New York until his death due to cancer in 1948, the Babe netted a small fortune by lending his name, image, and testimonial statements to dozens of products. A majority of them are listed below.

- White Owl Cigars
- Wheaties cereal
- Quaker Puffed Wheat and Puffed Rice cereal
- Spalding baseballs and mitts
- A.J. Reach baseballs and mitts
- Sinclair gasoline & oil
- Esso gasoline
- Tydol Ethyl gasoline
- Mrs. Sherlock's Bread
- Babe Ruth All-American Underwear
- Ruth's Home Run candy
- Girl Scout cookies
- Red Rock Cola
- Babe Ruth gum
- Babe Ruth nickel cigars
- Bambino tobacco
- Louisville Slugger bats
- Old Gold cigarettes
- Raleigh cigarettes
- Kaywoodie pipe tobacco
- Pinch-Hit tobacco

- Barbasol shaving cream
- McLoughlin union suits
- Remington shotguns
- Murphy-Rich soap
- Sports Kings gum
- Muffets Whole Wheat Biscuits
- Babe Ruth Fro-Joy ice cream
- Dr. Reed's Cushion Shoes
- The Talbot Company
- S.J. Beckwith & Company hardware
- Horace Partridge Co. (sporting goods)
- Grafonola Co. phonographs
- Babe Ruth's Baseball Game (produced by the Milton Bradley Company)
- Babe Ruth Doll (produced by the Sterling Doll Company)
- Ford, Cadillac, Packard, Chevy, Chrysler, Auburn, Studebaker, and Nash autos

Appendix V

Babe Ruth Annual Salary

- 1914: $1,800 (minors), $2,500 (majors)
- 1915: $3,500
- 1916: $3,500
- 1917: $5,000
- 1918: $7,000
- 1919: $10,000
- 1920: $20,000
- 1921: $30,000
- 1922: $52,000
- 1923: $52,000
- 1924: $52,000
- 1925: $52,000
- 1926: $52,000
- 1927: $70,000
- 1928: $70,000
- 1929: $70,000
- 1930: $80,000
- 1931: $80,000
- 1932: $75,000
- 1933: $52,000
- 1934: $35,000
- 1935: $25,000

Appendix VI

Babe Ruth Chronology

- **1895** Ruth is born in Baltimore, Maryland.
- **1902** Ruth is sent to live in St. Mary's Industrial School for Boys. He will learn the fundamentals of baseball there and begin his journey to the major leagues.
- **1914** Ruth signs with the Baltimore Orioles (of the International League) and receives his famous nickname, "Babe." His contract is sold to the Red Sox in July. He records his first major-league win as a pitcher and gets his first hit. He marries Helen Woodford at season's end.
- **1915** The Babe smashes his first homer. He wins 18 games and appears as a pinch hitter in the World Series. The Red Sox beat the Phillies in five games.
- **1916** The Babe wins more than 20 games on the mound. He wins his first World Series start. It's the longest complete game in Series history to that point, lasting 14 innings.
- **1917** Ruth wins 24 games for the BoSox.
- **1918** Ruth gradually makes the switch from pitcher to outfielder. He appears in 95 games and leads the AL in homers with 11. In the World Series, he completes a string of 29.2 scoreless innings—a record that will later be broken.
- **1919** The Babe hits 29 homers—a single-season record—and completes the switch to the outfield. Additionally, he homers in every AL park—a feat previously unmatched.
- **1920** Ruth's contract is sold to the Yankees. He blasts 54 homers, breaking his own record.
- **1921** The Babe raises the single-season home run record to 59. He hits his first World Series homer.

- **1922** Ruth is suspended by Commissioner Kenesaw Mountain Landis for his participation in a barnstorming tour.
- **1923** Yankee Stadium opens and Ruth is the first to homer there. He hits three homers in the World Series as the Yankees capture their first championship.
- **1925** Ruth develops an "intestinal abscess" and requires surgery. He is later suspended by Manager Miller Huggins for his excessive partying and recurrent insubordination. In his absence, the Yankees fall to seventh place.
- **1926** In Game 4 of the World Series, the Babe clubs three homers. It's a record that will be tied several times but never broken during the 20th century.
- **1927** Ruth reaches the peak of his slugging potential with 60 homers. The Yankees sweep the Pirates in the World Series.
- **1928** Ruth matches his own record of three homers in one World Series game. Once again, it comes at the expense of the Cardinals.
- **1929** The Babe's first wife dies tragically. He marries Claire Hodgson. On the ball field, he hits his 500th career homer.
- **1931** Ruth hits career homer number 600.
- **1932** The Yankees beat the Cubs in the World Series. It's the last championship of Ruth's career. In Game 3 of the series, he allegedly calls his own shot off Chicago hurler Charlie Root. The validity of the event will be an endless source of debate among fans and historians in subsequent years.
- **1933** Baseball's first All-Star Game is played in Chicago. Ruth is the star of the show with a home run and a nifty catch in the outfield that preserves an AL win.
- **1934** The Babe collects career homer number 700. He also plays in his last All-Star Game.
- **1935** Ruth returns to Boston with the Braves. On the last productive day of his career, he smashes three homers in a game against the Pirates. He performs horrendously overall and quits before the All-Star break.

- **1936** The Babe is included in the Hall of Fame's inaugural class along with Walter Johnson, Ty Cobb, Christy Mathewson, and Honus Wagner. The induction ceremony won't take place until 1939.

- **1938** Ruth accepts a job as coach of the Dodgers during the second half of the season. He is not rehired the following year.

- **1947** Babe Ruth Day ceremonies are held at Yankee Stadium. Ruth delivers a farewell speech to more than 58,000 fans.

- **1948** Ruth's number 3 is retired by the Yankees in a ceremony commemorating the 25th anniversary of Yankee Stadium. On August 16, Ruth succumbs to cancer at the age of 53.

- **1961** Roger Maris breaks Ruth's single-season home run record with 61 blasts.

- **1974** Ruth's career home run mark falls to Hank Aaron, who retires with 755.

APPENDIX VII

BABE RUTH'S FAVORITE HOME RUN VICTIMS

(* Denotes Hall of Famer)

PITCHER	HR TOTAL
Rube Walberg	17
Hooks Dauss	14
Lefty Stewart	13
Milt Gaston	13
Howard Ehmke	13
George Uhle	12
Earl Whitehill	11
Tommy Thomas	11
Ted Lyons*	10
George Earnshaw	10
Eddie Rommel	10
Hod Lisenbee	10
Walter Johnson*	10
General Crowder	9
Tom Zachary	9
Lefty Grove*	9
Jake Miller	9
Sam Gray	9
Red Faber*	9

Appendix VIII

Babe Ruth's Longest Homers

- In 1917, Ruth became the first player to hit a ball into the centerfield bleachers at Fenway Park. The dimensions of the stadium were changed in later years, but in the early 1900s, the distance was well over 500 feet.
- During spring training in 1919, the Babe hit a long blast in an exhibition game at Plant Field in Tampa, Florida. It landed on the railing of a horse racing track that circled the stadium. Estimates of the drive vary from 540 to 612 feet.
- During the 1919 regular season, Ruth reportedly slammed a pitch over the right field roof at the Polo Grounds. Joe Jackson, playing for Cleveland, was said to have hit the top of the roof in a 1913 game. But Ruth's clout allegedly cleared the roof on the fly.
- On July 18, 1921, the Babe went deep against Bert Cole of the Tigers at Navin Field in Detroit. By some accounts, the ball hit a parked car on Plum Street some 600 feet away then bounced/rolled another 250 feet. Many consider this to be the longest verifiable home run in major-league history.
- On July 31, 1921, the Babe launched a drive over the right-center field roof at the Polo Grounds. The blast, surrendered by Ray Caldwell of the Indians, was believed to be around 560 feet.
- During a 1926 barnstorming stop at Artillery Park in Wilkes-Barre, Pennsylvania, the Babe challenged a local pitcher to throw him his best fastball. Ruth blasted the pitch out of the stadium and beyond an adjacent running track. Estimates of the distance vary from 600 to 650 feet.
- In a 1929 exhibition game at Sing Sing Correctional Facility, Ruth hit a ball over the center field wall. It sailed past a watchtower and

traveled around 620 feet. Prior to then, no ball had ever exited the stadium by way of center field.

- In a 1934 spring training game at St. Petersburg, the Babe drilled an offering from Huck Betts of the Braves out of Waterfront Park and onto the second story porch of the West Coast Inn, where players were staying. That shot is believed to have carried at least 610 feet—probably even farther.

- The last homer of Ruth's career was a memorable one. It came off of Guy Bush of the Pirates at Forbes Field in Pittsburgh. It hit a house on Bouquet Street some 540 feet away. Some sources claim the blast was closer to 600 feet.

Bibliography

Aadrianse, Katherine. "Baseball behind Bars." National Baseball Hall of Fame. https://baseballhall.org/discover/short-stops/baseball-behind-bars.

Aaron, Hank, and Lonnie Wheeler. *I Had a Hammer: The Hank Aaron Story*. New York: Harper Perennial, 2007.

"Address to Fans on Babe Ruth Day at Yankee Stadium." American Rhetoric. https://www.americanrhetoric.com/speeches/baberuthfarewelltobaseball.htm.

Adomites, Paul, and Saul Wisnia. "Babe Ruth Discovers Baseball." How Stuff Works. https://entertainment.howstuffworks.com/babe-ruth3.htm.

———. "Babe Ruth's First Spring Training." How Stuff Works. https://entertainment.howstuffworks.com/babe-ruth6.htm.

———. "Babe Ruth's Power Swing." How Stuff Works. https://entertainment.howstuffworks.com/babe-ruth19.htm.

Ahrens, Mark. "Christy Walsh—Baseball's First Agent." *Books on Baseball* [blog], August 4, 2010. http://www.booksonbaseball.com/2010/08/christy-walsh-baseballs-first-agent/.

Amernic, Jerry. "How Babe Ruth Beat a Pandemic Twice." *New York Daily News*, May 3, 2020.

"Anyway, I Had a Better Year Than He Did." Quote Investigator, December 28, 2014. https://quoteinvestigator.com/2014/12/28/better-year/.

Aubrecht, Michael. "'Pride' of the Yankees." Baseball Almanac, November 2003. https://www.baseball-almanac.com/articles/aubrecht8.shtml.

"The Babe and Brother Matthias." uCatholic.com, April 4, 2016. https://ucatholic.com/blog/the-babe-and-brother-matthias/.

"Babe & Little Ray Kelly." Babe Ruth Central. http://www.baberuthcentral.com/kids-clubhouse/babe-ray-kelly/.

"Babe Ruth and Lou Gehrig Comedy Album." Babe Ruth Central. http://www.baberuthcentral.com/babe-ruth-lou-gehrig-comedy-album/.

"Babe Ruth Catches Ball from Airplane. Seventh Attempt Gives Him World's Record." *New York Times,* July 22, 1926.

"Babe Ruth Cigar." Baseball Reliquary. https://www.baseballreliquary.org/about/collections/babe-ruth-cigar-partially-smoked/.

"Babe Ruth's Longest Home Run." *Northeastern Journal*, March 7, 2014.

"Babe Ruth Plays after Day in Jail." *New York Times*, June 9, 1921.

Babe Ruth Quote Page. Baseball Almanac. https://www.baseball-almanac.com/quotes/quoruth.shtml.

Babe Ruth Quote Page. Brainy Quote. https://www.brainyquote.com/authors/babe-ruth-quotes.

"Babe Ruth Stories You Might Not Want to Tell Your Children." CooperToons. https://www.coopertoons.com/caricatures/CKftPI_baberuth_bio.html#baberuth_stories.

The Babe Ruth Story.Rotten Tomatoes. https://www.rottentomatoes.com/m/babe_ruth_story.

"Babe Ruth, The Slugger Who Went from Boyhood Chaos to Baseball Stardom." *New York Times*, August 16, 2016.

"The Babe's House Is For Sale, Cigar Burns and All." *Newsday*, May 7, 2012.

Bales, Jack. "The Show Girl and the Shortstop: The Strange Saga of Violet Popovich and Her Shooting of Cub Billy Jurges." *Baseball Research Journal* (Fall 2016).

"Baseball and PEDs: A 120-Year History." *Joy of Sox* [blog], February 15, 2009. http://joyofsox.blogspot.com/2009/02/baseball-peds-120-year-history.html.

"Baseball History: Babe Ruth's 1921 Suspension." *Call to the Pen* [blog], December 18, 2011. https://calltothepen.com/2011/12/18/baseball-history-babe-ruths-1921-suspension/.

"Baseball's Golden Days in Hot Springs." Hot Springs Arkansas Historic Baseball Trail Website, May 3, 2013. http://www.hotspringsbaseballtrail.com/untold-stories/baseballs-golden-days-in-hot-springs/.

Belluck, Pam. "Hoping a Soggy Piano Can Lift the Curse." *New York Times*, September 30, 2002.

Berger, Ralph. "Earle Combs." SABR Biography Project. https://sabr.org/bioproj/person/62bcbcbd.

———. "Moe Berg." SABR Biography Project. https://sabr.org/bioproj/person/moe-berg/.

———. "Ping Bodie." Society for American Baseball Research Biography Project. https://sabr.org/bioproj/person/712236b9.

Beschloss, Michael. "Babe Ruth Knocked Out." *New York Times*, May 16, 2014.

Bond, Mike. "The 1927 Yankees Are Still a Murderer's Row Now They're Our Best Team Ever." Thakoni, April 7, 2020. https://thakoni.com/the-1927-yankees-are-still-a-murderers-row-now-theyre-our-best-team-ever/.

Bryson, Bill. "Babe Ruth's Summer of Records." *Daily Beast*, September 29, 2013. https://www.thedailybeast.com/babe-ruths-summer-of-records.

Carey, Charles. "Walter Johnson." Society for American Baseball Research Biography Project. https://sabr.org/bioproj/person/0e5ca45c.

Castonguay, Matthew. "Ty Cobb Beat Babe Ruth . . . at Golf." SwingU Clubhouse, July 27, 2014. https://clubhouse.swingu.com/lifestyle/ty-cobb-once-beat-babe-ruth-at-golf/.

Christensen, Jen. "Besting Ruth, Beating Hate: How Hank Aaron Made Baseball History." CNN, April 8, 2014. https://www.cnn.com/interactive/2014/04/us/hank-aaron-anniversary/.

Clair, Michael. "Babe Ruth and Walter Johnson Once Played Each Other in a Star-studded Game on Halloween." MLB (CUT4 Blog). https://mlb.com/cut4/babe-ruth-and-walter-johnsons-1924-halloween-game/c-155304596, October 31, 2015.

Considine, Bob, with Babe Ruth. *The Babe Ruth Story*. New York: Signet, 1992.

Constrovince, Anthony. "These 9 Pitchers Dominated Babe Ruth." MLB, April 14, 2020. https://www.mlb.com/news/pitchers-who-owned-babe-ruth.

Cook, William A. *Waite Hoyt: A Biography of the Yankees' Schoolboy Wonder.* Jefferson, NC: McFarland, 2004.

Corrigan, Daniel. "Babe Ruth Had a Home Run Taken Away from Him." *The Scorecrow* [blog], June 24, 2020. https://thescorecrow.com/2020/06/24/babe-ruth-had-a-home-run-taken-away-from-him/.

Creamer, Robert. *Babe: The Legend Come to Life.* New York: Fireside, 1992.

Crowther, Bosley. "The Current Screen." *Washington Post*, August 7, 1948.

"The Curse of the Bambino." Babe Ruth Central. http://www.baberuthcentral.com/babesimpact/legends/the-curse-of-the-bambino/.

"The Curse of the Bambino." Baseball Almanac. https://www.baseball-almanac.com/poetry/po_tcotb.shtml.

Deezen, Eddie. "Babe Ruth: The Ladies Man." Mental Floss, August 16, 2012. https://www.mentalfloss.com/article/31471/babe-ruths-final-years.

———. "Babe Ruth's Final Years." Today I Found Out, December 23, 2013. http://www.todayifoundout.com/index.php/2013/12/babe-ruth-ladies-man/.

Dickson, Paul. *The New Dickson Baseball Dictionary: A Cyclopedic Reference to More Than 7,000 Words, Phrases and Slang Expressions That Define the Game, Its Heritage, Culture and Variations.* New York: Harcourt Brace, 1999.

"Did Babe Ruth Ever Bat Right-Handed?" *Baseball Researcher* [blog], October 12, 2018. http://baseballresearcher.blogspot.com/2018/10/did-babe-ruth-ever-bat-right-handed.html.

Dilbert, Ryan. "Recalling Babe Ruth's Stint as a Pro Wrestling Referee." *Bleacher Report*, August 6, 2015. https://bleacherreport.com/articles/2507385-recalling-babe-ruths-stint-as-a-pro-wrestling-referee.

Dixon, Mark. "How Babe Ruth's Career Almost Ended One Night on Baltimore Pike." *Mainline Today.* https://mainlinetoday.com/life-style/how-babe-ruths-career-almost-ended-one-night-on-blatimore-pike/, May 17, 2017.

Dow, Bill. "Babe Ruth's Greatest Practical Joke Happened in Detroit." *Vintage Detroit* [blog], February 5, 2011. https://www.vintagedetroit.com/blog/2011/02/05/babe-ruth%E2%80%99s-greatest-practical-joke-happened-in-detroit/.

Doyle, Jack. "Babe Ruth and Tobacco, 1920s–1940s." *Pop History Dig.* https://www.pophistorydig.com/topics/babe-ruth-tobacco-1920s-1940s/, September 25, 2010.

———. "The M & M Boys: Summer of 1961." *Pop History Dig.* https://www.pophistorydig.com/topics/maris-mantle-home-run-race-1961, August 21, 2018.

Dufresne, Chris. "The Babe in Boomtown." *Los Angeles Times*, June 2, 2008.

Eig, Jonathan. *Luckiest Man: The Life and Death of Lou Gehrig.* New York: Simon and Schuster, 2005.

"Eiji Sawamura." Baseball's Greatest Sacrifice. http://www.baseballsgreatestsacrifice.com/biographies/sawamura_eiji.html.

Eisenberg, John. *The Streak: Lou Gehrig, Cal Ripken Jr., and Baseball's Most Historic Record.* E-book. New York: Houghton Mifflin Harcourt, 2017.

Finkel, Jan. "Pete Alexander." SABR Biography Project. https://sabr.org/bioproj/person/79e6a2a7.

Fitts, Robert K. *Banzai Babe Ruth: Baseball, Espionage and Assassination during the 1934 Tour of Japan.* Lincoln: University of Nebraska Press, 2012.

Fitzpatrick, Frank. "Separating Babe Ruth Truth from Fiction." *Philadelphia Inquirer,* June 10, 2016.

Francis, Bill. "At Home on the Road." National Baseball Hall of Fame. https://baseballhall.org/discover-more/history/barnstorming-tours.

———. "Ball Hit for Ruth's 60th Home Run Part of Baseball Lore in Cooperstown." National Baseball Hall of Fame. https://baseballhall.org/discover/short-stops/babe-ruths-60th-home-run-ball.

———. "Big Star on the Big Screen." National Baseball Hall of Fame. https://baseballhall.org/discover-more/stories/short-stops/big-star-on-the-big-screen.

———. "100 Years Later, Sale of Ruth Remains Pivotal Point in History." National Baseball Hall of Fame. https://baseballhall.org/discover/sale-of-ruth-to-yankees-shook-baseball-world.

Freedman, Lew. *The Day All the Stars Came Out: Major League Baseball's First All-Star Game.* Jefferson, NC: McFarland, 2010.

Frick, Ford, "From the Press Box: The Law of Brick." ESPN, April 26, 2016. https://1927-the-diary-of-myles-thomas.espn.com/the-law-of-brick-owens-4afb2eb0b7fa.

"From a Babe Ruth Fan—Another Called Shot That Wasn't." Babe Ruth Central. http://www.baberuthcentral.com/babe-ruth-fan-call-shot-1932/.

Frommer, Harvey. *A Yankee Century.* New York: Berkley, 2002.

Fuchs, Alfred H. "Babe Ruth Sees a Psychologist: Science Sought to Discover the Secret of his Baseball Prowess." *American Psychological Association* 40, no. 10 (November 2009).

"Full Text of Lou Gehrig's Farewell Speech." *Sports Illustrated,* July 4, 2009. https://www.si.com/mlb/2009/07/05/gehrig-text.

Fullerton, Hugh. "From the Archive Why Babe Ruth is the Greatest Home Run Hitter." *Popular Science.* https://www.popsci.com/scitech/article/2006-10/archive-why-babe-ruth-greatest-home-run-hitter/, October 23, 2006.

Gaff, Alan D. "Babe Ruth and Betsy Bingle." Alan D. Gaff website, November 23, 2019. https://www.alandgaff.com/post/babe-ruth-and-betsy-bingle.

Gergen, Joe. "Dahlgren Recalls Decline of Gehrig 50 Years Ago." *Los Angeles Times,* July 9, 1989.

Glueckstein, Fred. "Tony Lazzeri." SABR Biography Project. https://sabr.org/bioproj/person/1b3c179c.

Goldman, Mike. "Play Ball." *Jacksonville.* https://jacksonvillemag.com/2015/06/19/play-ball/, June 19, 2015.

Goldman. Steven. "Forgiving, Forgetting, and Bob Shawkey's 46-Year Yankee Exile." *Vice.* https://www.vice.com/en/article/nzxnqx/forgiving-forgetting-and-bob-shawkeys-46-year-yankees-exile, April 14, 2016.

————. "Throwback Thursday: The Year Babe Ruth Lost It and Grew Up." *Vice*. https://www.vice.com/en/article/nzxzbq/throwback-thursday-the-year-babe-ruth-lost-it-and-grew-up, June 23, 2016.

Goldstein, Richard. "Julia Ruth Stevens, Babe Ruth's Daughter, Dies." *New York Times*, March 9, 2019.

————. "Ray Kelly, Babe Ruth's Little Pal, Dies." *New York Times*, November 14, 2001.

Goodspeed, John. "In the Babe's Own Words?" *Baltimore Sun*, July 20, 1992.

Gowdy, Kristin. "Babe Ruth Hits His 30th Home Run of the Season Breaking His Own Single Season Record." National Baseball Hall of Fame. https://baseballhall.org/discover/inside-pitch/ruth-hits-30th-of-season.

"The Greatest Man Ruth Ever Knew Was a Canadian." Cooperstowners in Canada, July 17, 2010. https://cooperstownersincanada.com/2010/07/17/the-greatest-man-that-babe-ruth-ever-knew-was-a-canadian/.

Green, Nelson. "Mike Cvengros." SABR Biography Project. https://sabr.org/bioproj/person/mike-cvengros/.

Gustkey, Earl. "The Babe's Farewell: Fifty Years Ago, an Unmatched Career Came to an Unhappy End." *Los Angeles Times*, June 2, 1985.

Guzzardi, Joe. "Babe Ruth Was a Better Pitcher Than Walter Johnson—For Two Years at Least." *Baseball Past and Present* [blog], August 11, 2010. https://baseballpastandpresent.com/mlb/babe-ruth-was-a-better-pitcher-than-walter-johnson-for-two-years-at-least/.

Hagerty, Tim. "Where Was Babe Ruth's Longest Home Run? A Six-City Mystery." *Sporting News*. https://www.sportingnews.com/us/mlb/news/babe-ruth-longest-home-run-new-york-yankees-sing-sing-tampa-wilkes-barre-fort-wayne-st-petersburg-detroit/1ch5kzxj84m791eu5r7kvkypip, October 31, 2016.

Hampton, Wilborn. *Up Close: Babe Ruth*. New York: Viking, 2009.

Harold, Zack. "Jackie Mitchell Couldn't Win. Skepticism Followed Baseball's Most Famous Female Pitcher until the Day She Died." *Lapham's Quarterly*. https://www.laphamsquarterly.org/roundtable/jackie-itchell-couldnt-win, March 28, 2018.

Harvey, Steve. "This Charge against Babe Ruth Was Off Base." *Los Angeles Times*, March 28, 2010.

Havilla, John. "Babe's Power Still Carries." *Hartford Courant*, April 23, 2006.

Heller, Billy. "Babe Ruth and Lou Gehrig Were Torn Apart by Women." *New York Post*, March 31, 2018.

Heller, Dick. "Correcting a Grave Injustice." *Washington Times*, July 5, 2008.

"The Historic Quest for Speed in Baseball." Scoutee Company Official Website, December 14, 2015.

Hofstetter, Fred. "The Screwball Pitch: What it is, How to Throw it and Pitchers Who Do." *Screwball Times* [blog], September 8, 2014. https://www.screwballtimes.com/extra-innings/screwball-pitch/.

Holmes, Dan. "A Player's Strike Almost Halted the 1918 World Series." *Baseball Egg* [blog], September 18, 2012. https://baseballegg.com/2012/09/18/a-players-strike-almost-halted-1918-world-series-before-game-five/.

——. "Rivalry Renewed: Ty Cobb and Babe Ruth Hit the Golf Course." *Baseball Egg* [blog], May 5, 2010. http://baseballegg.com/2010/05/01/ rivalry-renewed-ty-cobb-and-babe-ruth-on-the-golf-course/.

——. "When the Tigers, Yankees, Cobb, and Ruth Brawled in Detroit at Navin Field," *Vintage Detroit* [blog]. https://www.vintagedetroit.com/when-the-tigers-yankees-cabb-and-ruth-brawled-in-detroit-at-navin-field,March 12, 2012.

Horowitz, Tony. "The Woman Who (Maybe) Struck out Babe Ruth and Lou Gehrig." *Smithsonian*. https://www.smithsonianmag.com/history/the-woman-who-maybe-struck-out-babe-ruth-and-;ou-gehrig-4759182/, July 2013.

Hoyt, Waite. *Babe Ruth as I Knew Him.* New York: Dell, 1948.

"Huggins Looks for Yankees to Get Jump, Hornsby Confident Cardinals Will Win." *New York Times*, October 2, 1926.

Jackson, Frank. "Bombing in the Bronx: The Babe Ruth Story." *Hardball Times* [blog], October 28, 2014. https://tht.fangraphs.com/bombing-in-the-bronx-the-babe-ruth-story/.

Jenkinson, Bill. *Baseball's Ultimate Power: Ranking the All-Time Greatest Distance Home Run Hitters.* Guilford, CT: Lyons, 2010.

"Joe McCarthy." National Baseball Hall of Fame. https://baseballhall.org/hall-of-famers/mccarthy-joe.

Johnson, Charles. "The Giants Evict Yankees." Elysian Fielders, September 23, 2013. http://www.elysianfielders.com/the-giants-evict-the-yankees/.

Kashatus, William C. *Baseball's All-Time Greatest Hitters, Lou Gehrig: A Biography.* Westport, CT: Greenwood, 2004.

Kelly, Matt. "The Deal That Changed the Game." National Baseball Hall of Fame (Official Website). https://baseballhall.org/discover-more/stories/short-stops/the-deal-that-changed-the-game.

——. "On Account of War." National Baseball Hall of Fame. https://baseballhall.org/ discover-more/stories/short-stops/1918-world-war-i-baseball.

——. "When the First Five Were Chosen." National Baseball Hall of Fame. https://baseballhall.org/discover-more/stories/baseball-history/ first-bbwaa-hof-election-1936.

Kimball, George. "Woods Saga Couldn't Fail to Make Headines." *Irish Times*, December 3, 2009.

Kivette, Andrew. "Carl Hubbell Strikes out Five Hall of Famers in Succession at the All-Star Game." National Baseball Hall of Fame. https://baseballhall.org/discover/ inside-pitch/carl-hubbell-strikes-out-five-hofers.

Klein, Christopher. "Babe Ruth v. Baby Ruth." History, September 25, 2014. https:// www.history.com/news/babe-ruth-v-baby-ruth.

Konicek, James. "This Week in Universal News: The War of the Worlds Broadcast, 1938." *Unwritten Record* [blog], October 27, 2014. https://unwritten-record.blogs.archives.gov/2014/10/27/ this-week-in-universal-news-the-war-of-the-worlds-broadcast-1938/.

Krantz, Les. *Yankee Stadium: A Tribute. 85 Years of Memories—1923–2008.* New York: HarperCollins, 2008.

Leavy, Jane. *The Big Fella: Babe Ruth and the World He Created.* New York: Harper Perennial, 2018.

———. "The Theme Music Behind the Curse of the Bambino." ESPN. https://www.espn.com/mlb/story/_/id/24994062/jane-leavy-babe-ruth-legend-piano-bottom-curse-bambino, October 16, 2016.

———. "Why on Earth Did Boston Sell Babe Ruth to the Yankees?" *New York Times*, December 30, 2019.

Leeke, Jim. "Ernie Shore." SABR Biography Project. https://sabr.org/bioproj/person/6073c617.

Leerhsen, Charles. *Ty Cobb: A Terrible Beauty.* New York: Simon and Schuster, 2015.

———. "Ty Cobb Ruled Baseball Until Babe Ruth Stole His Spotlight." *Sports Illustrated.* https://www.si.com/mlb/2015/05/08/book-excerpt-ty-cobb-babe-ruth-detroit-tigers, May 11, 2015———.

"The Legend of Babe Ruth's West Coast Inn Home Run—The Longest Ever Hit in a Major League Game." Babe Ruth Central. http://www.baberuthcentral.com/legend-babe-ruths-west-coast-inn-home-run/.

Leggett, William. "A Tortured Road to 715." *Sports Illustrated.* https://vault.si.com/vault/1973/05/28/a-tortured-road-to-715, May 28, 1973.

Leventhal, Josh. *The World Series: An Illustrated Encyclopedia of the Fall Classic.* New York: Black Dog & Leventhal, 2001.

Liepa, John. "George Pipgras." SABR Biography Project. https://sabr.org/bioproj/person/d53de130.

Lindberg, James. "Ed Wells." SABR Biography Project. https://sabr.org/bioproj/person/ed-wells/.

Livacari, Gary. "Casey Stengel's Inside-the-Park Home Run Wins Game 1 of the 1923 World Series 94 Years Ago This Week!" *Baseball History Comes Alive* [blog]. https://www.baseballhistorycomesalive.com/casey-stengels-inside-the-park-home-run-wins-game-one-of-the-1923-world-series-94-years-ago-this-week, October 12, 2017.

Lowitt, Bruce. "Oh, Henry! Aaron Swings Past Ruth." *St. Petersburg Times*, December 25, 1999.

Lynch, Mike. "June 13, 1924: Yankees Win Forfeited Game in Detroit as 'All Hell Breaks Loose.'" SABR Games Project. https://sabr.org/gamesproj/game/june-13–1924-yankees-win-forfeited-game-in-detroit-as-all-hell-breaks-loose/.

Macht, Norman. *Babe Ruth.* New York: Chelsea House, 1991.

———. "Hy Myers." SABR Biography Project. https://sabr.org/bioproj/person/dca1fee6.

Maese, Rick. "A Buried Past." *Baltimore Sun*, February 6, 2008.

Mallory, Mary. "Hollywood Heights: 'Babe Comes Home' Ushers in Baseball Season." *Los Angeles Daily Mirror*, March 28, 2016.

Martin, Andrew. "Babe Ruth Arrested for Violating Child Labor Laws Prior to Historic 1927 Season." *Seamheads* [blog], February 3, 2012. http://seamheads.com/blog/2012/02/03/babe-ruth-arrested-for-violating-child-labor-laws-prior-to-historic-1927-season/.

———. "Going Back in Time: Ty Cobb Picks His All-Time Team." *Top Level Sports.* https://medium.com/top-level-sports/going-back-in-time--baseball-legend-ty-cobb-picks-his-all-time-team-a5f209a71bbd, December 28, 2019.

Martin, Brian. *The Man Who Made Babe Ruth: Brother Matthias of St. Mary's School.* Jefferson, NC: McFarland, 2020.

McBurney, Christian. "Babe Ruth and Lou Gehrig Play an Exhibition Game in Providence, Kids Go Nuts." Online Review of Rhode Island History. http://smallstatebighistory.com/babe-ruth-and-lou-gehrig-play-an-exhibition-game-in-providence-kids-go-nuts/.

McCarten, John. "The Current Screen." *Washington Post,* August 7, 1948.

McDonald, Anna. "Pruett Heir Remembers Ruthian Legacy." ESPN, March 2, 2014. https://www.espn.com/blog/sweetspot/post/_/id/44743/pruett-heir-remembers-ruthian-legacy.

McMillan, Ken. *Tales from the Yankee Dugout.* Champaign, IL: Sports Publishing, 2001.

McMurray, John. "Babe Ruth: Brooklyn Dodgers Coach." *Baseball Research Journal* (Fall 2015). https://sabr.org/journal/article/babe-ruth-brooklyn-dodgers-coach-4/.

———. "Joe McCarthy." SABR Biography Project. https://sabr.org/bioproj/person/joe-mccarthy/.

———. "McMurray: 100 Years Later, Looking Back at Ernie Shore's Perfect Game." Society for American Baseball Research, Deadball Era Committee Newsletter, February 2017.

Mead, William B., and Paul Dickson. *Baseball: The President's Game.* New York: Walker, 1997.

"Miller Huggins." National Baseball Hall of Fame. https://baseballhall.org/hall-of-famers/huggins-miller.

Miller, Randy. "Yankees Mount Rushmore: Picking 4 Best Bombers of 1920s: Babe Ruth, Lou Gehrig and . . ." NJ.com, April 24, 2020. https://www.nj.com/yankees/2020/04/yankees-mount-rushmore-picking-4-best-bombers-of-1920s-babe-ruth-lou-gehrig-and.html.

Millikin, Mark R. *Jimmie Foxx: The Pride of Sudlersville.* Lanham, MD: Scarecrow Press, 2005.

Montville, Leigh. *The Big Bam: The Life and Times of Babe Ruth.* New York: Doubleday, 2006.

Morris, Peter. "Eddie Bennett." SABR Biography Project. https://sabr.org/bioproj/person/eddie-bennett/.

Murnane, T. H. "Babe Ruth Beat Walter Johnson in Great Pitching Duel." *Boston Globe,* August 16, 1916.

Nack, William. "The Colossus." *Sports Illustrated,* August 24, 1998.

Neft, David S., et al. *The Sports Encyclopedia: Baseball 2000.* New York: St. Martin's Griffin, 2000.

"1922: Yankees Go Home" *This Great Game: The Online Book of Baseball.* http://www.thisgreatgame.com/1922-baseball-history.html.

1933 All-Star Game Box Score and Summary. Baseball Almanac. https://www.baseball-almanac.com/asgbox/yr1933as.shtml.

Nodjimbadem, Katie. "Babe Ruth Hit a Home Run with Celebrity Products Endorsements." *Smithsonian.* https://www.smithsonianmag.com/smithsonian-institution/how-babe-ruth-hit-home-run-celebrity-product-endorsements-180960038, August 10, 2016.

Norris, Luke. "The Little-Known Story of How Babe Ruth Almost Went to the Cincinnati Reds." *Sporstcasting,* April 21, 2020. https://www.sportscasting.com/the-little-known-story-of-how-babe-ruth-almost-went-to-the-cincinnati-reds/.

Nowlin, Bill. "Sammy Vick." SABR Biography Project. https://sabr.org/bioproj/person/sammy-vick/.

Packel, Charlie, and Julia Beth Stevens. *Babe and The Kid: The Legendary Story of Babe Ruth and Johnny Sylvester.* Charleston, SC: Arcadia, 2007.

Pastorek, Whitney. "Fever Pitch Ending Is Changed after Red Sox Win." *Entertainment Weekly.* https://ew.com/article/2004/11/12/fever-pitch-ending-changed-after-red-sox-win/, November 12, 2004.

Pegler, Westbrook. "All-Star Game Just What Doctor Ordered for Baseball." *Chicago Tribune,* June 19, 1933.

Pipp, Wally. "Bad Day for Babe Ruth." *Sports Illustrated.* https://vault.si.com/vault/1962/07/30/bad-day-for-babe-ruth, July 30, 1962.

Posnanski, Joe. "Did Babe Ruth Actually Hit 715 Home Runs?" MLB, June 7, 2018. https://www.mlb.com/news/did-babe-ruth-hit-715-homers-c280173404.

The Pride of the Yankees. IMDB. https://www.imdb.com/title/tt0035211/.

"Red Faber." National Baseball Hall of Fame. https://baseballhall.org/hall-of-famers/faber-red.

Rice, Grantland. "Landis Center of Angry and Puzzled Mob." *New York Tribune,* October 6, 1922.

Rice, Stephen V. "Bob Shawkey." SABR Biography Project. https://sabr.org/bioproj/person/bob-shawkey/.

Ritter, Lawrence. *The Glory of Their Times.* New York: Macmillan, 1966.

Robbins, Mike. *The Yankees vs. Red Sox Reader.* New York: Carroll & Graf, 2005.

Roberts, Randy, and Johnny Smith. *War Fever: Boston, Baseball and America in the Shadow of the Great War.* New York: Basic Books, 2020.

Roger Maris Quote Page. Baseball Almanac. https://www.baseball-almanac.com/quotes/quomari.shtml.

Rogers Hornsby Quote Page. Baseball Almanac. https://www.baseball-almanc.com/quotes/quohorn.shtml.

Rothman, Lily. "Read Babe Ruth's 1948 Obituary: 'He Was Unforgettable Even When He Struck Out.'" *Time,* August 16, 2018. https://time.com/5250916/babe-ruth-anniversary/.

Ruth, Babe. *Babe Ruth's Own Book of Baseball.* New York: Putnam, 1928.

"Ruth to Get $15,000 as Coach for Brooklyn: Baseball Writers Believe the Babe Is Likely to Be Manager Not Later Than 1939." *Boston Globe,* June 19, 1938.

Ruth Pirone, Dorothy. *My Dad, The Babe: Growing Up with an American Hero.* Boston: Quinlan Press, 1988.

"Ruth's Childhood." Babe Ruth Central. http://www.baberuthcentral.com/babe-ruth-biography/ruths-childhood/

Sandomir, Richard. "Legacy of Earning Power: Babe Ruth: Dead 41 Years, He Lives on in Endorsements That Bring Heirs Hundreds of Thousands." *Los Angeles Times*, December 22, 1989.

———. "Reversing Course on Reports About a Classic." *New York Times*, February 8, 2013.

Sarnoff, Gary. "The Day Babe Ruth Came to Sing Sing." *National Pastime* (2007): Baseball in the Big Apple.

Scher, Jon. "Oldest Living Ballplayer Tells All." *Duke* (September/October 2008).

Schwartz, Evan Scott. "5 Seedy Stories You Don't Know about Babe Ruth's Sex Life." MTV News, July 11, 2014.

Scoggins, Chaz. "This Baseball Stunt Goes Way Back." *Lowell Sun*, July 8, 2012.

Sharkey-Gottlieb, Simon. "Flashback: 100 Years Ago, Babe Ruth Threw a Combined No-Hitter." The Score, June 23, 2017. https://thescore.com/mlb/news/1323524.

Sheehan, Stephen. "Babe Ruth's Life Was More Tragic Than You Think." *Sportscasting*, April 19, 2020. https://www.sportscasting.com/babe-ruths-life-is-more-tragic-than-you-think/.

Shirley, Daniel. "Mark Koenig." SABR Biography Project. https://sabr.org/bioproj/person/560d9b03.

Shouler, Kenneth. "The King of Swings: Babe Ruth Revolutionized Baseball While Indulging in a Passion for Wine, Women and Cigars." *Cigar Aficionado* (Spring 95). https://www.cigaraficionado.com/article/the-king-of-swings-6087.

Shuman, Ik. "Champion Yankees Return from West." *New York Times*, September 28, 1926.

Smelser, Marshall. *The Life That Ruth Built: A Biography*. New York: New York Times, 1975.

"Smiling Eddie Bennett, Mascot Who Helped Yankees to Three World Series, Dead." Associated Press, January 18, 1935.

Spaeder, Ryan. "August 25, 1915: Babe Ruth Begins 'Domination' of Ty Cobb with First Strikeout." *Sporting News*, August 25, 2017.

"Stan Coveleski." National Baseball Hall of Fame. https://baseballhall.org/hall-of-famers/coveleski-stan.

Stanton, Tom. *Ty and The Babe: Baseball's Fiercest Rivals, A Surprising Friendship and the 1941 Has-Beens Golf Championship*. New York: Thomas Dunne, 2007.

Steadman, John. "Fifty Years After his Death, Babe Ruth Still Captivates as Man, Myth, Legend." *Los Angeles Times*, August 16, 1998.

Steinberg, Steve. "Miller Huggins." SABR Biograhy Project. https://sabr.org/bioproj/person/7b65e9fa.

Stewart, David O. "Babe Ruth Built the Best Brand Ever." David O. Stewart website. https://davidostewart.com/2017/04/06/babe-ruth-built-the-best-brand-ever/, April 6, 2017.

Stewart, Wayne. *Baseball's Greatest Hitters. Babe Ruth: A Biography*. Westport, CT: Greenwood Press, 2006.

Stout, Glenn. *Yankees Century*. New York: Houghton Mifflin, 2002.

"Ten Commandments for Success in Baseball." Baseball Almanac. https://www.baseball—almanac.com/legendary/lijoemc.shtml.

Terleska, Sofie. "Best of Nine: The Brief Life of the Extended World Series." Reddit. https://www.reddit.com/r/baseball/comments/6pme83/best_of_nine_the_brief_life_of_the_extended_world/.

https://ucatholic.com/blog/the-babe-and-brother-matthias/

Thorn, John. "Why Were They Called Murder's Row? How the 1927 Yankees Got Their Name." ESPN, August 26, 2016. https://1927-the-diary-of-myles-thomas.espn.com/why-were-they-called-murderers-row-47cfd21c3be4.

Thornley, Stew. "Twin City Ballparks." Stew Thornley website. https://stewthornley.net/twincityballparks.html.

Tomasik, Mark. "How Dizzy Dean Got the Best of his Matchup with Babe Ruth." *RetroSimba* [blog], April 24, 2015. https://retrosimba.com/2015/04/24/how-dizzy-dean-got-the-best-of-his-matchup-with-babe-ruth/.

"Two Killed When Fans Stampede in Yankee Stadium." Associated Press, May 29, 1929.

Vardeman, Johnny. "Relatives of Slugger's Wife Claire Clear Up Myths." *Gainesville Times*, July 12, 2015.

Verducci, Tom. "Love, Loss and Baseball: Letters from the Hub, Chapters VI–IV, The 1918 Season Begins and the Killer Arrives." *Sports Illustrated*, June 22, 2020. https://www.si.com/mlb/2020/06/22/boston-babe-ruth-1918-spanish-flu.

Wagenheim, Kal. *Babe Ruth: His Life and Legend*. E-book. New York: Open Road Media, 2014.

Walker, James R., and Pat Hughes. *Crack of the Bat: A History of Baseball on the Radio*. Lincoln: University of Nebraska Press, 2015.

Wancho, Joseph. "August 16, 1920: Ray Chapman Suffers Fatal Blow to His Skull on Pitch From Carl Mays." Society for American Baseball Research Games Project. https://sabr.org/gamesproj/game/august-16–1920-ray-chapman-suffers-fatal-blow-his-skull-pitch-carl-mays.

Ward, Arch. "Chicago to See Baseball's Biggest Game." *Chicago Tribune*, May 19, 1933.

Warren, Lee. "PCL Tales: Joe Sprinz's Attempt to Catch a Baseball from a Blimp." *SB Nation* [blog], March 11, 2014. https://www.minorleagueball.com/2014/3/11/5491812/pcl-tales.

Weekes, William. "Babe's Specialty Gets Needed Runs." Associated Press, July 7, 1933.

Weintraub, Robert. *The House That Ruth Built: A New Stadium, the First Yankees Championship and the Redemption of 1923*. E-book. New York: Little, Brown, 2011.

———. "The Sultan of Twat: Babe Ruth's Swinging First Few Years with the Yankees." *Deadspin* [blog], April 14, 2011. https://deadspin.com/the-sultan-of-twat-babe-ruths-swinging-first-few-years-5792180.

"Wife's Death Opened Secrets to Personal Life of Babe Ruth." *RetroSimba* [blog], January 7, 2019. https://retrosimba.com/2019/01/07/wifes-death-opened-secrets-to-personal-life-of-babe-ruth/.

"Wilkes Baseball Field Determined to be Home of Babe Ruth's Longest Shot." Wilkes University News. www.wilkes.edu/about-wilkes/campus/sports-facilities/babe-ruths-longest-homerun.aspx.

Wolf, Gregory H. "Charlie Root." SABR Biography Project. https://sabr.org/bioproj/person/charlie-root/.

———. "Guy Bush." SABR Biography Project. https://sabr.org/bioproj/person/guy-bush/.

Wolf, Thomas. *The Called Shot: Babe Ruth, the Chicago Cubs and the Unforgettable Major League Baseball Season of 1932*. Lincoln: University of Nebraska Press, 2020.

Wood, Allan. "Babe Ruth." SABR Biography Project. https://sabr.org/bioproj/person/9dcdd01c.

———. *Babe Ruth and the 1918 Red Sox*. Bloomington: IN, iUniverse, 2000. Kindle version.

Zirin, David. *Welcome to the Terrordome: The Pain, Politics and Promise of Sports*. Chicago: Haymarket, 2007.

END NOTES

INTRODUCTORY QUOTES
Babe Ruth Quote Page, Baseball Almanac. https://www.baseball-almanac.com/quotes/quoruth.shtml.

Babe Ruth Quote Page, Baberuth.com/quotes.

Brainyquote.com.

Bob Considine with Babe Ruth, *The Babe Ruth Story* (New York: Signet Books, 1992), xiii.

ESPN Classic Sports Century: Babe Ruth (ESPN Original Entertainment, 2000), https://www.youtube.com/watch?v=5GkZRw21kho.

Lawrence Ritter, *The Glory of Their Times: The Story of the Early Days of Baseball Told by the Men Who Played It* (New York: Macmillan, 1968), 82, 137, 260.

Sports of the 20th Century: Babe Ruth (HBO Studios, 1998), https://www.youtube.com/watch?v=CGThVd9sInU.

PART 1: A CHRONOLOGICAL JOURNEY THROUGH THE BABE'S LIFE AND CAREER
[1] Stephen Sheehan, "Babe Ruth's Life Was More Tragic Than You Think," *Sportscasting*, April 19, 2020, https://www.sportscasting.com/babe-ruths-life-is-more-tragic-than-you-think/.

[2] Leigh Montville, *The Big Bam: The Life and Times of Babe Ruth* (New York: Doubleday, 2006), 36.

[3] Paul Adomites and Saul Wisnia, "Babe Ruth's First Spring Training," How Stuff Works, https://entertainment.howstuffworks.com/babe-ruth6.htm.

[4] Ibid.

[5] Montville, *The Big Bam*, 54.

[6] "Wife's Death Opened Secrets to Personal Life of Babe Ruth," *RetroSimba* [blog], January 7, 2019, https://retrosimba.com/2019/01/07/wifes-death-opened-secrets-to-personal-life-of-babe-ruth/.

[7] Joe Guzzardi, "Babe Ruth Was a Better Pitcher Than Walter Johnson—For Two Years at Least," *Baseball Past and Present* [blog], August 11, 2010, https://baseballpastandpresent.com/mlb/babe-ruth-was-a-better-pitcher-than-walter-johnson-for-two-years-at-least/.

[8] Bill Francis, "100 Years Later, Sale of Ruth Remains Pivotal Point in History," National Baseball Hall of Fame, https://baseballhall.org/discover/sale-of-ruth-to-yankees-shook-baseball-world.

[9] Ibid.

[10] Matt Kelly, "The Deal That Changed the Game," National Baseball Hall of Fame, https://baseballhall.org/discover-more/stories/short-stops/the-deal-that-changed-the-game.

[11] "The Curse of the Bambino," Baseball Almanac, https://www.baseball-almanac.com/poetry/po_tcotb.shtml.

[12] Montville, *The Big Bam*, 108.

[13] Joseph Wancho, "August 16, 1920: Ray Chapman Suffers Fatal Blow to His Skull on Pitch From Carl Mays," Society for American Baseball Research Games Project, https://sabr.org/gamesproj/game/august-16–1920-ray-chapman-suffers-fatal-blow-his-skull-pitch-carl-mays.

[14] Ralph Berger. "Ping Bodie," Society for American Baseball Research Biography Project, https://sabr.org/bioproj/person/712236b9.

[15] Allan Wood. "Babe Ruth." SABR Biography Project, https://sabr.org/bioproj/person/babe-ruth/

[16] Montville, *The Big Bam*, 124.

[17] Norman Macht, *Babe Ruth* (New York: Chelsea House, 1991), 22.

[18] Montville, *The Big Bam*, 121.

[19] Glenn Stout, *Yankees Century* (New York: Houghton Mifflin, 2002), 99.

[20] Sofie Terleska, "Best of Nine: The Brief Life of the Extended World Series." Reddit, https://www.reddit.com/r/baseball/comments/6pme83/best_of_nine_the_brief_life_of_the_extended_world/.

[21] Stout, *Yankees Century*, 101.

[22] Bill Francis, "At Home on the Road," National Baseball Hall of Fame, https://baseballhall.org/discover-more/history/barnstorming-tours.

[23] Ibid.

[24] Stephen Goldman, "Throwback Thursday: The Year Babe Ruth Lost it and Grew Up," *Vice*, https://www.vice.com/en/article/nzxzbq/throwback-thursday-the-year-babe-ruth-lost-it-and-grew-up, June 23, 2016.

[25] "Baseball History: Babe Ruth's 1921 Suspension," *Call to the Pen* [blog], December 12, 2011, https://calltothepen.com/2011/12/18/baseball-history-babe-ruths-1921-suspension/.

[26] Goldman, "Throwback Thursday."

[27] Ibid.

[28] Robert Creamer, *Babe: The Legend Come to Life* (New York: Fireside, 1992), 270.

[29] Grantland Rice, "Landis Center of Angry and Puzzled Mob," *New York Tribune*, October 6, 1922.

[30] Eddie Deezen, "Babe Ruth: The Ladies Man," Today I Found Out, December 23, 2013.

[31] Robert Weintraub, "The Sultan of Twat: Babe Ruth's Swinging First Few Years with the Yankees," *Deadspin* [blog], April 14, 2011.

[32] Ibid.

[33] Evan Scott Schwartz, "5 Seedy Stories You Don't Know About Babe Ruth's Sex Life," MTV News, www.mtv.com/news/1865973/seedy-stories-babe-ruths-sex-life/, July 11, 2014,.

[34] Weintraub, *"The Sultan of Twat: Babe Ruth's Swinging First Few Years With the Yankees."*

[35] Kal Wagenheim, *Babe Ruth: His Life and Legend,* E-book, (New York: Open Road Media, 2014).

[36] Ibid.

[37] Les Krantz, *Yankee Stadium: A Tribute. 85 Years of Memories—1923–2008* (New York: HarperCollins, 2008), 108.

[38] Randy Miller, "Yankees Mount Rushmore: Picking 4 Best Bombers of 1920s: Babe Ruth, Lou Gehrig and . . ." NJ.com, April 24, 2020, https://www.nj.com/yankees/2020/04/yankees-mount-rushmore-picking-4-best-bombers-of-1920s-babe-ruth-lou-gehrig-and.html .

[39] Alan D. Gaff, "Babe Ruth and Betsy Bingle," Alan D. Gaff website, November 23, 2019, https://www.alandgaff.com/post/babe-ruth-and-betsy-bingle.

[40] Jonathan Eig, *Luckiest Man: The Life and Death of Lou Gehrig* (New York: Simon and Schuster, 2005), 39.

[41] Stout, *Yankees Century,* 107.

[42] Gary Livacari, "Casey Stengel's Inside-the-Park Home Run Wins Game 1 of the 1923 World Series," *Baseball History Comes Alive* [blog], https://www.baseballhistorycomesalive.com/casey-stengels-inside-the-park-home-run-wins-game-one-of-the-1923-world-series-94-years-ago-this-week, February 12, 2016.

[43] Lawrence Ritter, *The Glory of Their Times* (New York: Macmillan, 1966), 61.

[44] Ibid., 41.

[45] Dan Holmes, "When the Tigers, Yankees, Cobb, and Ruth Brawled in Detroit at Navin Field," *Vintage Detroit* [blog], https://www.vintagedetroit.com/when-the-tigers-yankees-cabb-and-ruth-brawled-in-detroit-at-navin-field, March 12, 2012.

[46] Tom Stanton, *Ty and The Babe: Baseball's Fiercest Rivals, A Surprising Friendship and the 1941 Has-Beens Golf Championship* (New York: Thomas Dunne, 2007), 244.

[47] Ibid.

[48] Charles Leerhsen, "Ty Cobb Ruled Baseball Until Babe Ruth Stole His Spotlight," *Sports Illustrated,* https://www.si.com/mlb/2015/05/08/book-excerpt-ty-cobb-babe-ruth-detroit-tigers, May 11, 2015.

[49] Charles Leerhsen, *Ty Cobb: A Terrible Beauty* (New York: Simon and Schuster, 2015), 326.

[50] Babe Ruth Quote Page, Baseball Almanac, https://www.baseball-almanac.com/quotes/quoruth.shtml.

[51] Leerhsen, *Ty Cobb: A Terrible Beauty,* 371.

[52] Montville, *The Big Bam,* 187.

[53] Ibid., 189.

[54] Jane Leavy, *The Big Fella: Babe Ruth and the World He Created* (New York: Harper Perennial, 2018), 268.

[55] Creamer, *Babe,* 284.

[56] Leavy, *The Big Fella,* 273.

[57] "Miller Huggins," National Baseball Hall of Fame, https://baseballhall.org/hall-of-famers/huggins-miller.

[58] Montville, *The Big Bam*, 99.

[59] Creamer, *Babe*, 293.

[60] Ibid., 294.

[61] "Miller Huggins," National Baseball Hall of Fame.

[62] Creamer, *Babe*, 297.

[63] Montville, *The Big Bam*, 214.

[64] Macht, *Babe Ruth*, 51.

[65] Stout, *Yankees Century*, 117.

[66] Ibid.

[67] Rogers Hornsby Quote Page, Baseball Almanac, https://www.baseball-almanc.com/quotes/quohorn.shtml.

[68] Ibid.

[69] "Huggins Looks for Yankees to Get Jump, Hornsby Confident Cardinals Will Win," *New York Times*, October 2, 1926.

[70] Ik Shuman, "Champion Yankees Return from West," *New York Times*, September 28, 1926.

[71] Marshall Smelser, *The Life That Ruth Built: A Biography* (New York: New York Times, 1975), 337–38.

[72] Montville, *The Big Bam*, 235.

[73] Ibid., 236.

[74] "Wilkes Baseball Field Determined to be Home of Babe Ruth's Longest Shot," Wilkes University News, www.wilkes.edu/about-wilkes/campus/sports-facilities/babe-ruths-longest-homerun.aspx.

[75] Leavy, *The Big Fella*, 233.

[76] Ibid., 234.

[77] Richard Sandomir, "Legacy of Earning Power: Babe Ruth: Dead 41 Years, He Lives on in Endorsements That Bring Heirs Hundreds of Thousands," *Los Angeles Times*, December 22, 1989.

[78] Bill Francis, "Big Star on the Big Screen," National Baseball Hall of Fame, https://baseballhall.org/discover-more/stories/short-stops/big-star-on-the-big-screen.

[79] Ibid.

[80] Mary Mallory, "Hollywood Heights: 'Babe Comes Home' Ushers in Baseball Season," *Los Angeles Daily Mirror*, March 28, 2016.

[81] Ibid.

[82] Ralph Berger, "Earle Combs," SABR Biography Project, https://sabr.org/bioproj/person/62bcbcbd.

[83] Daniel Shirley, "Mark Koenig," SABR Biography Project, https://sabr.org/bioproj/person/560d9b03.

[84] Fred Glueckstein, "Tony Lazzeri," SABR Biography Project, https://sabr.org/bioproj/person/1b3c179c.

[85] Ibid.

[86] Wayne Stewart, *Baseball's Greatest Hitters: Babe Ruth: A Biography* (Westport, CT: Greenwood Press, 2006), 86.

[87] Eig, *Luckiest Man*, 92.

[88] Ibid., 95.

[89] "1927: The Yankee Juggernaut." *This Great Game*, https://thisgreatgame.com/1927-baseball-history/.

[90] Bill Francis. "Ball Hit for Ruth's 60th Home Run Part of Baseball Lore in Cooperstown," National Baseball Hall of Fame, https://baseballhall.org/discover/short-stops/babe-ruths-60th-home-run-ball.

[91] Stewart, *Baseball's Greatest Hitters*, 86.

[92] John Liepa, "George Pipgras," SABR Biography Project, https://sabr.org/bioproj/person/d53de130.

[93] William B. Mead and Paul Dickson, *Baseball: The President's Game* (New York: Walker, 1997), 68.

[94] Creamer, *Babe*, 312–13.

[95] Smelser, *The Life That Ruth Built*, 384.

[96] John Goodspeed, "In the Babe's Own Words?" *Baltimore Sun*, July 20, 1992.

[97] Stewart, *Baseball's Greatest Hitters*, 89.

[98] Montville, *The Big Bam*, 291.

[99] Richard Goldstein, "Julia Ruth Stevens, Babe Ruth's Daughter, Dies," *New York Times*, March 9, 2019.

[100] Steve Steinberg, "Miller Huggins," SABR Biography Project, https://sabr.org/bioproj/person/7b65e9fa.

[101] Ibid.

[102] Ibid.

[103] Creamer, *Babe*, 347.

[104] Montville, *The Big Bam*, 294.

[105] "Two Killed When Fans Stampede in Yankee Stadium," Associated Press, May 29, 1929.

[106] "Anyway, I Had a Better Year Than He Did," Quote Investigator, December 28, 2014, https://quoteinvestigator.com/2014/12/28/better-year/.

[107] Montville, *The Big Bam*, 300.

[108] "Anyway, I Had a Better Year Than He Did."

[109] Stephen V. Rice, "Bob Shawkey," SABR Biography Project, https://sabr.org/bioproj/person/bob-shawkey/.

[110] William A. Cook, *Waite Hoyt: A Biography of the Yankees' Schoolboy Wonder* (Jefferson, NC: McFarland, 2004), 113–14.

[111] William C. Kashatus, *Baseball's All-Time Greatest Hitters: Lou Gehrig: A Biography* (Westport, CT: Greenwood, 2004), 55.

[112] Creamer, *Babe*, 352.

[113] Tony Horowitz, "The Woman Who (Maybe) Struck out Babe Ruth and Lou Gehrig," *Smithsonian*, https://www.smithsonianmag.com/history/the-woman-who-maybe-struck-out-babe-ruth-and-;ou-gehrig-4759182/, July 2013.

[114] Ibid.

[115] Brian Cronin, "Sports Legend Revealed: Did a Female Pitcher Strikeout Babe Ruth and Lou Gehrig?" *Los Angeles Times*, February 23, 2011.

[116] Horowitz, "The Woman Who (Maybe) Struck out Babe Ruth and Lou Gehrig."

[117] Cronin, "Sports Legend Revealed: Did a Female Pitcher Strike Out Babe Ruth and Lou Gehrig?"

[118] Zack Harold, "Jackie Mitchell Couldn't Win. Skepticism Followed Baseball's Most Famous Female Pitcher until the Day She Died," *Lapham's Quarterly*, March 28, 2018.

[119] Horowitz, "The Woman Who (Maybe) Struck out Babe Ruth and Lou Gehrig."

[120] "Joe McCarthy," National Baseball Hall of Fame, https://baseballhall.org/hall-of-famers/mccarthy-joe.

[121] John McMurray, "Joe McCarthy," SABR Biography Project, https://sabr.org/bioproj/person/joe-mccarthy/.

[122] Montville, *The Big Bam*, 304.

[123] McMurray, "Joe McCarthy."

[124] "Ten Commandments for Success in Baseball," Baseball Almanac, https://www.baseball-almanac.com/legendary/lijoemc.shtml.

[125] Stewart, *Baseball's Greatest Hitters*, 96.

[126] Mike Robbins, *The Yankees vs. Red Sox Reader* (New York: Carroll & Graf, 2005), 349.

[127] Smelser, *The Life That Ruth Built*, 444.

[128] Jack Bales, "The Show Girl and the Shortstop: The Strange Saga of Violet Popovich and Her Shooting of Cub Billy Jurges," *Baseball Research Journal* (Fall 2016).

[129] Smelser, *The Life That Ruth Built*, 446.

[130] Babe Ruth Quote Page, Baseball Almanac.

[131] Creamer, *Babe*, 361–62.

[132] Montville, *The Big Bam*, 312.

[133] Gregory H. Wolf, "Charlie Root," SABR Biography Project, https://sabr.org/bioproj/person/charlie-root/.

[134] Eig, *Luckiest Man*, 156.

[135] Ibid., 113–14.

[136] Leavy, *The Big Fella*, 122.

[137] Billy Heller, "Babe Ruth and Lou Gehrig Were Torn Apart by Women," *New York Post*, March 31, 2018.

[138] John Eisenberg, *The Streak: Lou Gehrig, Cal Ripken Jr., and Baseball's Most Historic Record*, E-book (New York: Houghton Mifflin Harcourt, 2017).

[139] Arch Ward, "Chicago to See Baseball's Biggest Game," *Chicago Tribune*, May 19, 1933.

[140] Westbrook Pegler, "All-Star Game Just What Doctor Ordered for Baseball," *Chicago Tribune*, June 19, 1933.

[141] Mark R. Millikin, *Jimmie Foxx: The Pride of Sudlersville* (Lanham, MD: Scarecrow Press, 2005), 151.

[142] Ibid.

[143] 1933 All-Star Game Box Score and Summary, Baseball Almanac, https://www.baseball-almanac.com/asgbox/yr1933as.shtml.

[144] William Weekes, "Babe's Specialty Gets Needed Runs," Associated Press, July 7, 1933.

[145] Montville, *The Big Bam*, 321.

[146] Smelser, *The Life That Ruth Built*, 457.

[147] Andrew Kivette, "Carl Hubbell Strikes out Five Hall of Famers in Succession at the All-Star Game," National Baseball Hall of Fame, https://baseballhall.org/discover/inside-pitch/carl-hubbell-strikes-out-five-hofers.

[148] Ralph Berger, "Moe Berg," SABR Biography Project, https://sabr.org/bioproj/person/moe-berg/.

[149] Montville, *The Big Bam*, 337.

[150] Gregory H. Wolf, "Guy Bush," SABR Biography Project, https://sabr.org/bioproj/person/guy-bush/.

[151] Stewart, *Baseball's Greatest Hitters*, 110.

[152] Earl Gustkey, "The Babe's Farewell: Fifty Years Ago, an Unmatched Career Came to an Unhappy End," *Los Angeles Times*, June 2, 1985.

[153] "Ruth to Get $15,000 as Coach for Brooklyn: Baseball Writers Believe the Babe Is Likely to Be Manager Not Later Than 1939," *Boston Globe*, June 19, 1938.

[154] John McMurray, "Babe Ruth: Brooklyn Dodgers Coach," *Baseball Research Journal* (Fall 2015), https://sabr.org/journal/article/babe-ruth-brooklyn-dodgers-coach-4/.

[155] Creamer, *Babe*, 403.

[156] Matt Kelly, "When the First Five Were Chosen," National Baseball Hall of Fame, https://baseballhall.org/discover-more/stories/baseball-history/first-bbwaa-hof-election-1936.

[157] Ibid.

[158] Joe Gergen, "Dahlgren Recalls Decline of Gehrig 50 Years Ago," *Los Angeles Times*, July 9, 1989.

[159] Ibid.

[160] "Full Text of Lou Gehrig's Farewell Speech," *Sports Illustrated*, July 4, 2009, https://www.si.com/mlb/2009/07/05/gehrig-text.

[161] Smelser, *The Life That Ruth Built*, 524.

[162] Richard Sandomir, "Reversing Course on Reports About a Classic," *New York Times*, February 8, 2013.

[163] *The Pride of the Yankees*. IMDB, https://www.imdb.com/title/tt0035211/.

[164] "Address to Fans on Babe Ruth Day at Yankee Stadium," American Rhetoric, https://www.americanrhetoric.com/speeches/baberuthfarewelltobaseball.htm.

[165] *The Babe Ruth Story*, Rotten Tomatoes, https://www.rottentomatoes.com/m/babe_ruth_story.

[166] Lily Rothman, "Read Babe Ruth's 1948 Obituary: 'He Was Unforgettable Even When He Struck Out,'" *Time*, August 16, 2018, https://time.com/5250916/babe-ruth-anniversary/.

[167] "Babe Ruth, The Slugger Who Went from Boyhood Chaos to Baseball Stardom," *New York Times*, August 16, 2016.

Part Two: Assorted Anecdotes

[1] Rick Maese, "A Buried Past," *Baltimore Sun*, February 6, 2008.

[2] "Babe Ruth Stories You Might Not Want to Tell Your Children," CooperToons.com, https://www.coopertoons.com/caricatures/CKftPI_baberuth_bio.html#baberuth_stories.

[3] Ibid.

[4] John Steadman, "Fifty Years After his Death, Babe Ruth Still Captivates as Man, Myth, Legend," *Los Angeles Times*, August 16, 1998.

[5] Ibid.

[6] Montville, *The Big Bam*, 66.

[7] Richard Goldstein, "Ray Kelly, Babe Ruth's Little Pal, Dies," *New York Times*, November 14, 2001.

[8] "Babe & Little Ray Kelly," Babe Ruth Central, http://www.baberuthcentral.com/kids-clubhouse/babe-ray-kelly/.

[9] Dorothy Ruth Pirone, *My Dad, The Babe: Growing Up with an American Hero* (Boston: Quinlan Press, 1988), 23.

[10] Ibid., 27.

[11] Montville, *The Big Bam*, 158.

[12] Pirone, *My Dad, The Babe*, 34.

[13] Nelson Green, "Mike Cvengros," SABR Biography Project, https://sabr.org/bioproj/person/mike-cvengros/.

[14] "Did Babe Ruth Ever Bat Right-Handed?" *Baseball Researcher* [blog], October 12, 2018, http://baseballresearcher.blogspot.com/2018/10/did-babe-ruth-ever-bat-right-handed.html.

[15] Ibid.

[16] "Babe Ruth Cigar," Baseball Reliquary, http://www.baseballreliquary.org/about/collections/babe-ruth-cigar-partially-smoked/.

[17] "Babe Ruth Catches Ball from Airplane. Seventh Attempt Gives Him World's Record," *New York Times*, July 22, 1926.

[18] Steve Harvey, "This Charge against Babe Ruth Was Off Base," *Los Angeles Times*, March 28, 2010.

[19] Andrew Martin, "Babe Ruth Arrested for Violating Child Labor Laws Prior to Historic 1927 Season," *Seamheads* [blog], February 3, 2012, http://seamheads.com/blog/2012/02/03/babe-ruth-arrested-for-violating-child-labor-laws-prior-to-historic-1927-season/.

[20] Ibid.

[21] Ibid.

[22] "Babe Ruth and Lou Gehrig Comedy Album," Babe Ruth Central, http://www.baberuthcentral.com/babe-ruth-lou-gehrig-comedy-album/.

[23] Bill Bryson, "Babe Ruth's Summer of Records," *Daily Beast*, September 29, 2013, https://www.thedailybeast.com/babe-ruths-summer-of-records.

[24] Bill Dow, "Babe Ruth's Greatest Practical Joke Happened in Detroit," *Vintage Detroit* [blog], February 5, 2011, https://www.vintagedetroit.com/blog/2011/02/05/babe-ruth%E2%80%99s-greatest-practical-joke-happened-in-detroit/.

[25] Gary Sarnoff, "The Day Babe Ruth Came to Sing Sing," *National Pastime* (2017): Baseball in the Big Apple1.

[26] Anthony Constrovince, "These 9 Pitchers Dominated Babe Ruth," MLB, April 14, 2020, https://www.mlb.com/news/pitchers-who-owned-babe-ruth.

[27] Anna McDonald, "Pruett Heir Remembers Ruthian Legacy," ESPN, March 2, 2014, https://www.espn.com/blog/sweetspot/post/_/id/44743/pruett-heir-remembers-ruthian-legacy.

[28] "The Greatest Man Ruth Ever Knew Was a Canadian," Cooperstowners in Canada, July 17, 2010, https://cooperstownersincanada.com/2010/07/17/the-greatest-man-that-babe-ruth-ever-knew-was-a-canadian/.

[29] "Babe Ruth's Longest Home Run," *Northeastern Journal*, March 7, 2014.

[30] Ibid.

[31] Mark Tomasik, "How Dizzy Dean Got the Best of his Matchup with Babe Ruth," *RetroSimba*, April 24, 2015, https://retrosimba.com/2015/04/24/how-dizzy-dean-got-the-best-of-his-matchup-with-babe-ruth/.

[32] Ibid.

[33] Pirone, *My Dad, The Babe*, 58.

[34] Dan Holmes, "Rivalry Renewed: Ty Cobb ad Babe Ruth Hit the Golf Course," *Baseball Egg* [blog], May 5, 2010, http://baseballegg.com/2010/05/01/rivalry-renewed-ty-cobb-and-babe-ruth-on-the-golf-course/.

[35] Ibid.

[36] Matthew Castonguay, "Ty Cobb Beat Babe Ruth . . . at Golf," SwingU Clubhouse, July 27, 2014, https://clubhouse.swingu.com/lifestyle/ty-cobb-once-beat-babe-ruth-at-golf/.

[37] Ibid.

[38] John McCarten, "The Current Screen," *Washington Post*, August 7, 1948.

[39] Bosley Crowther, "The Current Screen," *New York Times*, July 27, 1948.

[40] Creamer, *Babe*, 423.

[41] Eddie Deezen, "Babe Ruth's Final Years," Mental Floss, August 16, 2012, https://www.mentalfloss.com/article/31471/babe-ruths-final-years.

[42] Pirone, *My Dad, The Babe*, 183.

[43] Ibid.

[44] Roger Maris Quote Page, Baseball Almanac, https://www.baseball-almanac.com/quotes/quomari.shtml.

[45] Kristen Gowdy, "Babe Ruth Hits His 30th Home Run of the Season Breaking His Own Single Season Record," National Baseball Hall of Fame, https://baseballhall.org/discover/inside-pitch/ruth-hits-30th-of-season.

[46] Jack Doyle, "The M & M Boys: Summer of 1961," *Pop History Dig*, https://www.pophistorydig.com/topics/babe-ruth-tobacco-1920s-1940s/, August 21, 2018.

[47] Roger Maris Quote Page, Baseball Almanac.

[48] Joe Posnanski, "Did Babe Ruth Actually Hit 715 Home Runs?" MLB, June 7, 2018, https://www.mlb.com/news/did-babe-ruth-hit-715-homers-c280173404.

[49] Jen Christensen, "Besting Ruth, Beating Hate: How Hank Aaron Made Baseball History," CNN, April 8, 2014, https://www.cnn.com/interactive/2014/04/us/hank-aaron-anniversary/.

[50] William Leggett, "A Tortured Road to 715," *Sports Illustrated*, May 28, 1973.

[51] Bruce Lowitt, "Oh, Henry! Aaron Swings Past Ruth," *St. Petersburg Times*, December 25, 1999.

[52] Hank Aaron and Lonnie Wheeler, *I Had a Hammer: The Hank Aaron Story* (New York: Harper Perennial, 2007), 367.

[53] Ibid., 373.